— Th

BED & BREAKFAST
Guide to Ireland

— The —
BED & BREAKFAST
Guide to Ireland
Over 300 of the Best B&B's

Elsie Dillard &
Susan Causin

Appletree Press

First published and printed by
The Appletree Press Ltd,
19-21 Alfred Street, Belfast BT2 8DL,
1991, 1993

British Library Cataloguing-in-Publication Data
A catalogue record for this book is available
from the British Library.

ISBN 0 86281 378 6

9 8 7 6 5 4 3 2

Contents

Our Favourite B&Bs

- Ballymagarry House, 46 Leeke Road, Portrush, Co Antrim
- The Cottage, 377 Comber Road, Dundonald, Belfast, Co Antrim
- Maddybenny Farm, 18 Maddybenny Park, Portrush, Co Antrim
- Oakhill Country House, 59 Dunmurry Lane, Belfast, Co Antrim
- Tessie's, Fernhill Farmhouse, Doolin Road, Lisdoonvarna, Co Clare
- Culdaff House, Culdaff , Inishowen, Co Donegal
- Tanner Cottage, 5 Main Street, Groomsport, Co Down
- Chestnut Lodge, 2 Vesey Place, Monkstown, Dun Laoghaire, Co Dublin
- Mandalay, 10 Gentian Hill, Salt Hill, Galway, Co Galway
- Moycullen House, Moycullen, Co Galway
- Beech Grove, Camp Road, Castleisland, Co Kerry
- Ceol na h'Abhann, Tralee Road, Ballygrennan, Listowel, Co Kerry
- Grangebeg, Dunlavin, Co Kildare
- Glencarne House, Carrick-on-Shannon, Co Roscommon
- Coopershill, Riverstown, Co Sligo
- Bansha House, Bansha, Co Tipperary
- Foxmount Farm, Halfway House, Waterford, Co Waterford
- Grove House, Blackhall, Mullingar, Co Westmeath
- Mornington House, Multyfarnham, Co Westmeath
- Newbay Country House, Wexford, Co Wexford

Introduction

We would like to thank Bord Failte Eireann and the Northern Ireland Tourist Board for their help in making this book possible.

It is easy to fall in love with Ireland. Even though we are not strangers to Ireland, once again we found ourselves overwhelmed with the warmth of welcome and the beauty of the countryside and thoroughly enjoyed our travels to every corner of the country. Our researches covered the four seasons, and we highly recommend a visit to Ireland in the off-season when it is easy to get around and there are still plenty of things to interest the visitor. There are limited motorway facilities in Ireland, but the roads are well maintained, even in the most rural areas, and are seldom crowded.

Every property listed in this book was personally visited by us. There are no charges whatsoever for inclusion in this guide. Our criteria for entry is based primarily upon the warmth of welcome and cleanliness of the property, with many other factors, of course, taken into consideration. We have covered most parts of the country, including areas not considered as tourist regions, in order to accommodate business travellers, visiting friends and family gatherings.

Children are welcome unless otherwise stated. Smoking is allowed unless we have mentioned that it is not permitted, and pets are only welcome outside unless altogether excluded as indicated.

Parking is always available unless mentioned otherwise. We have included information on the number of ground-floor rooms, which is helpful for the elderly or infirm. Almost all bedrooms have washbasins and if other facilities in bedrooms, such as hairdryers, TVs, phones or tea/coffee-making services are available, this too has been mentioned. Unlicensed premises often allow guests to bring their own wine.

When booking, confirm prices; although at the time of publication these figures were correct, prices may vary. It is advisable when booking to also verify specifics such as child reductions, single supplements, special break prices, opening times, meals and dietary requirements, and whether a deposit is required. Obtaining driving directions is also recommended.

Wherever possible we have given the names of the owners. However, it is possible that change of ownership may have occurred, which could lead to significant differences in the standard of accommodation, welcome, cleanliness and price.

At the time of publication, and to the best of our knowledge, the facts in this book were correct. However, changes do occur for which we cannot be responsible. Visitors may want to read *Discover Ireland,* Aer Lingus's most popular holiday brochure, which includes a variety of programmes for touring Ireland.

We would welcome any comments you have on your personal experiences about properties in this book and we would be delighted to receive your recommendations for consideration for future inclusion. Please send your comments and recommendations to Elsie Dillard and Susan Causin, 48 Nursery Road, Great Cornard, Sudbury, Suffolk CO10 3NJ or, in North America, to PO Box 5107, Redondo, Washington 98054.

Note: A single supplement refers to the practice of charging a single visitor who stays in a double room the single-room rate plus a small additional charge.

The prices listed for accommodation in the Republic of Ireland are given in Irish pounds (punts). The prices listed for accommodation in Northern Ireland are given in pounds sterling (British pounds). Prices and exchange rates fluctuate, so be sure to check the rates when you book your reservation, as well as the method of payment. Some establishments may not accept credit cards. All prices refer to prices per person.

Dublin and the East

County Dublin

From above Killakee, on the northern slopes of the Dublin Mountains, there is a wonderful view of both city and county. You can see to the north east the majestic sweep of Dublin Bay, the beautiful peninsula of Howth Head, and to the south of the bay, South Killiney Head. The city stretches across the plain, divided by the River Liffey, and the large green patch in the north west is Phoenix Park, one of Europe's finest city parks, covering some 290 acres.

The county north of Howth has long sandy beaches and fishing villages, which in spite of their proximity to the city still retain their character and charm, and a wealth of archaeological sites. The castle at Howth dates from 1464, but has been altered over the centuries. The gardens, which are open to the public, are famous for their rhododendrons and eighteenth-century formal garden. Malahide Castle, which originally belonged to the Talbot family from 1185 to 1976 when the property was sold to Dublin County Council, now houses a large part of the National Portrait Collection.

To the south of the Liffey, Blackrock and Dalkey retain their village identity, and the popular Victorian holiday resort of Dun Laoghaire is one of the main sea-gateways to Ireland.

The city of Dublin is beautifully situated and the people have a friendliness and wit which captivates most visitors. Relatively speaking, it is a small and compact city. The city centre, stretching between Parnell Square and St Stephen's Green north to south and Dublin Bay and Phoenix Park east to west, can be covered easily by foot. Most points of interest in the city lie between these boundaries. Like any capital European city there is so much to see that it would take weeks to do it full justice, not just the principal sights of churches, museums and galleries, but to have the time to browse and absorb the atmosphere, the people, shops, theatres and pubs. Amongst the sights that come top of the list to visit are the National Museum, the National Gallery and the Municipal Gallery, as well as St Patrick's Cathedral dating from 1190, Christ-church Cathedral, restored in the nineteenth century, St Michan's, where intact bodies still lie in vaults, the fine eighteenth-century church of St Anne's, and St Werburgh's Church.

Dublin Castle, with its beautifully decorated State Apartments, was used by the British for state functions and since 1938 has been the scene of the inauguration of the presidents of Ireland. The GPO in O'Connell Street is where the Free Republic was proclaimed and the Custom House is one of the most impressive buildings in Dublin. Parliament House, now the Bank of Ireland, was built in 1785 by James Gandon, Dublin's most famous architect. The Book of Kells is kept in the Library at Trinity College, which is a restful spot away from the bustle of the city.

DUBLIN CITY

Ariel House

52 Lansdowne Road, Ballsbridge, Dublin 4, Co Dublin
Tel: (01) 685512, Fax: (01) 685845

A Victorian residence in an excellent location close to the city centre. Ariel House has recently been completely

refurbished and has new furniture, baths and showers, curtains, carpets and beds, although much of its former character has been preserved. There is a new addition which houses 20 period Victorian bedrooms. All bedrooms are equipped with TVs, direct dial telephones and hairdryers.

Very high standards pervade throughout the house, which cleverly combines the graciousness of a bygone era with all modern comforts. The owners, Michael and Marese, take great pride in their hotel and have created an informal, relaxed and friendly atmosphere. There are antique furnishings in the public rooms and beautifully decorated porcelains. The Garden Restaurant is a pleasant spot for dinner. Ariel House has a wine licence, enabling guests to enjoy a glass of wine with their meal. If you are looking for a special place to stay, this would make an excellent choice. Reservations recommended. Located 1 mile (1½ km) south east of the city centre, 4 minutes by rapid rail. All major credit cards accepted.

OWNER Michael O'Brien OPEN All year, except Christmas
ROOMS double/family/twin (all en suite) TERMS B&B IR £35.00-£45.00 p.p.; reductions for children; single supplement IR £10.00; evening meal at restaurant prices

Brian and Mary Bennett's

31 Leeson Close, Dublin 2, Co Dublin
Tel: (01) 765011, Fax: (01) 762929

A rare find in the centre of Dublin, number 31 is tucked away just off Leeson Street, an oasis of peace and quiet in this busy area. Built by the famous Dublin architect Sam Stephenson as his home, this spacious house has many interesting features. The low entrance opens up into a spacious drawing-room with a sunken sitting area featuring a bar, fireplace, high ceilings and tall windows. There are terraces and patios – 2 of the bedrooms have their own – and different levels. Breakfast can be served either in the upstairs dining-room or in the enclosed conservatory. The comfortable bedrooms all have phones, bathrooms and tea- and coffee-making facilities. This bed and breakfast has only been open for business since the summer of 1991, when Brian and Mary Bennett moved here from Monkstown.

OWNERS Brian and Mary Bennett OPEN All year, except Christmas ROOMS 5 double/twin (all en suite) TERMS B&B IR £29.00 p.p., single IR £40.00

Egan's House

779 Iona Park, Glasnevin, Dublin 9, Co Dublin
Tel: (01) 303611/305283, Fax: (01) 303312

Egan's House is a pleasant Victorian red-brick house with an attractive exterior full of window boxes. The bedrooms are well appointed, all with bathrooms, TVS, hairdryers, telephones and hospitality trays. There are 2 lounges for guests' use, one with a pool table. Both continental or cooked breakfasts are available at an extra charge, and evening meals can be served by arrangement. Egan's House has a wine licence. There is a good bus service to the town, so if you wish to avoid the parking and driving problems in Dublin, you can take the bus. Dublin airport is 4 miles (6 km) away. Visa and Access cards accepted.

OWNERS John and Betty Egan   OPEN All year   ROOMS 5 double, 15 twin, 4 single, 1 family (all en suite)   TERMS B&B IR £23.50-£26.25 p.p.; reductions for children; single supplement IR £8.00

Elva

5 Pembroke Park, Ballsbridge, Dublin 4, Co Dublin
Tel: (01) 602931, Fax: (01) 605417

An impressive Victorian residence in a central location, just 5 minutes from the town centre. There is a good bus service into town. The entry door has some beautiful stained glass work and leaded windows, and other original features include decorative ceiling cornices, fireplaces in the bedrooms and lounge. The bedrooms all have TVS, hairdryers, telephones and tea- or coffee-making facilities. There are antique funishings throughout the house and the atmosphere is warm and friendly. Pleasant hosts and personal attention guaranteed.

OWNER Sheila Matthews   OPEN 1 February–1 November
ROOMS 1 double/single/family   TERMS B&B IR £20.00-£25.00 p.p.

Glenogra House

64 Merrion Road, Ballsbridge, Dublin 4, Co Dublin
Tel: (01) 683661, Fax: (01) 683698

Glenogra House is a beautifully appointed Georgian residence in an excellent location, close to the city centre, Dart and all amenities. The house has recently been completely refurbished to a high standard of comfort in pleasing fabrics and colours. The bedrooms are a good size, and all have TVS, telephones, hairdryers, a trouser press and tea- and coffee-making facilities. The dining-room, where breakfast only is served, is rather ornate, with pillars, a fireplace and a decorative ceiling. Mr and Mrs McNamee offer all the facilities of a hotel, combined with the warmth and personal service of a private residence. There is a wine licence and off-street car parking is available. No smoking in the dining-room and no pets. Visa and Access cards accepted.

OWNERS Seamus and Cherry McNamee   OPEN All year, except Christmas and New Year   ROOMS 7 double, 2 twin (all en suite)   TERMS B&B IR £35.00 p.p.; reductions for children; single supplement IR £15.00

Glenveagh

31 Northumberland Road, Ballsbridge, Dublin 4, Co Dublin
Tel: (01) 684612

14

Glenveagh is a Georgian house retaining many original features, including beautiful cornices and a ceiling rose. There are antique furnishings, including a grandfather clock in the hallway. The bedrooms are well appointed, all en suite with TVS, hairdryers, direct dial telephones and writing desks. The house is spacious, beautifully maintained and extremely comfortable, combining the facilities of a hotel with the warmth and friendliness of a private house. Joe and Bernadette are a gracious couple who enjoy welcoming people to Dublin and are happy to offer advice. There is an excellent bus service to town and the house is minutes from the Dart station. Off-street parking available. No smoking in the dining-room and no pets. Visa and Access cards accepted.

OWNERS Joe Cunningham   OPEN All year, except Christmas
ROOMS 5 double, 4 twin, 2 family (all en suite)
TERMS B&B IR £25.00 p.p., single IR £35.00; reductions for children

Greenmount

124 Howth Road, Dublin 3, Co Dublin
Tel: (01) 339522

A spacious Victorian house standing in its grounds with splendid mature trees and a lawn. There is a garden with furniture which guests are welcome to use on pleasant days. The house is spacious and there is a warm, informal atmosphere. There are no en suite rooms, but all the bedrooms have wash basins and there are 2 bathrooms exclusively for guests' use. Greenmount has one enormous family room; children are welcome and a cot is provided. There is a large lounge/dining-room where freshly prepared breakfasts are served; special diets and vegetarians catered for. The lounge has a marble Georgian fireplace, rescued from a house in the process of being demolished. Located 10 minutes from the city centre; guests are advised to leave their cars at the B&B and take the local bus to town. Pets by arrangement. TV on request.

OWNERS Mrs Gladys Duggan   OPEN All year, except Christmas
ROOMS 2 double/twin/family   TERMS B&B IR £19.00 p.p.; babies free; children under 12 IR £7.00

Haddington Lodge

49 Haddington Road, Ballsbridge, Dublin 4, Co Dublin
Tel: (01) 600974

A Georgian house in a good location, close to Jury's Hotel and 15 minutes' walk from the town centre. All the rooms have been completely refurbished and are individually decorated with soft, restful colours. Each bedroom has an electric blanket, and some rooms overlook a pretty courtyard with shrubs and trees. Haddington Lodge started life as 2 separate houses, but they were cleverly converted into one house 4 years ago when Mrs Egan opened up the premises for guests. The TV lounge is quite small and leads onto the dining-room where breakfasts are served. Vegetarians catered for if prearranged. There is some private parking; street parking is also available. No pets. There is a self-catering unit available. Special off-season breaks upon request.

OWNER Mrs Mary Egan OPEN 16 January-16 December
ROOMS 4 twin, 1 family (all en suite) TERMS B&B IR £18.00 p.p.;
reductions for children; single supplement IR £14.00

× Joyville Guest House

24 St Alphonsus Road, Drumcondra, Dublin 9, Co Dublin
Tel: (01) 303221

Owners Roma and John Gibbons are a most gracious couple who extend a warm welcome in their pleasant red-brick Victorian house. Joyville is situated opposite St Alphonsus Convent and Church, 1 mile (1¹/2 km) to the town centre. There is a good local bus service; guests would be well advised to take local transport to avoid the parking and traffic problems. Street parking is available. The bedrooms are average in size, spotlessly clean, with orthopaedic beds. There are no en suite rooms, but there are 2 shower rooms and 2 WCs exclusively for guests' use. There is a family lounge, with a lovely marble fireplace, which guests are welcome to share. No pets. Four miles from the airport and 1 mile (1¹/2 km) to the city centre.

OWNERS Roma and John Gibbons OPEN All year
ROOMS 1 double, 3 twin TERMS B&B IR £13.00 p.p.; no
reductions for children; single supplement IR £4.00

Parknasilla

15 Iona Drive, Drumcondra, Dublin 9, Co Dublin
Tel: (01) 305724

A friendly welcome awaits one at this small Edwardian
detached house located in a quiet residential street. Mrs
Ryan is a friendly, chatty person who likes to make sure her
guests have everything they need. The location is excellent
for both the centre and the airport, with many buses
travelling in each direction. The accommodation is simple
but comfortable, with a TV lounge and breakfast room. No
smoking in the dining-room.

OWNER Mrs Teresa Ryan   OPEN All year, except Christmas
ROOMS 1 double, 1 twin, 2 family (2 en suite)   TERMS B&B
IR £14.00-£16.00 p.p.; reductions for children; single supplement
IR £4.00

Nora and Padraig Sheridan's

45 Upper Drumcondra Road, Dublin 9, Co Dublin
Tel: (01) 360714

A warm and friendly welcome awaits you at this creeper-
covered Victorian house set back off the road. This is an
excellent location for either the airport or downtown Dublin
and there is a frequent bus service. An extremely high
standard prevails; the rooms are immaculate, individually
decorated with pretty pastel wallpaper. Freshly prepared
substantial breakfasts are served in the cosy dining-room,
which has bright, attractive table-cloths. The B&B has been
in operation for 7 years, when the Sheridan's took over the
house and completely refurbished it. Mr Sheridan has done
all of the work himself and the result is a most charming
property offering all the facilities of a hotel with personal
service at reasonable prices. On the main road en route to
the airport in Drumcondra, 2 miles (3 km) to the city. No
pets.

OWNERS Nora and Padraig Sheridan   OPEN All year, except
Christmas   ROOMS 2 double, 1 twin, 2 family (all en suite)
TERMS B&B IR £16.00 p.p.; reductions for children; single
supplement IR £2.00

17

Chestnut Lodge

2 Vesey Place, Monkstown, Dun Laoghaire, Co Dublin
Tel: (01) 2807860, Fax: (01) 2801466

A delightful terraced Regency building facing a park, with a pleasant walled back garden and only minutes from Dun Laoghaire. Nancy Malone, who used to work in television, started doing bed and breakfast a few years ago. The house has beautifully proportioned rooms, with high, ornate ceilings on the ground floor. It is a most comfortable, elegantly furnished and well-equipped house, and the bedrooms all have TVs and telephones. Breakfast, which includes home-made preserves and bread, is beautifully presented in the dining-room/sitting-room, and there is also a separate drawing-room. Located between Salthill and Dun Laoghaire – access into central Dublin is quick on the Dart train service. Highly recommended as a Dublin base, or as a touring point from Dun Laoghaire.

OWNERS Nancy Malone   OPEN All year   ROOMS 3 double, 2 twin (4 en suite)   TERMS B&B IR £22.00 p.p., single IR £27.50

X *Ivylea*

220 Swords Road, Santry, Dublin 9, Co Dublin
Tel: (01) 369430

A modern, clean and homely property on the main airport road, situated 1½ miles (2½ km) from the airport and 2 miles (3 km) from the city centre. There are plenty of buses from the house to town. The bedrooms are freshly decorated, all have tea- and coffee-making facilities and TV. The front of the house and driveway have recently been redesigned for easier access, and there is an enclosed private car park. New to the area is a shopping complex and leisure centre. Tressa Brazil keeps very busy, so advance reservations are recommended.

OWNER Tressa Brazil   OPEN All year   ROOMS 1 double, 1 single, 2 family (2 en suite)   TERMS B&B IR £15.00 p.p.; reductions for children; single supplement IR £5.00

Rosmeen House

13 Rosmeen Gardens, Dun Laoghaire, Co Dublin
Tel: (01) 2807613

A beautifully appointed, turn-of-the-century Spanish-style villa set in its own grounds, in a quiet cul-de-sac, minutes from the ferry, bus and train. The house has recently been refurbished. The bedrooms are prettily decorated and a good size, with comfortable beds. There is one en suite ground-floor room. There is a well-furnished, comfortable lounge, a separate dining-room and a lovely antique grandfather clock in the hallway. Joan Murphy is a very friendly host, ably assisted by her sister Maureen. Excellent breakfasts are served, and continental or vegetarian breakfasts are available. Plenty of parking. No smoking in the dining-room or lounge and no pets.

OWNER Joan M Murphy   OPEN 1 January–mid December
ROOMS 1 double/twin/single/family (2 en suite)   TERMS B&B
IR£16.00–£18.50 p.p.; reductions for children; single supplement IR£5.00

Counties Louth and Meath

The Boyne Valley cuts right through the centre of this area – one of the most historic and evocative places in Irish history, which for thousands of years was the centre of power. Innumerable remains from every century lie scattered across this fertile green valley.

Dominating the town of Trim are the ruins of King John's Castle dating from 1172, the largest Anglo-Norman castle in Ireland. The Duke of Wellington's family came from here, as did the family of Bernardo O'Higgins, a prominent figure in Chilean history.

Apart from a few earthworks, there is not much left to see at the Hill of Tara, the seat of Ireland's kings since prehistoric times. Imagination is needed to conjure up the sight of great buildings and a mass of warriors and nobles who inhabited this place in days gone by.

At the attractive village of Slane the old castle overlooks the river and a little further along the valley is Brugh na Boinne, the Palace of the Boyne, an enormous cemetery with graves dating back to the Neolithic era, the main sites of which are at Newgrange, Knowth and Dowth.

The pretty village of Kells, which is in the Blackwater

Valley, was the site of the settlement of the Columban monks, who moved here from Iona in 807. St Columba's house still stands, and in the church is a copy of the famous Book of Kells.

Monasterboice and Mellifont are the sites of two ancient ecclesiastical centres, and at Drogheda one can see the preserved head of St Oliver Plunkett, former Archbishop of Armagh, in the Church of St Peter.

The Cooley Peninsula is an attractive and unspoilt area with lovely views, and the old town of Carlingford has lots of historical sites, including King John's Castle.

ARDEE

Red House

Ardee, Co Louth
Tel: (041) 53523

This attractive red-brick Georgian house is approached off the main Dundalk to Ardee road through parklike grounds. It is a relaxed, informal place with very friendly owners and a welcoming atmosphere. There is a large entrance hall, formal dining-room, comfortable sitting-room and enormous bedrooms. Outside, one end of the stable courtyard has been turned into an indoor swimming pool and sauna, and beyond is a hard tennis court. Guests are welcome to bring their horses and dogs, and local attractions include Newgrange, the oldest building in Europe. An 18-hole golf course is 1 mile (1½ km) away.

OWNERS Jim and Linda Connolly   OPEN All year   ROOMS 3 double (1 en suite)   TERMS B&B IR £30.00-£35.00 p.p.; reductions for children; single supplement IR £5.00; evening meal IR £18.00

BALTRAY

Aisling House

Baltray, Drogheda, Co Louth
Tel: (041) 22376

Aisling House is in a peaceful spot adjacent to the beach and 100 yards from the Louth Golf Club and Restaurant. The house is bright and clean and the bedrooms all have TVs and are simply furnished. There is a lovely bright lounge to relax in. Breakfasts are served in the dining-room, which overlooks the garden. The golf club restaurant is open to non-golfers and there are several other eating establishments close by. An ideal base for touring the Boyne Valley. No smoking in the dining-room. Located on the Boyne road 3 miles (4¹/2 km) from Drogheda.

OWNER Mrs Josephine McGinley   OPEN 1 March–1 October
ROOMS 1 double, 3 twin, 1 family (3 en suite)   TERMS B&B IR £12.00-£15.00 p.p.; single supplement IR £4.00

CARLINGFORD

Shalom

Glan Road, Carlingford, Co Louth

Tel: (042) 73151

Built as a family home in 1978 and added onto a couple of times, Shalom is an interestingly shaped house, with all sorts of angles and strange-shaped rooms. It is located close to the shore and near the outer end of the harbour. The 2 dining-rooms, where breakfast only is served, are on the upper floor to take advantage of the sea view. The house has a friendly, welcoming atmosphere, with modern fittings and strong colours. All rooms have tea- and coffee-making facilities and TVS. No pets in the house.

OWNERS Jackie and Kevin Woods   OPEN All year, except Christmas   ROOMS 4 double, 1 twin, 1 family (all en suite)   TERMS B&B IR £13.00-£16.00 p.p.; reductions for children

Viewpoint

Omeath Road, Carlingford, Co Louth

Tel: (042) 73149

A modern house, built by the owners as their own home, standing above the road on the edge of Carlingford and enjoying spectacular views over the town, harbour and across to the Mourne Mountains. All the bedrooms are motel style, with their own entrances, bathrooms, TVS and tea- and coffee-makers. They are comfortably furnished, some with views, and mostly painted in dark colours (one completely black, which is one of the most popular rooms). A new dining-room is being built to take better advantage of the surrounding views. No pets. Visa accepted.

OWNERS Marie and Paul Woods   OPEN All year   ROOMS 6 double (all en suite)   TERMS B&B IR £15.00-£18.00 p.p.; reductions for children

Faulty Piers

Smithstown, Drogheda, Co Meath

Tel: (041) 29020

Handy for travellers, this unassuming little bungalow lies just off the main Dublin to Belfast road and is only 30 minutes from the Dublin airport. The bedrooms are small, neat and freshly decorated, and the en suite rooms have very small shower rooms. There is rural countryside to the back of the house. The dining-room is for breakfast only and both a smoking and non-smoking lounge are provided. Smoking is discouraged outside the lounge; no pets.

OWNER Noeleen and Tom Dunne   OPEN Easter–October
ROOMS 4 double, 1 single, 1 family (4 en suite)   TERMS B&B
IR £12.00-£13.50 p.p.; reductions for children

Harbour Villa

Mornington Road, Drogheda, Co Louth

Tel: (041) 37441

Sheila and Tommy Dwyer offer a true Irish welcome at Harbour Villa, their vine-covered old-style country home on the River Boyne, just a mile (1½ km) from Drogheda. The gardens are lovely and there is a garden house containing a sun-lounge where guests can relax, away from the wind, and admire the flowers. There is a grass tennis court for guests' use. The bedrooms are small, clean and simply furnished. The comfortable lounge has the original marble fireplace. There are no TVs here; instead, people are encouraged to chat, enjoy the scenery or take a walk in the countryside. No pets. Located on the L21 east of Drogheda.

OWNER Mrs Sheila Dwyer   OPEN All year   ROOMS 2 double, 1 twin   TERMS B&B IR£14.00 p.p.; single supplement IR£4.00

DULEEK

Annesbrook

Duleek, Co Meath

Tel: (041) 23293, Fax: (041) 23024

An impressive gate and a long wooded drive bring you to

Annesbrook, an interesting house, the core of which is seventeenth century with additions added at different periods. The pedimented portico of the house and the ballroom were added on to impress George IV when he came here in 1821. Another distinguished visitor was William Thackeray. However, the formal hospitality of those days has been replaced by a relaxed and welcoming family atmosphere. All of the bedrooms are spacious and comfortable, with folders detailing events of local interest and suggested walks and drives to places of interest. Each bedroom has tea- and coffee-making facilities and hairdryers. The reception rooms have big log fires. Evening meals must be ordered prior to 11.30 am and feature home-grown organic vegetables picked fresh daily from the walled garden. There is a wine licence. No smoking in the dining-room and no pets. French spoken. The house can be found 4½ miles (6½ km) north of Ashbourne on the L144. Visa, Access and Eurocard accepted.

OWNER Kate Sweetman   OPEN 1 May–1 September
ROOMS 5 double/twin/family (all en suite)   TERMS B&B
IR £22.00-£25.00 p.p.; reductions for children; single supplement
IR £6.00; evening meals by arrangement

DUNDALK

Krakow

190 Ard Easmiunn, Dundalk, Co Louth
Tel: (042) 37535

A modern detached bungalow 1 mile (1½ km) from town on a quiet street, within walking distance of the railway station. The atmosphere is friendly and breakfast is served family-style in the pretty dining-room. Mrs Witherow, who was formerly in hotel management, enjoys contact with people and is always happy to assist guests to ensure their stay is enjoyable. There is a comfortable TV lounge. Guests are welcome to use the garden. Evening meals are available if prearranged and vegetarians are catered for. No pets. Signposted on Ecco Road.

OWNER Marian Witherow OPEN All year ROOMS 2 double, 2 twin, 1 family, 1 single (2 en suite) TERMS B&B IR £12.00-£13.50 p.p.; reductions for children; single supplement IR £15.00; evening meal IR £10.50

DUNSHAUGHLIN

Gaulstown House

Dunshaughlin, Co Meath

Tel: (041) 259147

A small, square, whitewashed, solidly built farmhouse standing in a small front garden. Gaulstown is located in a rural, peaceful scene and is surrounded by fields of grazing sheep. There is quite an extensive range of farm buildings to the rear of of the house. Mrs Delany is a most friendly lady who has won all kinds of prizes for her baking. Evening meals might well include home-reared lamb. The rooms are fresh and bright, there is a comfortable drawing-room and everything is clean and tidy. No smoking and pets outside only.

OWNER Kathryn Delany OPEN 1 April– 1 November ROOMS 1 double/twin/family (all en suite) TERMS B&B IR £13.00-£15.00 p.p.; reductions for children; evening meal IR £11.00

KELLS

Lennoxbrook

Carnaross, Kells, Co Meath

Tel: (046) 45902

A substantial farmhouse standing just off the main road in its own grounds. The back part of the house is over 200-years old, and the surrounding farmland is let out. Mrs Mullan looks after 3 small children and runs the bed and breakfast, while her husband runs a pub in Navan. The house is well lived in, the bedrooms are plain but comfortable and evening meals are available if booked in advance. No smoking except in the drawing-room. The house is on the main road between Virginia and Kells.

OWNER Pauline Mullan OPEN All year, except Christmas

ROOMS 2 double, 1 twin, 1 triple, 1 single
TERMS B&B IR £12.50-£15.00 p.p.; reductions for children;
evening meal IR £10.00

NAVAN

Gainstown House

Navan, Co Meath

Tel: (046) 21448

An attractive country house dating from the early nineteenth
century and standing in pleasant lawned gardens,
surrounded by 200 acres of pastureland. A patio at the rear
of the house overlooks the garden. Pleasantly decorated, the
drawing-room (with open fireplace) leads off the large
entrance hall; evening meals are served in the dining-room.
The house is located 2 miles (3 km) from Navan, 1 mile (1
1/2 km) off the Navan to Trim road and signposted on the
N3. Fishing, golf, swimming and riding are all available
locally. No pets.

OWNER Mrs Mary Reilly OPEN Easter–1 October ROOMS 3
family (1 en suite) TERMS B&B IR £13.00 - £17.00 p.p.;
reductions for children; evening meal IR £13.00

Lios na Greine

Bailis, Athlumney, Navan, Co Meath

Tel: (046) 28092

Lios na Greine, meaning "enclosure of the sun", is a neo-
Georgian style house in a sunny location. It is set back off
the road, 1 mile (11/2 km) from the town centre on the
Duleek to Ashbourne airport road. The house is immaculate
and the decor is of a high standard, with matching wallpapers, fabrics and cosy duvets. There is a comfortable TV
lounge, where tea is served in the evening. Breakfast is
served family style in the bright and cheerful dining-room,
as are evening meals (advance notice required). There is one
room on the ground floor and a pleasant garden with
furniture for guests' use. An ideal base for exploring
Newgrange and the Boyne Valley.

OWNER Mrs Mary Callahan OPEN 1 April–1 October ROOMS 1
double/twin/family TERMS B&B IR £13.00 p.p.; reductions for
children; single supplement IR £5.00; evening meal IR £13.00,
high tea IR £10.00

County Wicklow

Lying just to the south of Dublin, this is an area of hills and mountains, lakes and streams – a pleasant, peaceful place to escape to after the bustle of the city.

From Dublin one comes first to Bray, a large seaside resort, and then to Enniskerry. Here one can visit the gardens of Powerscourt Estate. The house, which had been one of the most beautiful in Ireland, was destroyed by fire in the 1950s, leaving only the shell still standing.

Glendalough is a beautiful, scenic place in the mountains, set between two small lakes, with the ruins of St Kevin's kitchen, the church and cathedral founded by St Kevin in 520. Just beyond is the small twelfth-century priory of St Saviour. The county town, Wicklow, is on the coast, and further south is Arklow, a popular resort and fishing centre.

At Blessington is Russborough House, a beautiful Palladian-style house containing a marvellous art collection, and the Poulaphouca Reservoir, which has been formed by damming the River Liffey.

ANNAMOE

Carmel's Bed and Breakfast

Annamoe, Co Wicklow
Tel: (0404) 45297

A warm and welcoming house set back off the main road in an acre of beautiful gardens. The house was built as a family home in 1970 by the Hawkins family and added onto in 1981. The bedrooms are clean and comfortable. There are no guests here; everyone is a family friend. Cups of tea or coffee are given upon arrival and/or during the evening. All of the bedrooms are on the ground floor, and with an addition to the back of the house 3 out of the 4 rooms are now en suite. This is a lovely spot in which to spend a few days. Close by is the Glendalough Fun Park, and hiking and walking can be enjoyed nearby. Mr and Mrs Hawkins are local people willing to assist with sightseeing and local events. No smoking in the dining-room. 3 miles (4¹/2 km) from Glendalough. Take the N11 from Dublin.

OWNER Carmel Hawkins OPEN 1 March–31 October ROOMS 1 double, 1 twin, 2 family (3 en suite) TERMS B&B IR £12.00-£14.00 p.p.; reductions for children; single supplement IR £5.00

Ballygriffin Farm

Arklow, Co Wicklow
Tel: (0402) 32251

David and Diana Lane are a friendly couple who have been welcoming guests to their delightful farmhouse for over 13 years. Ballygriffin is a mixed farm in an enviable position, surrounded by glorious countryside. David and Diana have created a warm and friendly atmosphere. Little wonder that most of the guests come here for long stays, and many give recommendations or are repeat visitors. The comfortable lounge leads onto the garden, where there is a hard tennis court. There are some interesting antique furnishings, including a seventeenth-century day bed and eighteenth-century chaise-longue. Wonderful home-cooking includes fresh eggs, home-grown produce, meats, home-made breads, dessert, and the farm speciality, shortbread. Vegetarian and special diets are catered for if prearranged. Wine licence. Baby-sitting by arrangement.

OWNERS David and Diana Lane OPEN 1 June–1 August ROOMS 2 double, 2 twin, 4 family (5 en suite) TERMS B&B IR £13.00 p.p.; reductions for children; no single supplement; evening meal IR £11.00

Fairy Lawn

Wexford Road, Arklow, Co Wicklow
Tel: (0402) 32790

An attractive brick-and-plaster house set back off the road. The owners, Mr and Mrs Kelly, do their own decorating, and the bright, airy bedrooms are all colour-coordinated with matching fabrics. Mr Kelly is a keen gardener, as evidenced by the beautiful landscaped gardens and colourful window boxes. Breakfast only is served, but there are lots of venues for meals in the area. There's a comfortable guest lounge with a TV. Situated 1/2 mile from Arklow on the N11 to Gorey.

OWNER Rita Kelly OPEN All year ROOMS 2 double/twin (2 en suite) TERMS B&B IR £12.50-£14.00 p.p.; reductions for children; single supplement IR £3.50

Lakevilla

Seaview Avenue, Ferrybank, Arklow, Co Wicklow
Tel: (0402) 32734

A modern house built in 1962 with later additions; a few minutes' walk to the beach and all amenities. The small garden is well maintained and the window boxes are a blaze of colour in summer. Una Dennehy is a cordial lady dedicated to ensuring that everything possible is done for her guests. The bedrooms are small but comfortable with plenty of wardrobe space. There is a comfortable guest lounge with TV. Tea- and coffee-making facilities are available on the landing. There is a pitch-and-putt course and leisure centre across the street and 2 golf courses within 2 miles (3 km). No pets. Self-catering available. The house is signposted on Ferrybank on the N11. All major credit cards accepted.

OWNER Una Dennehy   OPEN 1 April–1 September
ROOMS 2 double, 1 twin, 1 family   TERMS B&B IR £12.50 p.p.; reductions for children; single supplement IR £4.00

ASHFORD

Bartragh

Inchanappa, Ashford, Co Wicklow
Tel: (0404) 40442

A small, neat one-storey house standing back from the main road. Simply furnished and decorated, the house is kept immaculately clean by Mrs Long. There is a small front-facing lounge with a fireplace, and the dining-room behind has separate tables, where breakfast only is served. Bartragh is located on the main N11 road on the ouskirts of Ashford in the Dublin direction. No pets.

OWNER Mrs Phyl Long   OPEN 1 March–1 October
ROOMS 3 double (2 en suite)   TERMS B&B IR £12.00-£14.00 p.p.; reductions for children; single supplement IR £5.00

GLENDALOUGH

Derrybawn House

Glendalough, Co Wicklow
Tel: (0404) 45134

About a mile (1 1/2 km) from Glendalough, Derrybawn

House is set in 90 acres of sheep-grazing land. Built on the site of a sixth-century monastic settlement, the house was burnt down during the 1798 Rising and rebuilt in the style of a north Italian villa in the early nineteenth century. There are some very attractive, compact rooms in the back wing of the house, furnished in pine, en suite and with double/twin beds. The rooms in the main part of the house are larger, but not all are en suite. Upstairs there is a large room with a full-size snooker table, armchairs and wood-burning stove, while on the ground floor one will find the formal dining-room, where evening meals are served by arrangement, and an attractive small sitting-room with an open fire. No children under 12.

OWNER Donald and Lucy Vambeck   OPEN All year, except Christmas   ROOMS double/twin (most en suite)   TERMS B&B IR £18.00-£22.50 p.p.; single supplement IR £5.00-£7.50; evening meal from IR £17.00

KILTEGAN

Beechlawn

Kiltegan, Co Wicklow
Tel: (0508) 73171

Originally a Church of Ireland rectory and later a farmhouse, Beechlawn was in a very bad state of repair when the Jacksons moved here from the neighbouring farm. With Mount Leinster to one side and the Wicklow Mountains to the other, the house has lovely views. Beechlawn is part of a beef farm, and the Jackson's son runs the adjoining dairy farm. The accommodation is simple, but comfortable, and very clean, with 2 large attic family rooms. One of the singles is on the ground floor; the dining-room has the original fireplace and 2 tables and there is a comfortable sitting-room. No smoking in the bedrooms and pets outside only. The house can be found in Kiltegan village.

OWNERS Mrs E Jackson   OPEN 1 March–1 November
ROOMS 1 double, 2 single, 2 family   TERMS B&B IR from £12.50 p.p.; reductions for children; evening meal IR £11.00, high tea IR £7.50

Avonbrae House

Rathdrum, Co Wicklow
Tel: (0404) 46198

Nestling in the foothills of the Wicklow Mountains, just
outside the village of Rathdrum, is Avonbrae. The
Geoghegan family are pleased to be your hosts in this
walker's paradise. The hiker will find tracks and boreens
(little roads) across mountains, over hills, beside the lake
and along the seashore. Detailed maps are provided with
discussions on each day's itinerary the night before, and the
Geoghegans specialise in conducting guided hill-walking
tours. A very inviting house with warm, comfortable
bedrooms, open fires, grass tennis court and a heated
swimming pool, open from Easter to the beginning of
November. The Geoghegan family have organised some
excellent 5- and 7-day holidays, breakfast and evening meal
and packed lunch included. Special rates for 6 or more.
Transport to and from Rathdrum railway station or bus can
be arranged. There is free fishing (mostly brown trout) close
by. The house is located 400 metres outside Rathdrum on
the Glendalough road. Visa, Access and American Express
cards accepted.

OWNER Mrs Dorothea Geoghegan   OPEN 1 April–mid November
ROOMS 1 double, 3 twin, 2 family (all en suite)   TERMS B&B IR
£19.00 p.p.; reductions for children; single supplement IR £5.00;
evening meal IR £13.00, packed lunch IR £3.00

ROUNDWOOD

Forest Way Lodge

Baltynanima, Roundwood, Co Wicklow
Tel: (01) 2818429

A long, low house built 20 years ago as 2 bungalows. Forest
Way Lodge is set in beautiful countryside in an isolated
position with spectacular views. All rooms face the front,
taking advantage of the wonderful landscape. In 1983
Grainne Foy bought Forest Way with her sister and
transformed the 2 semi-detached bungalows into a single
house. There is a large sitting-room/dining-room with a
fireplace and a kitchen which guests are welcome to use at
any time to make tea or coffee. The owners have their own

kitchen at the other end of the house. It is a relaxed, informal place, the emphasis being on activities and the outdoors. With access to 4,000 acres of forest, this is a wonderful place for walking and painting. The Grainnes give riding lessons, have a cross-country course and take people out trekking; guests are welcome to bring their own horses. They also run riding courses for children aged between 10 and 16. Evening meals are by arrangement and no pets are allowed. The property can be found 1 1/2 miles (2 1/2 km) from Roundwood, the highest village in Ireland, on the Lough Dan road.

OWNERS Mrs Grainne Foy   OPEN All year   ROOMS 2 single/family
TERMS B&B IR from £14.00 p.p.; evening meal IR £12.50

WICKLOW

Bella Vista

St Patrick's Road Upper, Wicklow, Co Wicklow
Tel: (0404) 67325

A modern, neat bungalow in a most spectacular position, with panoramic views of Wicklow Harbour. The lounge and dining-room both overlook the harbour, and although there is a TV in the lounge, guests seem to prefer just to sit and relax and enjoy the scenery. The spotless bedrooms are comfortable, with firm beds. It's a 10-minute walk to the town centre, a little longer on the return as it is uphill all the way. Everything is cooked fresh daily: home-made desserts, soups and breads; evening meals are served. Eithne is a friendly lady; a cup of tea with home-baking is offered upon arrival. Mr Wright has a good sense of humour, is very knowledgeable about the area and enjoys planning itineraries for guests. No pets.

OWNER Mrs Eithne Wright   OPEN 1 June–1 September
ROOMS 2 double, 1 twin (1 en suite)   TERMS B&B IR£12.50-
£14.50 p.p., reductions for children; single supplement IR£5.00;
evening meal IR£15.00

Lissadell House

Ashtown, Wicklow, Co Wicklow
Tel: (0404) 67458

A modern house built in the Georgian style, Lissadell is surrounded by its own grounds in a quiet, peaceful spot on the outskirts of Wicklow. The Klaues used to live just down the road and built this house for themselves in 1982. They are a most friendly couple and the house has a welcoming, homely atmosphere. The rooms are plainly decorated and furnished, and there is a simple sitting-room and dining-room where home-cooked meals are served. No smoking in the bedrooms and pets outside only. The house is signposted off the Wexford to Wicklow road.

OWNER Mrs Patricia Klaue   OPEN 1 March–1 December
ROOMS 4 family (2 en suite)   TERMS B&B IR from £14.00-£16.00 p.p.; reductions for children; single supplement IR £4.00; evening meal IR £14.00

Silver Sands

Dunbur Road, Wicklow, Co Wicklow
Tel: (0404) 68243

A modern, friendly bungalow which has a reputation of possibly being one of the warmest houses in Ireland, in both temperature and welcome. The bungalow has magnificent views of the Sugar Loaf Mountains and the sea. The spacious bedrooms are tastefully decorated, with TVS and hairdryers and there are 3 en suite rooms on the ground floor. Guests share the family lounge. Mr and Mrs Doyle are a down-to-earth, friendly couple, always willing to help plan outings to local events and places of interest. Breakfasts and evening meals are served in the bright dining-room overlooking the sea. Home-cooking includes traditional Irish recipes and home-made breads and desserts. Baby-sitting is available. Electric blankets on all beds. No smoking in the dining-room. No pets. Drive through Wicklow town, take the Coast road; Silver Sands is on the right, 500 yards from the monument.

OWNER Mrs Lyla Doyle   OPEN All year   ROOMS 4 double, 1 twin (3 en suite)   TERMS B&B IR £13.00 - £15.50 p.p.; reductions for children; single supplement IR £6.00; evening meal IR £13.00

The Old Rectory

Wicklow, Co Wicklow
Tel: (0404) 67048, Fax: (0404) 69181

The Old Rectory, a delightfully quiet country house set in an acre of landscaped grounds, is early Victorian in architectural style, lovingly restored by the present owners. The house is warm and elegant with period furniture, pretty furnishings, lovely plasterwork and log fires. Delightful touches, such as beribboned original paintings and bowls of pot-pourri are everywhere and the standard of housekeeping is excellent. The bedrooms all have TVs, telephones and hairdryers, and a tea and coffee tray accompanied by a daily newspaper is provided. Meals are served in the newly refurbished dining-room, which is in the style of a Victorian orangery. Linda's cooking blends old-fashioned taste with fresh simplicity, featuring seafood, organically grown vegetables, interesting salads and home-made desserts. Vegetarians are catered for. Golf, walking and garden-visiting holidays are offered, and house parties can be taken by arrangement. Reservations are essential. Wine licence. No smoking in the restaurant. No pets. The house can be found on the N11, 1 mile (1¹/2 km) on the Dublin side of town. All major credit cards accepted.

OWNER Paul and Linda Saunders   OPEN Easter–mid October
ROOMS 3 double, 2 twin, (all en suite)   TERMS B&B IR £41.00 p.p.; reductions for children; single supplement IR £20.00; evening meal IR £25.00

The South and South West

County Cork

Ireland's largest county is like a miniature of the whole country in terms of its history and scenery. It has a spectacular coastline alternating between long sandy beaches and wild, rugged cliffs, high rocky mountains, corn-covered farmland and sub-tropical gardens.

Cork is a bustling, cosmopolitan, friendly city founded by St Finbar in the sixth century on some dry land in the Great Marsh of Munster – Cork meaning "a marsh". The appearance of much of the city is nineteenth century, with elegant wide streets. Because of its watery origins Cork is still a city of bridges. The city expanded uphill, on the north side of which is the Tower of Shandon, with its two faces and famous chime of bells. St Finbar's Cathedral is built on the site of Finbar's monastery, its French Gothic spires dominating the city.

The famous Blarney stone – kissing it gives you the gift of the gab – is at the castle, in the small village of Blarney, one of the largest and finest tower houses in Ireland.

Nineteenth-century Cobh, with its Gothic cathedral, is Cork's harbour, some 15 miles from the city. Beyond, travelling west along the coast, is Kinsale, popular with yachtsmen, an attractive old town packed with people enjoying its many restaurants and old buildings. There are marvellous cliffs at the Old Head of Kinsale and the remains of a fifteenth-century castle, and a lovely sandy beach at Garrettstown.

Youghal, which is a most attractive seaside town and has many interesting things to see, including the Clock Gate and St Mary's Collegiate Church, is known for its association with the potato. Sir Walter Raleigh is said to have planted the first potato in his garden during the time he was mayor of the town. Nearby is Shanagarry with its pottery, where William Penn lived, and Ballycotton, a small fishing village.

The coastal scenery west of Skibbereen is particularly beautiful and the view from Gabriel Mountain, which can easily be climbed, is spectacular. Garinish Island has a wonderful garden, which can be visited most days. Bantry House at Bantry is a most interesting house to visit and has a superb view; and Castle Hyde, a Georgian house close to Fermoy and former home of Douglas Hyde, first president of the Irish Republic, is one of the most beautiful houses in Ireland. Macroom is set in glorious countryside, particularly beautiful being the road across the pass of Keimaneigh and through the forest of Gougane Barra.

BANDON

Glebe Country House

Ballinadee, Bandon, near Kinsale, Co Cork

Tel: (021) 778294

This small, elegant Georgian rectory is in the centre of
Ballinadee next to the church. Gill and Tim Bracken bought
the house about 3 years ago and converted the basement for
themselves and their 2 small children. Guests have the run
of the rest of the house, which includes an attractive dining-
room with one large table for breakfast and smaller,
individual tables for evening meals. Good home-cooked
meals feature home-grown vegetables and an interesting
wine selection. The family rooms are particularly large and
all 3 contain telephones, tea- and coffee-making facilities,
hairdryers and bathrobes. The charming small library leads
into the very attractive garden, beyond which there are 2
self-catering apartments converted from old coach houses.
Visa and Access cards accepted.

OWNER Tim and Gill Bracken   OPEN All year, except Christmas
ROOMS 1 double, 2 family (all en suite)   TERMS B&B IR £20.00-
£25.00 p.p.; reductions for children; evening meal IR £16.50

BANTRY

Ard na Greine

Newtown, near Bantry, Co Cork

Tel: (027) 51169

A country house owned by Mrs Phyllis Foley, who is always
happy to advise guests on what to see and do. Complimen-
tary tea and refreshments are offered upon arrival. The
house is set in mature grounds, with panoramic views of the
countryside. This is a peaceful and restful location and an
ideal base for touring West Cork and south Kerry. Mrs
Foley is a keen golfer and is willing to prearrange golfing
holidays for guests. Evening meals, which must be arranged,
are tasty, with the emphasis on old-fashioned home-style
cooking. No pets. The house is located 300 metres from the
N71, 1 mile (1 1/2 km) from Bantry.

OWNER Mrs Phyllis Foley   OPEN 1 April–1 October
ROOMS 2 double, 1 twin, 1 family   TERMS B&B IR£13.00 p.p.;
reductions for children; single supplement IR£5.00; evening meal
IR£11.00, high tea IR £8.00

37

Ballylickey Manor House

Ballylickey, Bantry Bay, Co Cork
Tel: (027) 50071, Fax: (027) 50124

On the boundary of Cork and Kerry, amidst sheltered lawns, flower gardens and parkland and bordered by sea, river and mountains, stands Ballylickey House, commanding a magnificent view over Bantry Bay. Built some 300 years ago by Lord Kenmare as a shooting lodge, Ballylickey has been the home of the Graves family for over 4 generations. This elegant residence is beautifully furnished, with many antiques, luxurious bedrooms, all with TV, phone, hairdryer and trouser press. Five suites include bedroom, drawing-room and bathroom. Eight of the rooms are in the manor house, and there are 4 delightful garden cottages around the swimming pool and gardens (pool open summer only). Fully licenced. There are 2 golf courses nearby and miles of mountainous coastline. Visa and Mastercard accepted.

OWNERS Mr and Mrs Graves OPEN 1 April–1 November
ROOMS 5 suites, 6 twin (all en suite) TERMS B&B IR £42.50-£47.25 p.p., suites IR £55.00-£75.00 p.p. plus 10% service charge; evening meal IR £26.00-£30.00

Bantry House

Bantry, Co Cork
Tel: (027) 50047, Fax: (027) 50785

Bantry House, overlooking Bantry Bay, is one of the finest stately mansions in Ireland. Purchased by the White family in 1739, it is furnished with the most wonderful collection of

pictures, furniture and works of art. The White family were also responsible for laying out the formal gardens. Both east and west wings of Bantry House provide newly refurbished accommodation, all with direct dial telephones. Facilities for residents include a sitting-room, billiard room and a balcony TV room overlooking the Italian garden with its fountain, parterres and "stairway to the sky". There is a wine licence and guests are welcome to help themselves to drinks from the bar. Bantry House is open to the public and residents are admitted at no extra charge. There is also a tea room and craft shop on the premises. Evening meals are sometimes available and must be booked by noon. No pets.Visa, Access and American Express cards accepted.

OWNERS Mr and Mrs Egerton Shellswell-White   OPEN All year
ROOMS 5 double, 3 twin (all en suite)   TERMS B&B IR £45.00-£50.00 p.p.; reductions for children; single supplement IR £10.00; evening meal IR £20.00

Dunauley

Seskin, Bantry, Co Cork
Tel: (027) 50290

A country house in an elevated position with magnificent views of Bantry Bay and the Caha Mountains – absolutely worth the mile drive from Bantry itself. The dining-room cum lounge is spacious and overlooks the panoramic view, as do 2 of the bedrooms. There are 4 bedrooms on the ground floor and they are simply furnished and comfortable. Breakfast is a feast, including freshly squeezed orange juice and drop scones. Dunauley was the national winner in 1990 of the Galtee Breakfast award. There is also a self-catering unit with its own entrance available. No smoking in the dining-room/lounge. Follow hospital signs upon arriving in Bantry until you see Dunauley signposted.

OWNER Rosemary McAuley   OPEN 1 May–1 September
ROOMS 2 double, 2 twin, 1 family (2 en suite)   TERMS B&B IR£15.00–£18.00 p.p.; reductions for children

Grove House

Ahakista, Durrus, near Bantry, Co Cork
Tel: (027) 67060

A 250-year-old white-washed stone farmhouse set amidst beautiful scenery on Sheep's Head Peninsula. An idyllic setting, perfect for nature lovers, with beautiful walks, bird watching, private beach for swimming or boating (a boat is provided) and, with advance notice, bicycle hire can also be arranged. There is a huge old log fireplace, and the dining-room has been extended to include a conservatory with a stone floor where visitors can enjoy the lovely view. Down-to-earth Mary O'Mahoney is a good cook, using home-grown vegetables from the garden, and when the fishing is good, fresh seafood. Light meals, as well as evening meals, can be provided upon request. Honey from the hives, soda scones and home-baked breads are all on the menu here. No smoking in the dining-room and no pets. Signposted from Durrus village.

OWNER Mrs Mary O'Mahoney   OPEN 1 May–1 September
ROOMS 2 double, 1 twin, 1 single, 1 family (1 en suite)
TERMS B&B IR £13.50-£16.00 p.p.; reductions for children; single supplement IR £4.00; evening meal IR £12.00

Hillcrest House

Ahakista, Durrus, Bantry, Co Cork
Tel: (027) 67045

Situated on the Sheep's Head Peninsula 7¹/2 miles (11 km) from Durrus, Hillcrest stands in a lovely position on top of a hill with wonderful views over the coast. Mrs Hegarty has run a bed and breakfast for years, most recently in the bungalow they used to live in on the farm. Hillcrest is an attractive old stone dairy farm which was renovated a few years ago. An extension has been built onto the house, linking it with the old barn, which now houses the large games room. There are flagstone floors, peat fires and quite spacious rooms, simply furnished and decorated. Mrs Hegarty is the recipient of the 1991 AIB Agri-Tourism award and the BHS 1991 regional award, and her daughter plays traditional Irish music on the tin whistle and accordion. Hillcrest is a 5-minute walk to a sandy beach; there is good sea fishing and mountain walking behind the house. Pets can be kept outside. Visa and Access cards accepted.

OWNER Mrs Agnes Hegarty   OPEN 1 April –1 November
ROOMS 2 double, 2 family (3 en suite)   TERMS B&B IR £13.50-£15.50 p.p., single IR £16.50; reductions for children; evening meal IR £11.50, high tea IR £8.50

Larchwood House Restaurant

Pearson's Bridge, Bantry, Co Cork

Tel: (027) 66181

The Vaughans built Larchwood House as their home 14 years ago. Two years ago Sheila decided to start a restaurant, and they began to build onto the house. The property runs down to the River Ouvane and enjoys splendid views of the Caha Mountains. The small restaurant seats about 20 people and is open to non-residents. There is a sitting-room outside the restaurant and the bedrooms are pleasant and good sized, 2 with their own entrances. Bedrooms have TVS and hairdryers. There is a wine licence and pets can be kept outside. Located about 3 miles (4½ km) from Bantry off the N71; signposted at Ballylickey. Visa, Access and Diners Club accepted.

OWNER Sheila Vaughan OPEN Easter–Christmas
ROOMS 1 double, 1 twin, 2 family (all en suite) TERMS B&B from IR£18.00 p.p.; reductions for children; evening meal à la carte

The Mill

Newtown, Bantry, Co Cork

Tel: (027) 50278

Ten years ago Mr and Mrs Kramer came to Bantry for a holiday and fell in love with the area. Returning to Holland, they sold their farm and have since made Ireland their home. The Mill is a chalet-style house, set back from the road in beautiful, landscaped gardens. The house has been totally refurbished; the delightful bedrooms have wicker and pine furnishings. Mr Kramer, a true craftsman, has made all the wardrobes, cabinets and dining-room tables. Most rooms are on the ground floor, and now all except one have en suite bathrooms. Evening meals are available if booked in advance, and there are plenty of excellent pubs and restaurants in the area. Close by there is golf, fishing, horse-riding and bicycles for hire. Laundry services available.

OWNER Tosca Kramer OPEN 1 April–1 October
ROOMS 2 double, 2 twin, 3 family (6 en suite) TERMS B&B IR £12.00 - £14.50 p.p.; reductions for children; single supplement IR £2.00; evening meal IR £12.00

Ashlee Lodge

Tower, Blarney, Co Cork
Tel: (021) 385346

The Callaghans built this immaculately kept house 11 years ago. Whitewashed and with a porticoed front porch, the house is 2¹/₂ miles (4 km) from Blarney on the Killarney side. There is a large open-plan sitting-room/dining-room with cathedral ceilings and fireplace, off of which is a pleasant little patio. Furnished with reproduction furniture, the house has been interestingly decorated. No pets.

OWNERS The Callaghan family   OPEN 1 April –1 November
ROOMS 2 twin, 3 family (3 en suite)   TERMS B&B IR £12.50-
£14.50 p.p., single rate extra charge; no reductions for children

Rosemount House

The Square, Blarney, Co Cork
Tel: (021) 385584

An ideal location for Blarney. Parking is usually difficult, particularly during high season, but Rosemount House offers private parking and is a 5-minute stroll to the castle. Mr Cronin completely renovated the house for resale, but after the work was finished Mr and Mrs Cronin decided to keep the house and start a bed-and-breakfast business. They have never regretted their decision. Mrs Cronin thoroughly enjoys her business, as do her guests, as evidenced by the many who return. The house is warm, the rooms clean and comfortable, each with their own telephone. There is a TV and video in the comfortable guest lounge. There is one en suite ground-floor room. No pets. The house can be found opposite the woollen mills.

OWNER Mrs Margaret Cronin   OPEN 1 March–1 October
ROOMS 2 double, 2 twin, 1 family (3 en suite)   TERMS B&B IR
£13.00 - £14.50 p.p.; reductions for children; single supplement
IR £5.00

Traveller's Joy

Tower, Blarney, Co Cork
Tel: (021) 385541

One of the nicest things about Traveller's Joy is Gertie

O'Shea, a warm, friendly lady who offers a home-from-home welcome. The bungalow is 2¹/2 miles (4 km) from Blarney, in a quiet location, set in an award-winning ³/4 acre garden with mature shrubs, colourful flowers and a fish pond. The rooms are large, basic and spotlessly clean. The family room is ideal, as there is a small room adjoining. The O'Sheas are happy to offer advice on local sightseeing and where to find the best Irish entertainment. There is a cosy guest lounge with TV. Evening meals are to be booked in advance. No smoking in the dining-room. Approximately 7 miles (10¹/2 km) from Cork on the R617.

OWNERS Sean and Gertie O'Shea   OPEN 1 April–1 November
ROOMS 1 double/ twin/ family   TERMS B&B IR £12.50-£14.50 p.p.; reductions for children; single supplement IR £5.00; evening meal IR £11.00, high tea IR £8.00

The White House

Blarney, Co Cork
Tel: (021) 385338

Owned by a most friendly couple who were in the hotel business for 15 years, the White House was purpose built by the Coughlans 6 years ago. It is an attractive whitewashed house, standing just above the road from Cork on the edge of Blarney, with views of the castle. The rooms are well decorated and attractive, with the dining-room at the back of the house overlooking a small garden with patio and fields. No pets.

OWNER Mr and Mrs Coughlan   OPEN All year, except mid December–mid January   ROOMS 2 double/twin/ family (4 en suite)   TERMS B&B IR £12.00-£14.00 p.p., single IR £17.00; reductions for children

Yvory House

Killowen, Blarney, Co Cork
(021) 381128

Yvory House is an attractive 3-year-old house, 1¹/2 miles (2¹/2 km) from Blarney, in a peaceful and pretty setting. The owner, Veronica Annis-Sisk, was persuaded to take in a few guests during a particularly busy time, reluctantly agreeing. However, she enjoyed the experience so much, meeting such interesting people, that she decided she had a great location in which to start her own business. The house is well appointed; all bedrooms are on the ground floor and are equippped with hairdryers. The guest lounge is most attractive; the marble fireplace was handmade from an Italian marble slab. There is an 18-hole golf course within 3 miles (4½ km) and a riding school 600 yards away. A pleasant 10-minute stroll to the town centre, longer on the way back as it is uphill. No pets.

OWNER Mrs Veronica Annis-Sisk   OPEN 1 April–1 October
ROOMS 3 double, 1 twin (4 en suite)   TERMS B&B IR£12.00–£14.00 p.p.; reductions for children; single supplement IR£16.00

BUTLERSTOWN

Sea Court

Atlantic View, Butlerstown, Co Cork
Tel: (023) 40151/40218

David Elder is an American. He visited Ireland several times, falling in love with the land of his ancestors, and he wanted to establish roots here, so 9 years ago he bought an old Georgian mansion. It dates from 1760 and stands in 10 acres of wooded grounds on the Seven Heads Peninsula. The house, which has been listed, was in a very rundown condition and the garden was completely overgrown. David Elder has taken on the challenge of restoration, adding modern comforts as financing permits, yet carefully preserving the character of the house. Most of the rooms have the original shutters, the bedrooms are spacious, furnished with antiques. Four rooms have sea views. David loves to cook, and breakfasts are sumptuous; they include his own scone recipe. Evening meals are available if booked by noon. The house is available for self-catering from the end of August through May.

OWNER David Elder   OPEN 10 June–20 August   ROOMS 3 double, 1 twin, 1 family (5 en suite)   TERMS B&B IR £18.50 p.p.; reductions for children; single supplement IR £13.50

CASTLELYONS

Ballyvolane House

Castlelyons, Co Cork
Tel: (025) 36349

Ballyvolane is a country house in a lovely setting, surrounded by its own farmland, wooded grounds and formal, well-maintained gardens. It was built in 1728 on the site of an older house and altered later to the Italianate style. When the Greens bought the house some 30 years ago, there was a lot of work to be done, and their own sitting-room/kitchen is still the old drawing-room. Guests have a choice of 5 comfortable en suite rooms, and there is one on the ground floor suitable for wheelchairs. The house has been elegantly furnished and decorated and there is both a drawing-room and large sitting area and piano in the hall. Evening meals are provided by arrangement, sometimes also for non-residents, and served either at the large dining-room table or at smaller tables for those who prefer eating on their own. One of the bathrooms contains a wonderful old bathtub, encased in wood and raised on 2 steps. Vegetables come from the garden. There is a croquet lawn and lovely walks; salmon fishing is also available. There is a wine licence and French is spoken. The house is signposted from Castlelyons. Visa and Access cards accepted.

OWNERS Merry and Jeremy Green   OPEN All year
ROOMS 3 double, 4 twin (all en suite)   TERMS B&B IR £33.00-£44.00 p.p.; single supplement IR £8.00; evening meal IR £20.00

CASTLEMARTYR

Swan Lake

Caherultan, Castlemartyr, Co Cork

Tel: (021) 667261

Bordering on the banks of Lough a Derra and surrounded by forestry, Swan Lake is highly recommended for its warm welcome and hospitality. The rooms are average in size, but are clean and functional. There is a cosy sitting-room with a TV, and hot drinks are provided upon request. Mrs Harty has a good sense of humour and enjoys chatting to guests and offering advice on local sightseeing. Weekly or day permits are available for fishing on the lake. There are lovely woodland walks and sandy beaches close by. Situated halfway between Youghal and Cork, signposted off the N25.

OWNER Mrs Margaret Harty   OPEN mid March–mid November
ROOMS 2 double, 1 twin (2 en suite)   TERMS B&B IR £13.00 p.p.; reductions for children; no single supplement; evening meal IR £12.00

Ard na Greine

Ballinascarthy, Clonakilty, Co Cork
Tel: (023) 39104

Reached down narrow lanes, Ard na Greine is a compact, square house standing in an elevated position with fine rural views. The comfortable bedrooms are on the small side, most with shower rooms, and there is a small sitting-room and dining-room. Mrs Walsh has won many awards, including the Galtee Irish Breakfast award in 1989/90 and the Agri-Tourism award in 1990. Signposted off the N71 Bandon to Clonakilty road. Visa accepted.

OWNER Norma Walsh OPEN All year ROOMS 4 double, 2 family (2 en suite) TERMS B&B IR £14.00-£16.00 p.p.; reductions for children; evening meal IR £14.00

Norday House

off Western Road, Clonakilty, Co Cork
Tel: (023) 33655

A secluded, cosy family home on ³/4 acre, set in a lovely garden bordered by trees. Colourful flowers abound in the pretty window boxes and hanging baskets. The whole house has recently been redecorated with new furnishings, and 2 extra rooms have been added to the back of the house. These 2 rooms cater particularly for families, one with a well-equipped kitchenette and the other with 2 bedrooms and 2 bathrooms. There is a comfortable guests' lounge, and the dining-room, serving excellent meals and featuring home-baked breads and fresh vegetables, faces the pretty garden. High tea must be ordered in advance. Horseback-riding can be arranged locally, and there are some lovely walks close by. Mrs McMahon has been in business for just over 10 years and is concerned that her guests are comfortable. Many visitors return on a regular basis for her special brand of hospitality. There is a sun-lounge for guests' use. The house can be found about 70 metres off the N71, and it is just a 2-minute walk from the town centre, where restaurants, a pub and a church can be found.

OWNER David and Noreen McMahon OPEN All year, except Christmas ROOMS 2 double/twin/family (4 en suite) TERMS B&B IR £12.50-£14.50 p.p.; reductions for children; single supplement IR £4.00; high tea IR £9.00

Youghals House

Inchydoney Road, Clonakilty, Co Cork
Tel: (023) 33349

Once the residence of the local bishop, this comfortable
Georgian house is set in extensive wooded grounds, with
lots of pretty shrubs and flowers, close to the sea. Mrs
Harrington, a kindly lady, has been running her business for
12 years. She loves meeting people, is from the area and is
always prepared to assist guests with information. The
spacious drawing-room has the original carved wall mirror
and window shutters. The front bedrooms overlook the
gardens. There is an antique grandfather clock in the hallway. Breakfasts are served family-style and include Mrs
Harrington's delicious home-made breads and scones.
Evening meals are available if booked in advance, and
vegetarian dishes can be provided. Mrs Harrington likes to
welcome her guests with afternoon tea in the drawing-room
or on fine days in the garden. No smoking in the dining-
room and no pets. The house is located 1 mile (1½ km)
from Youghal and is signposted at the roundabout on the
eastern side of town.

OWNER Mrs Frances Harrington OPEN mid March–1 September
ROOMS 1 double, 2 twin TERMS B&B IR £12.00 p.p.; reductions
for children

CORK

Lotamore House

Tivoli, Cork, Co Cork
Tel: (021) 822344, Fax: (021) 822219

Lotamore House, an impressive Georgian manor, is set in
extensive grounds with magnificent views of Blackrock
Castle and Harbour. The house retains the atmosphere and
furnishings of an elegant home, with window shutters, a
beautiful oval ceiling rose and decorations. There are several
antiques of interest, including a gold-leaf marble hatstand.
The well-appointed bedrooms, all with TVs and telephones,
are colour-coordinated, 5 of which are on the ground floor,
one large enough for wheelchair access. The spacious
drawing-room has a marble fireplace; a most enjoyable place
to relax in after a busy day. Light snacks are also available.
Lotamore House is a very popular place with business
people and tourists, so early reservations are recommended.

Situated in a peaceful spot just off the dual carriageway in the direction of Dublin and Waterford, 4 minutes' drive to the city centre. Visa and American Express cards accepted.

OWNER Mrs Harty   OPEN All year   ROOMS 12 double, 8 twin, 1 single, 1 family (all en suite)   TERMS B&B IR £22.00-£25.00 p.p.; reductions for children

COURTMACSHERRY

Travara Lodge

Courtmacsherry, Co Cork
Tel: (023) 46493

Travara Lodge is a Georgian residence nestling in the sheltered foothills of Courtmacsherry and overlooking its magnificent bay. The house was named after the intrepid men of Travara who manned one of the first lifeboats out of Courtmacsherry in 1825. Mandy Guy is a hard-working entrepreneur who follows her dream. Recognising its potential, she purchased the house in a very dilapidated condition, and extensive restoration was undertaken. The main house is now restored, and the latest plans are to convert some of the outbuildings into 3 en suite rooms. Mandy studied at the Alex Gardiner Cordon Bleu School in Dublin and has quickly built up an enviable reputation for excellent, imaginative evening meals. The restaurant specialises mainly in local seafood, and vegetarian and special diets are catered for. Off season, evening meals require advance notice. An ideal location for bird-watching, golf, riding, cycling, deep-sea angling, beaches and watersports. There are bicycles for hire and drying-room facilities. Travara Lodge can be found in the village of Courtmacsherry. Visa and Access cards accepted.

OWNER Mandy Guy   OPEN Easter–1 November   ROOMS 2 double, 4 twin, 1 family (5 en suite)   TERMS B&B IR £13.50-£16.50 p.p.; reductions for children; evening meal IR £14.00, packed lunch IR £2.50

DOUGLAS

Riverview

Douglas Village, Cork, Co Cork
Tel: (021) 893762

Riverview is a Georgian-style house built in the Victorian era

48

in Douglas village. It is located near the police station on the
number 7 bus route, 2 miles (3 km) from Cork. The rooms
are all a good size, with modern furnishings, comfortable
beds and TVS. There is a warm, civilised atmosphere, and
Mr and Mrs Edwards are a charming couple, offering guests
personal service. The lounge-cum-dining-room has the
original fireplace and an antique chaise-longue. There is one
ground-floor room. Breakfast only is available, but there are
lots of good pubs and restaurants close by. No pets.

OWNER Mrs Catherine Edwards   OPEN All year, except Christmas
ROOMS 1 double/twin/family (3 en suite)   TERMS B&B IR £15.00
p.p.; reductions for children; single supplement IR £5.00

KILLEAGH

Ballymakeigh House

Killeagh, Co Cork

Tel: (024) 95184

This is a truly delightful place. Ballymakeigh House is a
charming 250-year-old farmhouse located in the rich
farmlands of East Cork. An intensive dairy farm, guests are
welcome to walk around the farm, observe cows being
milked, or relax with a book in the sunny conservatory.
There is a hard tennis court (coaching available on request),
and a games room with snooker and table tennis. Michael
and Margaret Browne are gracious hosts and are proud of
their Agri-Tourism award in 1987. Margaret also received
the Housewife of the Year award. Furnishings include
marble tables, wrought-iron chairs and log fireplaces. The
public rooms and bedrooms have recently been redecorated
and upgraded, with all bedrooms now en suite and containing their own hairdryers. The kitchen has been extended
and an extra room added, and the gardens are taking shape.
Excellent evening meals are served, featuring fresh vegetables, herbs and fruit from the garden, and fresh cream and
milk from the farm. Vegetarian and special diets catered for.
There is a wine licence. A marvellous spot in peaceful and
tranquil surroundings, convenient to beaches, Fota Wildlife
Park, Trabolgan Leisure Centre and Blarney Castle. No
smoking in the dining-room and pets outside only.

OWNER Mrs Margaret Browne   OPEN 1 February–1 November,
Christmas by arrangement   ROOMS 6 family (all en suite)
TERMS B&B IR £18.00–£20.00 p.p.; reductions for children; single
supplement in July and August IR £4.00; evening meal IR £16.00

Hilltop

Sleaveen Heights, Kinsale, Co Cork
Tel: (021) 772612

An attractive and immaculate modern bungalow on a quiet
residential street overlooking the harbour. The front bedroom with the view is the most sought after, and the en suite
facilities are cleverly concealed behind louvred doors. Mrs
McCarthy was in the baking and catering trade for many
years prior to starting the bed-and-breakfast business, and,
as a result, guests here enjoy the best in home-made breads,
etc. Breakfasts are served in the bright, sunny dining-room
overlooking the harbour. There is a sunny patio and a cosy
lounge where guests congregate after a busy day of
sightseeing, and tea and coffee are served all day on request.
Just a pleasant 5-minute walk to the town centre, with lots
of good eating places.

OWNERS Michael and Maura McCarthy   OPEN All year
ROOMS 4 double, 2 family (all en suite)   TERMS B&B IR £15.00
p.p.; reductions for children; single supplement IR £17.00

Murphy's Farmhouse

Kinsale, Co Cork
Tel: (021) 772229

If you are looking for farmhouse accommodation in Kinsale,
Murphy's farm is the only one in the area, a turn-of-the-
century house situated on 80 acres of mixed farming.
Kinsale is half a mile away. The house has been in the

family for 3 generations. Mrs Murphy and her daughter run the B&B and her son takes care of the farm. The family have their own private quarters close by, and guests have the run of the house. The one non en suite bedroom has its own private bathroom one floor down. The house is warm and inviting, decorated to a high standard with pretty wall-papers. The lounge has the original fireplace, and there are 2 antique jugs and 2 firescreens. Tasty breakfasts are served in the dining-room, which has freshly polished wooden floors. No smoking in the bedrooms. Not suitable for children; a peaceful retreat for adults.

OWNER Mrs Eileen Murphy   OPEN 1 April–1 October
ROOMS 3 double, 1 twin (3 en suite)   TERMS B&B IR £14.00 p.p.; single supplement IR £4.00

MACROOM

Findus House

Ballyvoige, Kilnamartyra, Macroom, Co Cork
Tel: (026) 40023

This poultry and dairy farm is approached down very narrow lanes in peaceful, lovely countryside. The house has been in the O'Sullivan family for some years and was built onto in 1981 to provide more accommodation. The lounge/dining-room is a long, narrow room with windows all around to take advantage of the extensive views. Findus House was awarded the regional Farmhouse of the Year award in 1989. There are 2 ponies to ride, entertainment and singing in local pubs, and the geologically interesting area of the Gearagh is nearby – an ancient forest system on an alluvial plain with an intricate tangle of narrow channels. No smoking in the dining-room. Visa, American Express and Access cards accepted.

OWNERS   The O'Sullivan family   OPEN 1 April–1 October
ROOMS   2 double, 1 twin, 3 family (4 en suite)
TERMS B&B IR £12.50-£14.00 p.p.; reductions for children; evening meal IR £13.00

SHANAGARRY

Ballymaloe House

Shanagarry, Co Cork
Tel: (021) 652531, Fax: (021) 652021

Ballymaloe House is part of an old Geraldine Castle which

has been rebuilt and modernised throughout the centuries, the fourteenth-century keep remaining in its original form. It is situated in the middle of a 400-acre farm, owned and run by the Allen family. Thirteen of the 29 bedrooms are in the main house; they vary in size and character as dictated by the old buildings. Five new large rooms lie on the north side, opening onto a lawn and stream. Eleven rooms surround the old coachyard beside the main house. Four of these are on the ground floor and have been designed to take wheelchairs. All rooms have telephones and hairdryers. Full of character, history and charm, Ballymaloe is a place in which to recover from the stresses of life. Evening meals are a formal affair. The food is always chosen for its quality; vegetables and salads are picked fresh that day. Lunch is also served, and there is a children's menu available. There is an extensive wine list, and Ballymaloe has a full licence. Restricted smoking in the dining-room and no pets. An excellent craft and kitchenware shop lies on the premises, and the Ballymaloe Cookery School is nearby. Visa and Access cards accepted.

OWNERS Myrtle and Ivan Allen OPEN All year, except Christmas ROOMS 15 double, 13 twin, 1 single (all en suite) TERMS B&B IR £50.00-£56.00 p.p.; single supplement IR £20.00; evening meal IR £31.00, lunch IR £16.00

SKIBBEREEN

Bow Hall

Castletownsend, Skibbereen, Co Cork

Tel: (028) 36114

Dating from the late seventeenth century, Bow Hall is right in the centre of the charming village of Castletownsend, its one steep street leading to the harbour and sea. The Vickerys are a delightful retired couple from New York state who have lived here for 15 years and have created a charming home. The bedrooms are light and spacious with some American furniture. Good home-cooked evening meals are served in the dining-room and the large drawingroom cum library has floor-to-ceiling bookshelves at one end with a fireplace at the other; all kinds of ornaments and knick knacks are found throughout the house. The slate-faced front of the house overlooks a very large and immaculately kept walled garden. Smoking only in the drawing-room. No pets.

OWNERS Mrs R Vickery OPEN All year ROOMS 1 double, 2 family (2 en suite) TERMS B&B IR £25.00-£28.00 p.p.; reductions for children; evening meal (including cost of B&B) IR £43.00

Whispering Trees

Baltimore Road, Skibbereen, Co Cork
Tel: (028) 21376

A comfortable, modern, detached house set back off the main road on the edge of town. The bedrooms are clean and comfortable and are furnished in a modern style with fitted wardrobes, all with hairdryers and tea- and coffee-making facilities. All rooms are now en suite. The TV lounge, which has a piano, is spacious and comfortable with fires lit on chilly days. Mrs O'Sullivan has been in business for over 6 years and is happy to assist guests with itineraries for local sightseeing. She is assisted by her daughter during the summer holidays. Whispering Trees is a good base for touring, and amenities include golf, fishing, sailing and walking. Breakfasts include home-baked bread and scones. No smoking in the dining-room. No pets. Visa and Access cards accepted.

OWNERS Michael and Kay O'Sullivan OPEN Easter–1 October ROOMS 3 double, 2 twin (all en suite) TERMS B&B IR £15.00 p.p.; reductions for children; single supplement IR £3.00

YOUGHAL

Mount Carmel

Ballyvergan, Killeagh Road, Youghal, Co Cork
Tel: (024) 92542

A pretty 100-year-old cottage with black-and-white shutters, set in 1½ acres of beautiful secluded gardens with a mani-cured lawn, 2 miles (3 km) from Youghal on the N25. The rooms are freshly decorated, clean and comfortable, and there are now 3 rooms en suite. They are a little on the small side, but this is more than compensated for by the five-star welcome and wonderfully friendly atmosphere created by Mr and Mrs Lynch. Mr Lynch is a talented gentleman who enjoys participating in the musical evenings that often happen on an impromptu basis in the evenings. Guests are encouraged to treat the house as their own home, and although they may arrive as guests they all leave as friends. The owners have been doing B&B for 25 years, with many repeat guests, so early reservations are highly recommended. No smoking in the dining-room and no pets.

OWNER Mrs Mary Lynch   OPEN 1 April–1 October
ROOMS 1 double, 1 twin, 2 single, 1 family (3 en suite)
TERMS B&B IR £13.00 p.p.; reductions for children; single supplement IR £3.00

County Kerry

Every tourist wants to visit Kerry to see for themselves the beauty of the landscape. The sea surrounds most of the county and it is the mixture of water and light which makes Kerry such a special place. There is an inconsistency in the weather – wind and rain from the Atlantic, misty drizzle or bright light and sunshine – making each day or part of a day different from the next and projecting a constantly changing pattern over the mountains, lakes and streams. Each type of weather brings its own peculiar beauty to the landscape.

The Killarney area is the most famous of Irish places of beauty. The town caters for large numbers of tourists and is full of hotels, yet the lakes, mountains and woods of the surrounding countryside remain unspoiled. Close to Killarney is the ruined fourteenth-century Ross Castle. From here one can hire a boat to Inisfallen Island and visit the ruins of the twelfth-century Augustinian Inisfallen Abbey. Muckross House is now a folk museum and has a most beautiful garden. From the Gap of Dunloe there is a marvellous view of the Black Valley. This is where huge torrents of water poured through the Gap at the end of the Ice Age.

The Ring of Kerry is a famous scenic drive around the Iveragh Peninsula. Killorglin is known for its annual horse and cattle fair, Puck Fair, held for two days in August, a great event with pagan origins when a wild mountain goat is captured and enthroned in the centre of town. Waterville is the principal resort on the Ring of Kerry, and at Cahirciveen one can see the ruins of a magnificent police barracks, which were meant to have been built in the north-west frontier of India, but the plans got mixed up. At Ballinskelligs, which is an Irish-speaking area, there are the ruins of a monastery and a fine beach with wonderful views. The Skelligs is a rocky island off the extreme western part of the Ring of Kerry which can be visited. It is a wonderful place for birds, notably kittiwakes, guillemots, petrel, shearwater and fulmar, and one can also see the ruins of the old monastery which stands 183 metres above the landing place and is approached by long flights of stone steps. There are also beehive huts, stone crosses, the Holy Well, oratories and cemeteries to see. A beautiful, peaceful spot in fine weather, but terrifying in a storm.

The Dingle Peninsula is made up of mountains, cliffs, glacial valleys, lakes and beaches and west of Dingle the scenery is wild and beautiful. Some 2,000 prehistoric and early Christian remains have been discovered and a little of the old Gaelic culture can be observed at the tip of the peninsula. The little village of Ventry was the scene of a great legendary battle and at Fahan lies the greatest collection of antiquities in Ireland: stone beehive huts, cave dwellings, standing and inscribed stones and crosses, souterrains, forts, cahers and a church. There are spectacular views around Slea Head, especially of the Blasket Islands and scattered rocks, all part of an exploded volcanic area, and it was around here that the film *Ryan's Daughter* was made. Beyond Ballyferriter, a mostly Irish-speaking village that attempts to preserve its Gaelic culture, is Gallarus, the most perfect example of early Irish building and dry rubble masonry.

The principle town of Kerry is Tralee, a trading and industrial centre. At Ardfert the cathedral, which was built in 1250 and has the ruins of its Franciscan Friary, is the most striking building.

ANASCAUL

Four Winds

Anascaul, Co Kerry

Tel: (066) 57168

Mrs O'Connor started doing bed and breakfast 13 years ago when a friend asked if she could help out during a busy season. She enjoyed meeting people and sharing her house and has been offering accommodation ever since. There is a view of the Anascaul Mountains from the front of the house and a clear view of Dingle and Ross Bay from the rear. The rooms are simply furnished and clean. There is an antique chaise-longue in the hallway. Located approximately mid-way on the Dingle/Tralee walk, 3^1/$_2$ miles (5 km) away from Anascaul Lake and close to the 4 mile (6 km)-long sandy Inch Beach. Drying facilities available. No pets. Five minutes' stroll to the village.

OWNERS Kathleen and P J O'Connor   OPEN 1 March–31 October
ROOMS 2 double/twin (2 en suite)   TERMS B&B IR £12.50 p.p.;
10% reduction for children; single supplement IR £4.00

BALLYBUNION

The Country Haven

Car Ferry Road, Ballybunion, Co Kerry
Tel: (068) 27103

This superb Georgian-style house is ideally situated on the
L105 road, 2 miles (3 km) from the golf course and a 10-
minute drive from the Tarbert car ferry. Mrs Eileen Walsh is
a friendly lady with a good sense of humour. The house sits
on a 160-acre beef farm and there are 19 acres of young
forest and a 4-mile designated walk. The spacious bedrooms
are of a very high standard, tastefully decorated with every
comfort. Two bedrooms are not en suite but have their own
bathrooms. There is one ground-floor en suite bedroom
with a small conservatory. The elegant drawing-room has a
marble fireplace, a Killarney antique marble wood fireplace
and a beautiful crystal chandelier. Early breakfasts are
prepared for golfers, with home-made scones, breads,
preserves and marmalade. The house has antique furniture
throughout and most bedrooms have sea views. This is a no
smoking house. Guests will be extremely comfortable here
and have easy access to golf courses and scenic countryside.

OWNER Mrs Eileen Walsh   OPEN All year, except Christmas
ROOMS 1 double, 2 twin, 1 family (3 en suite)   TERMS B&B IR
£16.00–£17.00 p.p.; 50% reduction for children under 12; no
single supplement

The 19th Green

Golf Links Road, Ballybunion, Co Kerry
Tel: (068) 27592

An immaculate bungalow in a superb location overlooking
the golf course and a 2-minute walk to the first tee. The
bedrooms are furnished with rich wood, pretty pastel fabrics
and lace curtains. The sitting-room with TV is pleasantly
furnished and has a new blue-and-pink carpet. Breakfast is
plentiful and is available as early as 4 am. Owners Mr and
Mrs Beasley are a most accommodating couple who go out
of their way to ensure their guests have everything they
need. Tea or coffee is offered upon arrival at no extra

charge. Garden furniture is available for guests' use on nice days. Plans to make the bedrooms en suite should be well underway by 1993. Not suitable for children. A phone is available. No pets.

OWNER Mrs Mary Beaseley   OPEN 1 April–1·December
ROOMS 1 double, 2 twin, 1 family (1 en suite)   TERMS B&B IR £13.00-£15.00 p.p.; single supplement IR £6.00

CAHERDANIEL

Moran Farm

Bunavalla, Caherdaniel, Co Kerry
Tel: (0667) 5208

A modern bungalow with the most spectacular views in Ireland, overlooking Derrynane and the Atlantic, and just 5 minutes' walk down to the sea. There are 2 clean sandy beaches where guests can swim, hike, boat or just relax and enjoy the beautiful scenery. The house is basic, simply furnished and has a homely welcoming atmosphere. All rooms are on the ground floor. Moran Farm is a working farm of sheep and cows, 8 miles (12 km) from Waterville, signposted off the Ring of Kerry road (Waterville/Caherdaniel road). Simple home-cooked wholesome evening meals are available by prior arrangment. There is a separate guest lounge. Smoking in the sitting-room only.

OWNER Mrs Nancy Moran   OPEN All year, except Christmas
ROOMS 1 double/twin/family (all en suite)   TERMS B&B IR £13.50 p.p.; 40% reduction for children; single supplement IR £8.00; evening meal IR £12.00

The Old Forge

Rathfield, Caherdaniel, Co Kerry
Tel: (0667) 5140

The Old Forge, built in 1983, is surrounded by 30 acres of rugged land with panoramic views of the Caha Mountains and Kenmare Bay. The property extends down to the sea, where there is a rocky cove for swimming, windsurfing and fishing. A restaurant and coffee shop is now in operation, and the Old Forge has been restored to a museum. The Fitzmaurices share the work: Reg cooks breakfast and Cathy cooks the evening meal, served in the dining-room which overlooks the view, as does the comfortable lounge. The rooms are clean and simply furnished. There is a wine licence. Trips to the Skelligs and fishing excursions can be arranged. Situated off the Ring of Kerry in a remote spot, 10 miles (15 km) from Waterville. Visa, Access and Mastercard accepted.

OWNERS Reg and Catherine Fitzmaurice   OPEN All year, except Christmas   ROOMS 3 double/twin (4 en suite)
TERMS B&B IR £13.00-£25.00 p.p.; 20% reduction for children; single supplement IR £5.00; evening meal IR £12.00

CARAGH LAKE

Glendalough House

Caragh Lake, Co Kerry

Tel: (066) 69156, Fax: (066) 69156

Glendalough House is a charming residence, just a short distance from the shores of Caragh Lake, built 122 years ago. It is a warm country house with mature gardens and views of the lake and Ireland's highest mountain range, the McGillycuddy's Reeks. It is furnished with antiques and there are several old paintings. An ideal spot for those looking for peace and tranquillity, the house is approached by a long private gravel drive, bordered with trees, shrubs and wild flowers. There is a pretty garden inhabited by a colourful peacock and pea-hen. Candle-lit dinners featuring Caragh salmon and succulent mountain lamb are served in the elegant dining-room. There are 2 comfortable lounges for guests, both have fireplaces. Local activities include golf, salmon and trout fishing, woodland walks and hill climbing; 5 golf courses are within easy driving distance. Not suitable for young children. Some German spoken. Wine licence. Take the Ring of Kerry road to Caragh Lake, turn off on left after 3^1/$_2$ miles (5 km); signposted from the road. Visa and Mastercard accepted.

OWNER Josephine Roder   OPEN 1 January–30 November
ROOMS 3 double, 2 twin (all en suite)   TERMS B&B IR £35.00 p.p.; single supplement available; evening meal IR £22.00

CASTLEISLAND

Beech Grove

Camp Road, Castleisland, Co Kerry
Tel: (066) 41217

Beech Grove is a 100-year-old farmhouse that has been
tastefully modernised over the years, on a 200-acre Hereford
cattle farm. This is a wonderful place for animal lovers and
families who love the outdoors. There are deer, pheasant,
goats and a host of wildlife. Pony rides are available for
children as well as a play area with a tree house and a 2 mile
(3 km)-walk around the farm into a high bog area. There is
a comfortable sitting-room, of predominantly red decor,
with an old-fashioned atmosphere and turf fires. Farm-fresh
breakfasts are served on separate tables in the dining-room,
with the original restored cornices and ceiling rose. Four-
course evening meals with fresh farm produce are served if
prearranged. There is a furnished sun porch overlooking the
scenic countryside, and during the summer months a tea
shop is open. Guests may bring their own wine. Hairdryers
are available. There is plenty to see and do in this area,
including visits to the Crag Cave, to Memory Lane Museum
and a wide choice of sports – where better to participate
than from Beech Grove Farm with its warm atmosphere and
its own ring fort. Three miles (4¹/₂ km) west of Castleisland
– signposted.

OWNERS The O'Mahoney family   OPEN 1 April–1 October
ROOMS 2 double, 2 twin, 1 family (4 en suite)   TERMS B&B
IR £12.50-£13.50 p.p.; reductions for children; single supplement
IR £2.50; evening meal IR £11.00

DINGLE

Ard na Greine House

Spa Road, Dingle, Co Kerry
Tel: (066) 51113

An attractive bungalow in a quiet location, just 5 minutes
from the town centre. Mary Houlihan wanted to ensure that
guests had everything they could need, and she has certainly
accomplished her goal. All the bedrooms, which are on the
ground floor, have TVS, tea-makers, electric blankets, iron
and ironing boards, and direct dial telephones. The beds
have Dorma-designed duvets and the rooms are bright and

attractive. There is a breakfast menu featuring smoked herring, salmon, home-baked breads, Irish cooked breakfast, etc. You certainly won't need lunch. Ard na Greine is very popular with tourists and walkers, and drying facilities are available. The house is extremely good value and the owners are most accommodating and friendly. The beautiful shamrock/harp tapestry displayed in the dining-room was hand-made by Mary's sister. No smoking in the dining-room. Pets outside only. Easily located, it is the third house past Hillgrove Hotel. All major credit cards accepted.

OWNER Mrs Mary Houlihan   OPEN All year, except Christmas
ROOMS 2 double, 1 twin, 1 family (all en suite)
TERMS B&B IR £15.00 p.p.; no reductions for children; single supplement IR £5.00

Devane's Farmhouse

Lisdargan, Lispole, near Dingle, Co Kerry
Tel: (066) 51418

A warm welcome awaits you at Devane's farm, a working dairy farm of 40 acres nestled at the foot of the mountains, with beautiful views all around. It is very popular with walkers and tourists as it is situated on the Dingle Way walk. The bedrooms are clean, a little small, but the owners are so hospitable, offering tea and home-baked bread and cake to guests, that room size seems unimportant. Another bedroom now has en suite facilities and there are tea-making facilities in the TV lounge. Hairdryers and a trouser press and iron are available upon request. Guests return here year after year, and visitors new to the property sometimes book in for a night and end up staying a week or more. Guests are welcome to enjoy the daily farm activities, watch the sheep grazing or walk in this beautiful area. The farmhouse is located on a small side road, but don't give up; just when you think you must have passed it the farm comes into view. A peaceful, tranquil setting. Pets outside only. Cot available. No smoking in the dining-room. Off the main Tralee to Dingle road.

OWNER Mary Devane   OPEN 1 April–1 November
ROOMS 2 double, 1 twin, 1 family (2 en suite)
TERMS B&B IR £16.50 p.p.; 25% reduction for children; single supplement IR £3.50; evening meal IR £13.00

Duinin

Conor Pass Road, Dingle, Co Kerry

Tel: (066) 51335

Duinin, meaning "little fort", is a friendly, modern family home with beautiful views of sea and mountains. There is a large front garden with a manicured lawn and lots of pretty flowers and shrubs; guests enjoy tea outside on warm days. The comfortable TV lounge has a video which guests may use. There is a separate lounge for reading or just relaxing in after a busy day. All of the bedrooms are on the ground floor, with modern furnishings, large fitted wardrobes and chairs. The front bedrooms have lovely views. Tasty breakfasts, with fresh-baked breads, are served in the sunny dining-room overlooking the harbour. Golf, fishing, boat trips, beaches, hill walking and excellent pubs and restaurants are close by. No smoking in the bedrooms. Located on the Conor Pass Road, half a mile from Dingle.

OWNERS Anne and Pat Neligan   OPEN mid March–1 November
ROOMS 3 double, 2 twin (all en suite)   TERMS B&B IR £14.50 p.p.; 20% reduction for children under 10; single supplement IR £4.00

Greenmount House

Gortonora, Dingle, Co Kerry

Tel: (066) 51414

Greenmount House, also known as Curran's bed and breakfast, is a comfortable house set in a peaceful location with lovely views, 5 minutes' stroll to town. A special feature here are the breakfasts, for which Mary Curran received the 1991 Certification of Merit award, featuring home-made muesli, breads, muffins, fresh juices, followed by a cooked breakfast, ordered from an extensive menu; vegetarians catered for. An additional bonus is that it is served in a lovely conservatory/dining-room which overlooks the town of Dingle and the beautiful bay. The tastefully decorated bedrooms all have TVs, clock radios, telephones, hairdryers and electric blankets. Snacks are available upon request. No smoking in the dining-room. No pets. On entering Dingle from Tralee/Killarney, turn right at roundabout, take first right, drive to the top of John Street; Greenmount House is the second bungalow on the left.

OWNERS Mary and John Curran   OPEN All year, except Christmas
ROOMS 6 bedrooms: double/twin/family (all en suite)
TERMS B&B IR£15.00 p.p.; reductions for children; single supplement IR£5.00

Kavanagh's Bed and Breakfast

Garfinney, Dingle, Co Kerry

Tel: (066) 51326

An attractive, modern, split-level home with a pretty front garden, set back off the road. The bedrooms are of a good size, tastefully and individually decorated in pastel shades, and with comfortable beds. Guests' bedrooms that are not en suite have keys to their private bathroom. A warm and welcoming atmosphere pervades here and your hosts are enthusiastic and accommodating. The house has been open for B&B for 4 years and is a very popular stop for cyclists and tourists. There is a TV lounge. There are several stairs to the approach of the house, so Kavanagh's is not suitable for people with a walking handicap. Situated in beautiful countryside, 1 1/2 miles (2 1/2 km) from Dingle. Visa and Access cards accepted.

OWNER Marguerite Kavanagh   OPEN Easter–31 October
ROOMS 4 double, 1 twin, 1 family (all en suite)
TERMS B&B IR£13.50 p.p.; 33% reduction for children; single supplement IR£4.50; high tea IR £9.00

KENMARE

Ardmore House

Killarney Road, Kenmare, Co Kerry

Tel: (064) 41406

Set in an attractive rose garden, this black-and-white shuttered bungalow is in a quiet cul-de-sac, less than 5 minutes' walk to the town centre. The back bedrooms overlook mountains and fields with grazing cattle. There is a well-furnished TV lounge, which was extended in 1991. Golf, fishing and hill walking are available locally. Toni and Tom are a friendly, accommodating couple, always willing to assist their guests in every way. Hot drinks are available on request, and freshly prepared breakfasts include home-made brown bread. Ardmore House offers good value accommodation in a quiet location. Pets outside only. Situated 1/2 km from the city centre on the main Kenmare to

Killarney road (N71), opposite Whyte's Esso Station. Visa, Access and Mastercard accepted.

OWNERS Toni and Tom Connor   OPEN 1 March–1 December
ROOMS 2 double/twin/ family (all en suite)   TERMS B&B IR £13.50 p.p.; 50% reduction for children; single supplement IR £2.00; evening meal IR £12.50

Ashgrove

Gortalinney South, Kenmare, Co Kerry
Tel: (064) 41228

A charming new country house set in peaceful surroundings of pasture and woodland with a view of the Caha Mountains. Lynne O'Donnell is a friendly lady who welcomes guests as friends into her family home. After evening meals, guests are welcome to relax in armchairs in front of the fire or, if preferred, join the family in their spacious and elegantly furnished TV lounge. Breakfasts are served in the Jacobean-style dining-room with its exposed beams, stone fireplace and log fire. Light snacks are available and tea and coffee can be requested most any time at no extra charge. There is one ground-floor en suite room with bath and shower. Satellite TV and a VCR are available for use. A hairdryer and iron are provided upon request. No smoking in the bedrooms. Two miles (3 km) from Kenmare – signposted on the Kenmare to Glengariff road. Pets outside only.

OWNER Mrs Lynne O'Donnell   OPEN Easter weekend; 1 May– 1 September   ROOMS 3 double, 1 twin, 1 family (3 en suite) TERMS B&B IR £15.00 p.p.; reductions for children under 10; 20% reduction for senior citizens in May/June/September; single supplement IR £4.00; evening meal IR £12.00

Ceann Mara

Kenmare, Co Kerry
Tel: (064) 41220

Ceann Mara is in a peaceful location overlooking Kenmare Bay. The views are breathtaking, and both the dining-room and lounge have views of the bay. Special facilities include a grass tennis court and rowing boat for guests' use. The bedrooms all have tea-makers and electric blankets. The welcome is warm: Mrs Hayes is a helpful host, and hill walking (offshoots of the Kerry Way) and lake fishing at special rates can also be arranged. There is an intimate

atmosphere here, which is enhanced by the log fires.
Evening meals include organically grown vegetables from
the garden; vegetarians are catered for by prearrangement.
There is a wine licence. No smoking in the dining-room.
Located 1 mile (1¹/₂ km) from Kenmare on the L62 road.

OWNER Mrs Theresa Hayes   OPEN 1 April-31 October
ROOMS 1 double, 3 twin, 1 family (4 en suite)   TERMS B&B
IR£13.00-£14.00 p.p.; reductions for children; no single supple-
ment; evening meal IR£12.00, high tea IR£9.00

Muxnaw Lodge

(on Castletownbere Road), Kenmare, Co Kerry
Tel: (064) 41252

This interesting eighteenth-century house stands in a lovely
position set in 3¹/₂ acres of beautiful landscaped grounds,
with an all-weather tennis court. The house has an informal,
lived-in atmosphere and is decorated with Laura Ashley
wallpapers, a Waterford crystal chandelier, antique furnishings and many items of interest. The comfortable TV guest
lounge has the original fireplace and window shutters. The
spacious bedrooms, refurbished in keeping with the character of the house, have lovely views, original fireplaces and
antique furniture; one bedroom has a brass bed. Telephones
and hairdryers are available upon request. Mrs Boland has 3
charming daughters, all musical, who are easily persuaded to
play the harp for guests. Evening meals are available if
prearranged. There is no licence, but guests may bring their
own wine. A peaceful and relaxing house and a wonderful
base for touring this beautiful area. Pets outside only. A
pleasant 10-minute stroll into town over the bridge.

OWNER Mrs H Boland OPEN All year ROOMS 3 double, 2 twin (all en suite) TERMS B&B IR £14.00 p.p.; no reductions for children; single supplement IR £2.00; evening meal IR £12.00

O'Donnells of Ashgrove

Gortalinney South, Kenmare, Co Kerry
Tel: (064) 41228

A charming, new country house set in peaceful surroundings of pasture and woodland with a view of the Caha Mountains. Lynne O'Donnell is a friendly lady who welcomes guests as friends into her family home. After meals, guests are welcome to relax in armchairs in front of the fire or, if preferred, join the family in their spacious and elegantly furnished TV lounge. Breakfasts are served in the Jacobean-style dining-room with its exposed beams, stone fireplace and log fire. Light snacks are also available, and tea and coffee can be requested most any time at no extra charge. There is one en suite ground-floor room with bath and shower. Satellite TV and video are available for guests' use. A hairdryer and iron are provided upon request. Pets outside only. No smoking in the bedrooms. Two miles (3 km) from Kenmare, signposted on the Kenmare-Glengariff road.

OWNER Mrs Lynne O'Donnell OPEN Easter weekend and 1 May–1 September ROOMS 3 double, 1 twin, 1 family (3 en suite) TERMS B&B IR £15.00 p.p.; 50% reduction for children under 10; 20% reduction for senior citizens in May/June/September; single supplement IR £4.00; evening meal IR £12.00

KILLARNEY

Clonalis House

Countess Road, Killarney, Co Kerry
Tel: (064) 31043

A luxurious Georgian-style residence within half a mile of the town centre. Owner Mr O'Connor designed the house, and there are cornices, a ceiling rose and an archway made by a local craftsman. The house is spacious, well furnished and there is a lounge with TV. Plentiful breakfasts are served in the dining-room at a large mahogany table overlooking the pretty garden. There is a fine display of crystal on the sideboard. Anne O'Connor takes great pride in her home and goes out of her way to ensure that her guests are comfortable and well-taken care of. This is a no smoking house. Evening meals are not served but there is a wide choice of restaurants and pubs in the town centre. Golf, fishing and mountain climbing are available locally. Clonalis is a family home in Roscommon, which is where the O'Connors descended from; many Americans of the same name find their way here.

OWNER Anne O'Connor   OPEN 1 April–1 October
ROOMS 2 double/twin (all en suite)   TERMS B&B IR £15.00 p.p.; no reductions for children; single supplement IR £2.00 - £4.00, depending on season

Fair Haven

Cork Road, Killarney, Co Kerry
Tel: (064) 32542

Fair Haven is a comfortable, warm country house set in an acre of land in peaceful scenic surroundings. The bedrooms are comfortable, simply furnished and spotlessly clean. The TV lounge has open fires and tea-makers, and guests may help themselves at any time at no extra charge. There's a separate, bright dining-room where freshly cooked breakfasts with home-baking are served. Anne Teahan is an extremely friendly lady who has been welcoming visitors since 1984. Fair Haven was named after the home town of an American who was the first guest – an excellent choice: it is an apt description. For guests who would enjoy a rest from driving, Anne Teahan can arrange tours of the Ring of Kerry and Dingle Bay at a cost of IR £10.00 p.p. Buses collect guests at the door. Reservations can also be made in advance for the Killarney Manor House Banquet, which started in 1990 – an excellent evening of food and entertainment. No pets. Smoking in the lounge only. Located on the N22 Cork road. One and a half miles (2½ km) from town and 1 mile (1½ km) from the roundabout near the Shell station.

OWNER Mrs Anne Teahan   OPEN 1 March–1 November
ROOMS 3 double, 2 twin, 1 family (5 en suite)
TERMS B&B IR £14.00 p.p.; 20% reduction for children; single supplement IR £5.00

Kathleen's Country House

Tralee Road, Killarney, Co Kerry
Tel: (064) 32810, Fax: (064) 32340

Kathleen's Country House is a delightful family-run guest house where traditional hospitality and courteous personal attention are assured. The house is extremely well maintained and was refurbished in 1991. The well-appointed en suite bedrooms have individually controlled central heating, radio/clock alarms, TVs and tea-makers. Breakfasts and evening meals are served in the spacious dining-room, with the emphasis on traditional, wholesome dishes using fresh garden produce in season. There is a wine licence, enabling guests to enjoy a glass of wine with their evening meal. Kathleen's combines the facilities of a first-class hotel with the comforts and warmth of an Irish home. The house motto is "Easy to get to, hard to leave!", endorsed by the many visitors who return again and again. There are two 18-hole golf courses within a 5-minute drive, and fishing, lovely country walks, cycling and swimming are all available close by. No pets. Special group rates upon request. Visa accepted.

OWNER Kathleen O'Regan Sheppard   OPEN 1 March–30 November   ROOMS 5 double, 9 twin, 2 family (all en suite) TERMS B&B IR £23.50-£27.50 p.p.; 50% reduction for children; single supplement IR £10.00; evening meal IR £15.50

Knockcullen

New Road, Killarney, Co Kerry
Tel: (064) 33915

Knockcullen, which means "hill on top", is an immaculate family home in a private location off the main road, situated 2 minutes' walk from town and the National Park. Marie O'Brien has been in business for 18 years; she started when her family had grown and she needed to do something to fill her time and her home. It has become a popular venue, many guests returning often for her special hospitality and the warm and welcoming atmosphere. The house is an ideal base for touring this scenic area. There's a pleasant lounge with TV, where guests can relax after a busy day and enjoy a cup of tea or coffee. Breakfasts only are served, but there are lots of good restaurants and pubs close by. Marie is interested in walking and mountain climbing and is pleased

to assist guests with information, and/or planned itineraries.
No pets. No smoking in the dining-room.

OWNER Mrs Marie O'Brien   OPEN 1 April–31 October
ROOMS 3 double, 1 twin (3 en suite)   TERMS B&B IR £13.00 p.p.;
33% reduction for children; single supplement IR £3.00

Linn Dubh

Aghadoe Heights, Killarney, Co Kerry
Tel: (064) 33828

A dormer bungalow surrounded by scenic countryside,
overlooking Killarney's lakes and mountains. The bedrooms
are nicely decorated, all with pine orthopaedic beds. There
are tea-making facilities on the landing. Carmella Sheehy is
an enthusiastic lady who decided to open up her home to
guests when her children were young; B&B meant that she
could stay at home with her children and still have the
opportunity to meet people. There's a comfortable lounge
with a TV, and a large, furnished patio area and spacious
garden for guests' use. Breakfasts and evening meals, if
prearranged, are served in the pleasant, bright dining-room.
A telephone is available. Situated off the N70 on the T61
Dingle road, signposted from there. No pets. Smoking in the
dining-room only.

OWNER Carmella Sheehy   OPEN 1 March–1 November
ROOMS 2 double/family (all en suite)   TERMS B&B IR£14.00 p.,p.;
30% reduction for children; single supplement IR£5.00; evening
meal IR£11.00

Montrose

Cork Road, Killarney, Co Kerry
Tel: (064) 31378

A modern two-storey house set back off the road within
walking distance of the town, bus and train station. Guests
are encouraged to leave their car at the house, thus avoiding
parking problems. The house has been well maintained, the
bedrooms are colour-coordinated and have orthopaedic
beds. The one non en suite bedroom has its own bathroom.
Breakfast only is served in the spotless dining-room, which
has pretty lace tablecloths. Mrs Sayers has been doing bed
and breakfast most of her life, starting off as a young girl.
She loves her vocation, and guests return here often. Local

tours can be arranged and the bus picks up visitors right at the door. No smoking in the dining-room. There is a 4-bedroom self-catering unit available.

OWNERS The Sayers family   OPEN All year, except Christmas
ROOMS 1 double, 1 twin, 2 family (1 en suite)
TERMS B&B IR £11.00-£15.00 p.p.; 25% reduction for children under 12; single supplement IR £3.00

Park Lodge Guesthouse

Cork Road, Killarney, Co Kerry

Tel: (064) 31539

This attractive guest house is on the main road in its own grounds, with horses grazing in the fields. The rooms are attractively decorated, colour-coordinated with nice furnishings and all have direct dial telephones, tea-makers and TVs. Hairdryers on request. There are several ground-floor rooms. Varied breakfasts are ordered off the menu and are served in the bright dining-room. The guest lounge has an open fire, and there is a beautiful piano. Mary Fleming is a most gracious lady who is assisted by her daughter. There is a wine licence. No pets. Situated on the N22 next to the Ryan Hotel, 1 mile (1½ km) from Killarney.

OWNER Mary Fleming   OPEN 1 March–1 November
ROOMS 20 double/twin/family (all en suite)
TERMS B&B IR £17.50 p.p.; 33% reduction for children; single supplement off season only, ask for rate

The 19th Green

Fossa, near Killarney, Co Kerry

Tel: (064) 32868

The 19th Green is an immaculate, well-maintained property situated in quiet and peaceful countryside, yet only a 5-minute drive from Killarney on the Killorglin Ring of Kerry road, close to the entrance to the Killarney Golf Club. High standards prevail here. The house is efficiently run, and the large bedrooms are tastefully decorated with comfortable, firm beds. There is a large, well-furnished TV lounge, which overlooks the mountains. Situated across the road from Killarney's two 18-hole championship courses, sited in mature woodlands and a short drive to the par 3 18th on Mahoney's Point. Tours can be arranged for the Ring of

Kerry, Dingle Peninsula, Blarney Castle, etc. Timothy and Bridget Foley are proud of the personal attention guests receive here and they make every effort to ensure that guests feel welcome and comfortable. An excellent base from which to play golf and tour this scenic area.

OWNERS Timothy and Bridget Foley   OPEN 1 January–20 December   ROOMS 3 double, 5 twin, 5 family (10 en suite)   TERMS B&B IR£16.00-£20.00 p.p.; 50% reduction for children; single supplement negotiable

Villa Marias

Aghadoe, Killarney, Co Kerry
Tel: (064) 32307

A dormer bungalow in a peaceful and quiet location, 2¹/₂ miles (4 km) from Killarney. The house is immaculate, the bedrooms well appointed and comfortable. There is a separate dining-room and a TV lounge with an open fireplace over which is displayed a fine Waterford Crystal sword. Mary Counihan has been established for 8 years and previously worked in the catering industry. She went into the B&B business in order to maintain her contact with people. Mary's first criteria is her guests' comfort, and a warm, friendly welcome is extended to everyone. Guests are greeted with a cup of tea or coffee and biscuits upon arrival. Although there are no en suite bedrooms, there are 2 bathrooms exclusively for guests' use. The spotless bedrooms each have a trouser press and hairdryer. Pets welcome. Located 1 mile (1¹/₂ km) from the golf course, signposted on the N17 Tralee road from Killarney.

OWNER Mrs Mary Counihan   OPEN 1 March–1 October   ROOMS 3 double, 1 twin   TERMS B&B IR£13.00 p.p.; 25% reduction for children; single supplement IR£5.00

LISTOWEL

Ceol na h'Abhann

Tralee Road, Ballygrennan, Listowel, Co Kerry
Tel: (068) 21345

Ceol na h'Abhann, which means "music of the river", aptly describes this charming thatched house nestled in the woods and overlooking the river. Owners Kathleen and Niall are a charming and welcoming couple who had the house built for their retirement. The rooms are spacious, well furnished and extremely comfortable. There is one ground-floor en suite bedroom and some rooms have river views. Excellent breakfasts are served in a large Georgian-style dining-room with fine linen and china. The sitting-room, with a beautiful Sanderson design wallpaper of birds and trees, has a TV, video and turf fires on chilly days. Guests can relax in the furnished conservatory or in the garden, which overlooks the River Feale. This is a delightful, tranquil spot to return to after a busy day of sightseeing or golfing at nearby Ballybunion. Ceol na h'Abhann is the recipient of the Ideal Kerry House award. Tea and scones are offered on arrival. No pets. No smoking in the bedrooms. Situated half a mile from Listowel.

OWNERS Niall and Kathleen Stack   OPEN 1 April–31 October
ROOMS 2 double, 1 twin, 1 family (3 en suite)
TERMS B&B IR £13.00-£15.00 p.p.; no reductions for children; single supplement IR £8.50 high season, negotiable other times

SNEEM

Avonlea House

Sneem, Co Kerry
Tel: (064) 45221

An immaculate, luxurious house set in scenic, rural sur-roundings. Mrs Hussey began her bed-and-breakfast busi-ness after a friend asked her to take her overflow of guests during high season. Mrs Hussey enjoyed the guests so much that she decided to do it full time. A most accommodating host, assisted by her children during the summer holidays. The modern bedrooms are warm and comfortable, and the TV lounge, with a real fire, has a piano which guests may play. The house is well maintained and an additional en suite family room has been added to one of the bedrooms. As well, one bedroom has a shower and there are 2 other bathrooms for guests' use. Hairdryers are available. Tea and coffee are provided upon request. Situated just one minute from the village, with several good restaurants and local pubs with entertainment during the season. Advance reser-vations recommended during high season. No smoking in the dining-room. Signposted from Sneem. Visa accepted.

OWNER Mrs Maura Hussey   OPEN 1 March–1 November
ROOMS 3 double/ twin (3 en suite)   TERMS B&B IR £11.00-£13.00 p.p.; 20% reduction for children; single supplement IR £15.00; cvening meal IR £11.00

Derry East Farmhouse

Sneem, Co Kerry
Tel: (064) 45193

Derry East is a working beef-suckling farm, situated ¹/2 mile from Sneem on the Ring of Kerry road on the Waterville side. This is a botanist's paradise, with its wild mountain landscape background and seafront. Derry East has its own hard tennis court and farm walks, and you can golf, hill walk, trout fish, shore angle, etc. The bedrooms are warm and comfortable and there is a bright, colourful dining-room. Turf fires glow brightly on chilly days. Evening meals are available, if prearranged, featuring home-grown vegetables, with vegetarian and special diets catered for. An ideal spot for a quiet and relaxing holiday. Mrs Teahan is a caring and considerate host offering guests a truly warm welcome and ably assisted by her children during the summer holidays, who are happy to play Irish music for guests. No pets. No smoking in the dining-room. Half a mile from Sneem on the N70 on the Waterville side.

OWNER Mrs Mary Teahan OPEN Easter–October ROOMS 1 double, 3 twin (3 en suite) TERMS B&B IR £12.00-£14.00 p.p.; 25% reduction for children; single supplement IR £6.00; evening meal IR £12.00

Hillside Haven

Tahilla, Sneem, Co Kerry
Tel: (064) 82065

Hillside Haven is a country house set in mature gardens with magnificent views of sea, mountains and glorious countryside.The 4 bedrooms, all on the ground floor, are spotlessly clean and comfortable. There is a separate lounge and cosy dining-room. Tasty evening meals are served (if prearranged): Irish stew, bacon and cabbage, home-baked breads and desserts; vegetarians are catered for. Breakfasts are served either in the dining-room or, if the guests prefer, outside in good weather. Helen Foley is an accommodating host; walking is one of her hobbies and she would be pleased to arrange walking holidays for small groups. Tea or coffee are available just about any time. Smoking in the lounge only. No pets. Located on route from Killarney into Kenmare; take Sneem road – N22 - 2¹/2 miles (4 km) past the Blackwater Bridge. The house is easily located on the right-hand side.

OWNER Mrs Helen Foley OPEN All year, except Christmas
ROOMS 2 double/family (all en suite) TERMS B&B IR £14.00 p.p.;
25% reduction for children; single supplement IR £3.00; evening
meal IR £12.00, packed lunch IR £5.00

Woodvale House

Pier Road, Sneem, Co Kerry
Tel: (064) 45181

Full of old-world atmosphere, Woodvale House is set in its
own grounds on the estuary of a river, in the award-winning
village of Sneem in the Ring of Kerry. In the middle of the
last century the house was built as a convent by the presen-
tation nuns, who taught in the local school until 1891. Since
that time it has been in the hands of the O'Sullivan family,
who have been careful to preserve the house's character,
while offering all modern comforts. There are 2 lounges,
one for reading or chatting to other guests, and a very
spacious TV lounge. There is access to the river, and fishing
enthusiasts may take trips out on the bay from Oysterbed
Pier. Just a pleasant 3-minute stroll into Sneem with its gaily
painted houses and landscaped greens. Mrs O'Sullivan is an
enthusiastic walker and is happy to assist with walking
itineraries. Smoking in the lounge only. Pets outside. Situated on the road to the pier from Sneem. Visa, Access and
Mastercard accepted.

OWNER Mrs Alice O'Sullivan OPEN All year, except Christmas
ROOMS 2 double, 1 twin, 3 treble (all en suite) TERMS B&B
IR £13.00 p.p.; 25% reduction for children; single supplement
IR £5.00; evening meal IR £12.00

TRALEE

Ard na Gaoite

Listellick North, Tralee, Co Kerry
Tel: (066) 23272

An immaculate modern house set back off the road in a
peaceful area, with magnificent views of the mountains. The
bedrooms are individually furnished and colour-coordinated, with large en suite bathrooms. The spacious, mostly
pine, family room overlooks the mountains. The TV lounge
is decorated with restful peach and grey colours. The
dining-room has rich wooden floors. The conservatory has
lots of flowers and plants, is furnished in wicker and is the

73

only area of the house where smoking is allowed. Majella Barrett is a charming and dedicated host whose goal is to ensure that her guests are comfortable and that their needs are met. Golf, horse-riding and beautiful beaches are close by. Two miles (3 km) from Tralee on the Aberdorney/Ballybunion road. Tralee is best known for its Rose of Tralee festival in August each year.

OWNER Majella Barrett   OPEN 1 May-31 October   ROOMS 2 double, 1 family, 1 single (all en suite)   TERMS B&B IR £14.00 p.p.; 50% reduction for children under 8; single supplement IR £4.00; evening meal IR £12.00

Brianville

Clogherbrien, Fenit Road, Tralee, Co Kerry
Tel: (066) 26645

A luxurious, modern bungalow bordered by flowers, and a scenic view of the mountains. The well-furnished lounge has a fireplace, TV and piano. The rooms have all been refurbished and each bedroom has a hairdryer. There is a lovely antique grandfather clock in the hallway. This is very much a family-run establishment, with Mrs Smith's daughter helping out during school holidays. All rooms are on the ground floor. There are some excellent seafood restaurants close by. On the Gateway to Tralee Bay, with golf, fishing and sailing all nearby. No pets. Visa and Access cards accepted.

OWNER Mrs Joan Smith OPEN All year, except Christmas
ROOMS 3 double, 1 twin, 1 treble (4 en suite)
TERMS B&B IR £14.50 p.p.; 33% reduction for children; single supplement IR £4.00

Cluain Mor House

Boherbee, Tralee, Co Kerry
Tel: (066) 25545

A well-built, attractive townhouse, set back off the main road, in a one-acre garden, with palm trees, shrubs and lawns. There are some interesting old farm implements displayed on the lawn: ploughs, a hay turner and a hay mower. Window boxes full of flowers decorate the front of the house. The bedrooms are well appointed, 4 of them with 100-year-old carved furniture. The cosy dining-room is tastefully decorated and the TV lounge has a fireplace and piano. A quiet and peaceful house within a few minutes' walk of all amenities, including the bus and the railway station. Excellent restaurants and entertainment are located close by. There is an 18-hole golf course within 5 miles (7^1/$_2$ km), and Kerry airport is 9 miles (13^1/$_2$ km) away. No pets. No smoking in the bedrooms.

OWNER Mrs Helen O'Shea OPEN All year, except Christmas
ROOMS 2 double/twin/family (3 en suite)   TERMS B&B IR £14.00
p.p.; 25% reduction for children; single supplement IR £2.00

Gleann Cuilinn House

Tralee Road, Cleeney, Tralee, Co Kerry
Tel: (064) 32101

Gleann Cuilinn means Holly Lane, named after the area on the Wicklow border where Anne O'Connor is from. Anne started her B&B in 1973 when she was asked to help out during the Killarney races. Anne and her husband are warm, friendly, outgoing people who really enjoy their guests and are happy to assist in planning what to see and do in the area. Tea and home-made scones are offered upon arrival in the family lounge, shared with guests. Mr O'Connor is retired and enjoys tending the beautiful gardens, featuring an old cast-iron crane and skillet. The bedrooms are airy and clean, all on the ground floor. A half-mile from Killarney. Not suitable for small children. Pets outside only. No smoking in the dining-room.

OWNER Mrs Anne O'Connor OPEN 1 January–1 November
ROOMS 2 double, 1 twin (1 en suite)   TERMS B&B IR £12.00 p.p.;
50% reduction for children; single supplement IR £3.00

Sea View House

The Spa, Tralee, Co Kerry
Tel: (066) 36107

A secluded Georgian residence in its own wooded grounds of 9^1/$_2$ acres, with sea views. The house has recently been completely refurbished and redecorated. There are no en suite rooms, but Sea View House has 2 bathrooms for guests' use as well as additional showers. The wide wooden staircase is original, and there are many antique furnishings throughout the house. The dining-room is extremely spacious, as is the TV lounge, which has a piano and fireplace; a fire is lit on chilly evenings. There are lots of interesting books for guests to read. The setting is idyllic and Sea View is one of the few houses in Ireland that has its own private beach, which guests have access to, just 50 yards from the house. Evening meals are not available, but there are several restaurants in the area. Evening meals must be ordered in advance. Located off the main Fenit Road, 4 miles (6 km) from Tralee.

OWNER Mrs K O'Donnell OPEN 1 April–1 November
ROOMS 1 double, 2 twin, 1 family, 1 single
TERMS B&B IR £14.00 p.p.; 10% reduction for children; single supplement IR £2.00

WATERVILLE

Benmore Farmhouse

Oughtive, Waterville, Co Kerry
Tel: (0667) 4207

A 200-year-old farmhouse on a 250-acre working sheep farm, situated in a remote area with spectacular mountain views. The farmhouse itself is quite basic, but the O'Sheas extend a five-star welcome. This is a popular property and advance reservations are highly recommended. Two of the bedrooms are in an annex, have their own entrance and share one bathroom. There's a comfortable lounge where musical evenings are a regular occurrence, as well as a slide show presented around the fire by Mr O'Shea whose interest is local history, local legends and archaeology. Fresh farm-style evening meals are served, if prearranged, using home-grown produce with delicious home-baking and desserts. Some people come just for the raisin bread. A sixth-century souterrain and old village ruins lie on the farm. There are private walks and spectacular mountain climbs close by. No pets. Signposted from Waterville.

OWNER The O'Shea family OPEN 1 April–1 November
ROOMS 2 double, 2 twin, 1 family (1 en suite)
TERMS B&B IR £12.00-£14.00 p.p.; 25% reduction for children; single supplement IR £4.00; evening meal IR £11.00

Sunset House

Waterville, Co Kerry
Tel: (0667) 4258

An attractive bungalow overlooking Ballinskelligs Bay on the edge of town. The house is clean and pleasantly furnished, with a large, spacious dining-room and lounge with a TV and piano. There is a pretty furnished patio for guest use. Mrs Fitzgerald began offering bed and breakfast over 14 years ago, adding more rooms for the many guests looking for accommodation. However, she still turns people away. Advance reservations are recommended, particularly during high season. Four rooms now have en suite facilities, and there are ample bathrooms for the other bedrooms. Evening meals are not available, but Mrs Fitzgerald would be happy to recommend local eating places serving good food at reasonable prices. Pets welcome by arrangement. Situated on the Ring of Kerry road, 3 minutes' walk to town.

OWNER Mrs Patricia Fitzgerald   OPEN Easter–30 November
ROOMS 1 double, 2 twin, 1 single, 1 family (4 en suite)
TERMS B&B IR £13.00-£26.00 p.p.; 25% reduction for children; single supplement off season only

County Waterford

Waterford is probably best known for its crystal factory, which has regular hours for visits. Situated in the south east of the country, it is reputedly one of the sunniest spots. Waterford has a pretty coastline and a more rugged interior, with good farmland. The Nire Valley is good for walking and pony trekking and has wonderful views.

Waterford city has much of interest to visit. Reginald's Tower, a massive circular fortress, is now the civic museum. Christ Church Cathedral, built in 1779, the French church, the Chamber of Commerce building, a lovely Georgian building, and the City Hall, which houses two old theatres, are all worth seeing. The International Festival of Light Opera is held in Waterford in September.

Dunmore East, Tramore, Annestown and Dungevan are all pleasant seaside spots, particularly Dunmore East, which resembles a Devon fishing village. Further south is the Irish-speaking village of Ring, where Irish scholars go to study.

St Declan's Oratory, built in the ninth century, and St Declan's Well and Temple Disert can be found at Ardmore. The cathedral which dates back to the twelfth century is known for its sculptured figures.

Four miles from Cappoquin is the Trappist Cistercian Abbey of Mount Melleray, which maintains the old rule of monastic hospitality, so it is quite in order to accept a meal if it is offered to you.

Lismore, which was at one time a great centre of learning, has one of Ireland's finest castles, originally built by King John in 1185 and at one time belonging to Sir Walter Raleigh. The gardens are open to the public. The medieval Cathedral of St Carthach is most attractive and was restored in 1633.

ARDMORE

Newtown View Grange

Ardmore, Co Waterford

Tel: (024) 94143

A 100-acre dairy farm in idyllic surroundings, with a lovely garden and views of sea and hills. The bedrooms are simply furnished and all have TVs and tea-making facilities. Mrs O'Connor, a friendly, cheerful lady, has won several cooking awards, including Gourmet Queen and a special award for seafood preparation. Excellent evening meals are served in the newly added dining-room, with its attractive pine wood ceiling. There is a cosy TV lounge and a hard tennis court. Close by is a sandy beach, deep-sea fishing, golf, horse-riding and a local swimming pool. Located off the Youghal/Dungarvan N25 road and signposted 200 metres off the N25. Visa and Access cards accepted.

OWNER Mrs Teresa O'Connor OPEN Easter–mid October
ROOMS 1 double, 4 twin, 1 family (all en suite)
TERMS B&B IR£14.00 p.p.; reductions for children; single supplement IR£4.00; evening meal IR £10.50

BALLYMACARBRY

Nire Valley Farmhouse

Ballymacarbry, Co Waterford
Tel: (052) 36149

Easy to find, Nire Valley Farmhouse stands beside a petrol station, which together with a small shop is also run by the Doocey family in the centre of Ballymacarbry. This is a square, whitewashed house at the foot of Deerpark Hill and is part of a sheep and cattle farm. There is one ground-floor en suite room, and the dining-room has windows all along the back opening out onto the patio. No smoking in the dining-room and no pets.

OWNERS The Doocey family OPEN Easter–1 October
ROOMS 2 double/family (2 en suite) TERMS B&B IR £12.00-£14.00 p.p.; reductions for children; single supplement IR £3.00; evening meal IR £12.00

CAPPOQUIN

Aglish House

Cappoquin, Co Waterford
Tel: (024) 96191

A period house on a working dairy farm in the Blackwater Valley lying between the Knockmealdown Mountains and the sea. Aglish House is very much a family home, with 6 children and 5 dogs, and has a relaxed atmosphere with very friendly hosts. All bedrooms have phones, TVs and hairdryers and there is a wine licence. Golf, deep-sea fishing, pony trekking and bike hire can be arranged locally. No smoking in the bedrooms and pets by arrangement only. Visa, Access and Eurocard accepted.

OWNERS Tom and Terry Moore   OPEN All year, except Christmas
ROOMS 2 double/twin/family (2 en suite)   TERMS B&B from IR
£15.00 p.p.; reductions for children; single supplement IR £3.00;
evening meal IR £14.00

DUNGARVAN

Ballyguiry Farm

Dungarvan, Co Waterford

Tel: (058) 41194

The Kiely family bought this property in 1940 for £1,200.
The original house is 300-years old, and the front façade
dates from the late Georgian period. Ballyguiry stands in a
wonderful position with superb views on a mixed farm, the
farm buildings being to the rear of the property. Mrs Kiely
has recently done up virtually the whole house, installing
quite a lot of reproduction plasterwork. An immaculately
clean home, Ballyguiry Farm caters predominantly for
families. It is signposted off the N25 south of Dungarvan.

OWNERS Kathleen Kiely   OPEN 1 March–1 December
ROOMS 1 double, 1 twin, 3 family (2 en suite)
TERMS B&B IR £13.00-£20.00 p.p.; reductions for children;
evening meal IR £10.00

Fáilte Guest House

Youghal Road, Dungarvan, Co Waterford

Tel: (058) 43216

This is a comfortable town house set in its own grounds
with views of the bay and less than a 5-minute walk to all
amenities, beaches and good restaurants. There are 2
beautiful and unusual antique clocks in the hallway. The
comfortable bedrooms are spotlessly clean, colour-
coordinated with plenty of wardrobe space. The
conservatory, which overlooks the bay, is an ideal spot for
playing cards, chatting to other guests or relaxing and
enjoying the view. The owners are a friendly, outgoing
family, all of whom play golf. Mr Spratt is currently building
an 18-hole championship golf course which will open in
June 1993. By the summer of 1993 special prices will apply
for a combination of room and golf. Not suitable for
children. Pets outside only. Safe private parking. Fáilte
Guest House is located opposite the police station on the
N25 Waterford to Cork road.

OWNER Mrs Nola Spratt   OPEN 1 March–1 November
ROOMS 1 double/twin/single/family (all en suite)
TERMS B&B IR £15.00 p.p.

Seaview

Windgap, Dungarvan West, Co Waterford
Tel: (058) 41583

An immaculate dormer bungalow in an elevated position,
with magnificent panoramic views of the bay and
Dungarvan. Mrs Fahey has been running her bed and
breakfast for over 19 years, and Seaview was one of the first
establishments in the area. Two of the comfortable
bedrooms have superb views. Mrs Fahey is very
knowledgeable about the area and is happy to assist guests
with itineraries, and there is lots of tourist information
available. Located 300 yards from the famous Seanchai
restaurant. No smoking in the bedrooms. No pets. 5 miles
(7¹/₂ km) west of Dungarven on the N25. This is a very
popular property, so early reservations are recommended.

OWNER Mrs Nora Fahey   OPEN All year   ROOMS 2 twin, 1 single,
2 family (3 en suite)   TERMS B&B IR £13.00 p.p.; reductions for
children; single supplement IR £5.00; evening meal IR £10.00,
high tea IR £7.00

The Old Rectory

Waterford Road, Dungarvan, Co Waterford
Tel: (058) 41394

Built in 1942, the Old Rectory sits in 2¹/₂ acres, with landscaped gardens, fruit trees and a fish pond. The house is in a
secluded, tranquil setting, an ideal retreat for guests wanting
to get away for a peaceful holiday. The bedrooms are large
and tastefully decorated in warm pastel shades. There is also
a guest lounge furnished in wicker with lots of plants,
leading onto the conservatory. Mr and Mrs Prendergast are
into sports and can assist guests with information on local
tennis and golfing facilities. Special-break angling holidays
can be arranged, including evening meals. No pets.

OWNER Mrs R Prendergast   OPEN All year, except Christmas
ROOMS 1 double, 2 twin, 1 family (2 en suite)
TERMS B&B IR £12.50 p.p.; reductions for children; single
supplement IR £4.00; evening meal IR £11.00, high tea IR £9.00

Church Villa

Dunmore East, Co Waterford
Tel: (051) 83390

A quaint, whitewashed period house, one of a row of cottages opposite the Church of Ireland and adjacent to the Ship bar and restaurant. The small cosy bedrooms are individually decorated, some with the original fireplaces. The light fixtures are Waterford crystal. There is a guest lounge with TV. Breakfasts only are served in the dining-room, which leads onto the patio. Lucy Butler is a friendly, outgoing lady who wants her guests to feel relaxed and very much at home. Evening meals are available at the adjacent restaurant. There are several other eating establishments close by. Minutes from the beach, harbour and close to the park for those interested in exploring the many caves there. No pets.

OWNER Mrs Lucy Butler   OPEN All year, except Christmas
ROOMS 3 double, 2 twin (5 with showers only)
TERMS B&B IR£13.50-£16.00 p.p.; reductions for children

Dunmore Lodge

Dunmore East, Co Waterford
Tel: (051) 83454

Formerly called the Cottage, this is one of the oldest houses in Dunmore East. Extremely attractive, it is located right in the centre of town yet is protected by its own grounds, with a pretty half-circular front garden and some outbuildings to the back. Dunmore is a low stone building with a porch and 20 very pronounced bow windows with wonderful views over the water. A long hallway stretches to the back of the house, ending with the kitchen, which has a small patio for sitting outdoors on fine days. The rooms are off to each side. Pets outside only.

OWNER Zoe Coffey   OPEN 1 April–1 October   ROOMS 2 double, 1 twin (all en suite)   TERMS B&B IR £15.00-£17.00 p.p.; single supplement IR £10.00

Castle Farm

Millstreet, Cappagh, Co Waterford
Tel: (058) 68049

Mountain Castle was the principal seat of the McGraths of Sliabh gCua, one of the two Gaelic families that owned land in this county before the arrival of Cromwell. The accommodations are in a restored wing of the fifteenth-century castle. The oldest section, with the original archway, contains the long, narrow dining-room with its 4-feet thick stone walls. The house is kept very warm and the rooms are plainly furnished and decorated. Castle Farm, which won the Agri-Tourism award in 1991, stands in lovely countryside with fine views and can be found down a lane beside the pub in Millstreet. There is a wine licence, and evening meals are available featuring organically grown vegetables. At breakfast guests are served milk from the farm and home-made jam. Guests can help themselves to tea or coffee in the kitchen. No smoking in the dining-room. Pets outside only. Signposted from the N72, Dungarven to Killarney road.

OWNER Mrs Joan Nugent   OPEN 1 March–1 November
ROOMS 3 double, 3 twin, 2 family (all en suite)
TERMS B&B IR £14.00-£17.00 p.p.; reductions for children; evening meal IR £11.00

NIRE VALLEY

Hanora's Country Cottage

Nire Valley, via Clonmel, Co Waterford
Tel: (052) 36134

An absolute haven of peace and tranquillity, Hanora's Cottage, a converted ancestral home, nestles at the foot of the Comeragh Mountains beside the Nire Church and old schoolhouse. The Nire River runs alongside. The cottage was recently refurbished, and the bedrooms are now individually and tastefully decorated in colour-coordinated fabrics and with pretty duvets. There is a sitting area with TV. Sumptuous breakfasts include freshly baked scones, home-made jams and muslei. Evening meals must be prearranged. Meals are served in the cosy dining-room where the fireplace has a 100-year-old "wheel": a device for getting the fire going. Eoinn, the son and also the chef,

completed his training under Darina Allen at Ballymaloe
Cookery School. Seamus Wall is past captain of Clonmel
Golf Club and would be happy to make all golfing
arrangements. A paradise for walkers and nature lovers,
where guests return often to relax and unwind in the beautiful surroundings. Maps and itineraries are provided. Smoking in the lounge only. Not suitable for children. Twenty
minutes' drive from Clonmel or Dungarvan; turn left off T27
at Ballymacarby (Melodys).

OWNERS Seamus and Mary Wall OPEN All year, except Christmas
week ROOMS 2 double, 3 twin, 3 family (6 en suite)
TERMS B&B IR £17.50 p.p.; single supplement IR £3.50; evening
meals à la carte

ROSSDUFF

Elton Lodge

Rossduff, Co Waterford

Tel: (051) 82117

A 200-year-old farmhouse, Elton Lodge has been in the
Richardson family for some 80 years. There are pleasant
gardens to the front, and at the back of the house is the
farmyard for the dairy farm which is run by Mr Richardson
and his son. The rooms have recently been redecorated and
furnished, and there is one twin en suite room off the
sitting-room. Eileen Richardson is a very friendly lady with 6
children. The house is located on the main Dunmore East
to Waterford road.

OWNER Mrs Eileen Richardson   OPEN 1 June–1 October
ROOMS 2 double, 1 twin, 1 family (all en suite)   TERMS B&B from
IR £14.00; reductions for children; evening meal IR £11.00

STRADBALLY

Park House

Stradbally, Co Waterford

Tel: (051) 93185

Approached along a quarter-mile drive through parkland
with grazing sheep and cattle, Park House is a 150-year-old
white farmhouse. It stands in extensive, beautifully landscaped gardens. Although the house is spacious it has a
cottage-style interior. All the rooms have lovely views and
are tastefully decorated. There are telephones and hairdryers
in each room. The furnishings are old fashioned and there is
an antique grandfather clock in the hallway. This is an
absolutely delightful property, the perfect combination of
peace and tranquillity and wonderful Irish hospitality.
Evening meals and high teas are available if prearranged;
vegetarians catered for. Good old-fashioned home-cooking,
farm-fresh produce and meats, brown bread and delicious
desserts are featured. Baby-sitting available. Six miles (9
km) from Dungarvan on the coast road to Tramore;
signposted.

OWNER Mrs P Connors   OPEN All year, except Christmas
ROOMS 3 double, 2 twin, 1 family (3 en suite)
TERMS B&B IR £12.00-£14.00 p.p.; reductions for children; single
supplement IR £4.00; evening meal IR £10.00, high tea IR £7.00

TRAMORE

Cliff House

Cliff Road, Tramore, Co Waterford

Tel: (051) 81497

This house, built 10 years ago by the owners, stands in its
own landscaped gardens overlooking the sea. The bedrooms, 2 of which are on the ground floor, are well
appointed and spotlessly clean, with attractive pastel print
duvets. All bedrooms now have their own bathrooms. This
is very much a family-run house, ably assisted by 15-year-
old Brian and 19-year-old Ciara during school holidays.
Both enjoy the opportunity to meet people who come to stay
at Cliff House from all over the world. A thoroughly

enjoyable place to stay: friendly people, a family atmosphere and, an added bonus, panoramic views. Within walking distance of town centre and adjacent to new leisure centre. Secure parking. No smoking in the bedrooms. No pets. Ten minutes to Waterford Glass Factory. The house is on the R675 Coast road.

OWNER Mrs Hilary O'Sullivan   OPEN 1 April–1 October
ROOMS 3 double, 2 twin, 1 family (5 en suite)
TERMS B&B IR £12.50–£14.50 p.p.; reductions for children; single supplement IR £5.00

Mountain View

Fena, Tramore, Co Waterford
Tel: (051) 96107

Mountain View, an idyllic newly thatched cottage, dates from the 1700s. The owners have lovingly restored the farmhouse to a most delightful and charming property. Furnished with traditional and period pieces, chintzy decor and satin bedspreads. The family room is very large indeed, combining 2 bedrooms, bathroom and sitting-room. Ideal for families or people wanting a little extra privacy. There is a colourful TV lounge with an additional sitting-room where sing-alongs of 10 take place in the evening. When wandering about please be careful: this is a "mind your head" house. Fresh home-style three-course meals are served in the cosy dining-room. All rooms are on the ground floor. Four miles (6 km) from Tramore, 1½ miles (2 km) to beaches. All major credit cards accepted.

OWNER Mrs E Rockett   OPEN late March–1 October
ROOMS 4 twin, 2 single, 4 family (7 en suite)
TERMS B&B IR £12.00–£13.50 p.p.; reductions for children; single supplement IR £3.00; evening meal IR £10.00

Rushmere House

Branch Road, Tramore, Co Waterford
Tel: (051) 81041

A Georgian-style house built in the late 1800s overlooking Tramore Bay. The rooms vary in size from small to spacious, the front rooms having views of the bay. Teddy and Rita McGivney purchased the house 14 years ago with the intention of starting a bed and breakfast. It is an ideal location and they have been busy with guests from the beginning. The TV lounge is small and cosy and the house is minutes from the beach and all amenities. Lots of good eating establishments close by. There are tea-making facilities in all the bedrooms. Ample parking across the street. No smoking in the dining-room. No pets.

OWNER Rita McGivney   OPEN 1 March–1 November
ROOMS   2 double/twin/family (4 en suite)
TERMS B&B IR £12.50-£14.50 p.p.; reductions for children; single supplement IR £3.00; evening meal IR £10.00

Venezia

Church Road Grove, Tramore, Co Waterford
Tel: (051) 81412

A well-maintained and comfortable town house on a quiet residential street, with a garden and car park to the front of the house. The bedrooms are a good size, individually decorated in blue, pink, green and peach, with modern, comfortable furnishings and fitted wardrobes. Excellent breakfasts are served in the bright dining-room which is nicely decorated with quality wallpapers. The lounge/dining-room has a cosy gas fire and a Kilkenny marble fireplace. Mrs St John is a charming host, trained in hotel management. The house is within walking distance of the beach and 10 minutes' drive to Waterford. No smoking and no pets. Some rooms on the ground floor.

OWNER Mrs St John   OPEN 1 April–1 September
ROOMS   1 double, 1 twin, 2 family (all en suite)
TERMS B&B IR £15.00 p.p.; reductions for children; single supplement IR £4.00

WATERFORD

Blenheim House

Blenheim Heights, Waterford, Co Waterford
Tel: (051) 74115

Set in a country lane in lovely countryside, Blenheim House was built in 1763 and stands in 4 acres of grounds. This grand Georgian house is furnished throughout with antiques and decorated to a high standard, cleverly combining the grandeur of the past with all modern comforts. The elegant bedrooms are spacious and comfortable, most of them with original fireplaces. The large lounge, with an open fire, overlooks the grounds and is a peaceful spot to unwind in.

The house derives its name from the Battle of Blenheim. The Waterford Glass factory is close by. Other local activities include golf, fine beaches and swimming. Horse-riding can be arranged. Situated 3½ miles (5 km) from Waterford city on the Passage East Road, just 7 minutes' drive from the Passage East car ferry.

OWNER Mrs Claire Fitzmaurice   OPEN All year   ROOMS 6 rooms (all en suite)   TERMS B&B IR£15.50 p.p.; reductions for children; no single supplement

Diamond Hill Guest House

Slieverue, Waterford, Co Waterford
Tel: (051) 32855/32254

A well-appointed and comfortable guest house in an elevated position in a quiet part of Waterford, situated in award-winning gardens. The modern bedrooms are well furnished, immaculate and are good sized. The upstairs bedrooms overlook the gardens, peaceful countryside and grazing cattle. There are 2 lounges; one has a TV. Evening meals are available in the restaurant, which has an excellent reputation for fine food. There is a menu for breakfast and Diamond Hill is fully licenced. Two miles (3 km) from Waterford, with golf, horse-riding, fishing and sandy beaches nearby. No smoking in the dining-room and no pets. Visa and Access cards accepted.

OWNERS John and Mary Malone   OPEN All year, except Christmas   ROOMS 5 double, 2 twin, 1 single, 2 family (all en suite)   TERMS B&B IR £14.00-£20.00 p.p.; reductions for children; evening meal à la carte

Foxmount Farm

Halfway House, Waterford, Co Waterford

Tel: (051) 74308

A lovely house in attractive countryside down a lane surrounded by a 250-acre farm, which is managed by Mr Kent and one of his sons. The Kents are a most welcoming, friendly couple and have been many years in the bed-and-breakfast business. In 1991 they were the winners of the Galtee National award. The drawing-room is most attractive and has an open fireplace; the dining-room has separate tables and a piano. The 2 front family-rooms are very large and offer lovely rural views. Although no bedroom is en suite, there are plenty of baths and showers to go around. The evenings have a party-like atmosphere, with excellent home-cooked meals using fresh food; afterwards it is but a short walk to the pub at the end of the lane. Amenities include a hard tennis court, table tennis, snooker and ponies to ride on – on leading rein only. The house is signposted off the Dunmore East to Waterford road.

OWNER Mrs Margaret Kent   OPEN 1 March–1 November
ROOMS 1 double, 2 twin, 2 family   TERMS B&B from IR £14.00 p.p.; reductions for children; single supplement IR £4.00; evening meal IR £12.00

Knockboy House

Dunmore Road, Waterford, Co Waterford

Tel: (051) 73484

A detached Georgian house set back off the road in an elevated position, with a pleasant garden. The house has been in the family since it was built 160 years ago. Very little is left of the original house other than a few outbuildings, as it has been modernised and added to over the years. Mrs Karmash is an accommodating host, and there is a relaxed home-from-home atmosphere here. The bedrooms are basic and clean, and 2 rooms have recently had bathrooms added onto them. There is a sun-porch overlooking the River Suir and a guest lounge with TV. No smoking in the dining-room. No pets. Situated 3 miles (4½ km) from Waterford and the beaches.

OWNER Mrs Jacinta Karmash   OPEN All year, except Christmas
ROOMS 2 double, 3 twin, 1 family (2 en suite)
TERMS B&B IR £15.00 p.p.; reductions for children; single supplement IR £5.00; evening meal IR £12.00

Lakefield House

Rossduff, Dunmore Road, Waterford, Co Waterford
Tel: (051) 82582

A large, modern house set in its own grounds about 200 yards off the Dunmore East to Waterford road. Lakefield overlooks Bellake, below the house, and there are views to the coast at Woodstown beach about 2 miles (3 km) away. The surrounding farmland is mostly tillage, but there are a few goats, sheep, chickens and ducks, as well as 2 ponies and a donkey. Most of the rooms have a view and there is a patio outside the drawing-room. Mrs Carney is a friendly lady who was previously in the hotel and restaurant management business. No smoking in the dining-room.

OWNER Cally Carney   OPEN All year, except Christmas
ROOMS 3 double, 1 twin, 1 family (all en suite)
TERMS B&B IR £14.00 p.p.; reductions for children; single supplement IR £3.00; evening meal IR £12.00

Moat Farmhouse

Faithlegg, Cheekpoint Road, Waterford, Co Waterford
Tel: (051) 82166

An attractive whitewashed building in a historic spot, surrounded by a cluster of low farm buildings. The main house has had a long strip added onto it, which mostly accommodates the guests, and there is an attractive garden to one side of the house. Moat Farmhouse has been in the Gough family for many generations and the gardens surround the site of an eighth-century castle. The mixed farm consists of tillage and cattle (greyhounds are also reared and trained here) and there is a new golf course almost next door. The bedrooms are very small and plain and there is a sitting/dining-room with piano.

OWNER The Gough family   OPEN mid March–1 November
ROOMS 2 double, 1 twin, 1 family (2 en suite)   TERMS B&B
IR £12.00-£13.00 p.p.; reductions for children; single supplement
IR £3.00; evening meal IR £12.00

County Wexford

The most south-easterly county and one of the main gateway points through the port of Rosslare; it is also the driest and warmest part of the whole country, an area of gentle hills, fertile farmland and a coastline of sandy beaches. Much of Wexford's history is associated with the Norman invasion and the 1798 rebellion.

The Wexford Festival, which takes place every October, is a world-renowned opera festival featuring lesser-known works and top international singers. The town throbs with an influx of opera lovers, and many fringe events take place at the same time. It is an attractive town with narrow, winding streets, and of particular interest to see are the Maritime Museum and the twelfth-century ruins of Selskar Abbey.

The castle at the attractive market town of Enniscorthy now houses the county museum, with an interesting folk section. Worth a visit are the thirteenth-century castle at Ferns, the old town of New Ross and Dunrody Abbey dating from 1182, near Campile. Nearby at Dunganstown is the Kennedy ancestral home.

BUNCLODY

Clohamon House

Bunclody, Co Wexford

Tel: (054) 77253 , Fax: (054) 77956

Clohamon is a delightful eighteenth-century house on 180 acres, surrounded by beech woods and gardens which

contain many rare trees and plants. There are garden walks and the fields in front run down a gentle hill to the River Slaney, where by special arrangement guests can fish for salmon and trout in season. The land is farmed as a dairy farm and is also home to the internationally renowned Connemara ponies. The bedrooms are tastefully decorated, with four-poster beds (including the single), all with matching fabrics. Each bedroom has a hairdryer and tea- and coffee-making facilities. The annex is more basic but ideal for someone who wants a little privacy. The study has a TV and telephone for guests' use. Organically grown vegetables are used in the excellent five-course meals, which are served by prior arrangement. The atmosphere here is informal; guests are treated like personal friends. Pets outside by arrangement. No smoking in the bedrooms. The house is signposted from Bunclody. Visa and Access cards accepted.

OWNERS Sir Richard and Lady Levinge   OPEN 1 February–mid November   ROOMS 3 double/twin/single (all en suite)
TERMS B&B IR £36.00-£45.00 p.p.; reductions for children; single supplement occasionally available

ENNISCORTHY

Ballinkeele House

Ballymurn, Enniscorthy, Co Wexford
Tel: (053) 38105

Built in 1840 this rather austere, large country house still belongs to the Maher family 4 generations later. It is approached up a long driveway and is set in 350 acres of farmland. Apart from the additions of such modern conveniences as bathrooms and heating, it remains much as it was built, with a distinctively Victorian flavour. The Mahers are a friendly couple, and Margaret produces an enormous breakfast which can include hot pancakes and home-made jams. The master bedroom, which has a four-poster bed, is the same shape as the drawing-room below, and the formal dining-room has one large table. Guests have use of the billiard room, hard tennis court and are welcome to walk around the estate. The Mahers also cater for shooting parties. No smoking in the bedrooms and pets outside only.

OWNERS John and Margaret Maher   OPEN 1 April–mid November
ROOMS 4 double/twin (all en suite)   TERMS B&B IR £25.00-£27.00 p.p.; reductions for children; single supplement IR £4.00; evening meal IR £15.00

Oakville Lodge

Ballycarney Road, Enniscorthy, Co Wexford

Tel: (054) 88626

A friendly, welcoming family home set in a ³/₄-acre garden in a quiet, peaceful location overlooking miles of countryside, including the River Slaney Valley, famous for its salmon and trout fishing. The gardens are landscaped with heathers, flowering shrubs and ornamental trees, with a background of beech, oak and holly trees. There is a conservatory for guests' use. Three of the comfortable bedrooms have their own individual porches. There are several stairs to the approach of the house and, for people with difficulties, these can be avoided by entering through a side door. All rooms are on the ground floor. No smoking in the dining-room. Located off the N80 road to Enniscorthy. Visa accepted.

OWNER Mrs Attracta Doyle OPEN 1 April–1 September
ROOMS 2 double/twin/ family (2 en suite, 3 with showers only)
TERMS B&B IR£13.00-£14.50 p.p.; reductions for children; single supplement IR£3.00

Woodville

Ballyhogue Road, Enniscorthy, Co Wexford

Tel: (054) 47810

A wistaria-covered 70-year-old farmhouse in a tranquil setting. There is a wonderful informal, friendly atmosphere, and guests are treated as friends. The bedrooms are comfortable, one with a marble washstand. The family room is very large and there is a cot for a small child. Although there is a guest lounge, Mrs Doyle welcomes guests into the family lounge, offering tea or coffee and delicious home-made scones. The guest lounge has a wooden ceiling and a fine display of silver. Both Mr and Mrs Doyle enjoy chatting to their guests and are a most accommodating, helpful couple. Excellent home-cooked evening meals are served, with large portions, fresh vegetables and tasty desserts. Smoking in the family lounge only. Pets outside. Forty minutes' drive to Rosslare. From the ferry take the first right immediately after the bridge, Ballyhogue Road; signposted from there.

OWNER Mrs Ann Doyle OPEN 1 March–1 October
ROOMS 1 double, 2 twin, 1 single (2 en suite) TERMS B&B
IR £13.00-£14.00 p.p.; reductions for children; evening meal
IR £11.00, high tea IR £7.00

Horetown House

Foulkesmill, Co Wexford
Tel: (051) 63771, Fax: (051) 63633

Horetown House is a lovely seventeenth-century house situated in beautiful parklands and tranquil countryside, amidst 150 acres of mixed farming. All of the rooms are fairly spacious and comfortable, with old-fashioned furnishings. Guests are offered tea or coffee upon arrival in the drawing-room where guests can relax around the log fire. There's a separate TV room. The paint is peeling a little here and there and the floors creak, but somehow it just seems to add to the charm. There are no en suite rooms at present, but there are plans to add these soon. The Cellar restaurant offers an imaginative menu and is very popular with the locals; reservations are required (children's meals available). An equestrian centre includes a large all-weather indoor arena and offers riding instruction for the beginner and the competent rider. No pets. Located 1 1/2 miles (2 1/2 km) east of Foulkesmill.

OWNERS The Young family OPEN mid March–mid January
ROOMS 7 double, 2 twin, 2 family TERMS B&B IR£15.00 p.p.; reductions for children

Riversdale House

Lower William Street, New Ross, Co Wexford
Tel: (051) 22515

A large modern house just 3 minutes from the town centre, surrounded by gardens which the Foleys only built a couple of years ago. Riversdale has lovely views over the town and the River Barrow and from the back it is particularly attractive at night, when the church is floodlit. This is a comfortable house with an upstairs lounge, and all the bedrooms and dining-room are on the ground floor. Mrs Foley is a friendly, chatty lady who teaches cookery classes and has won the National Housewife of the Year award. No smoking in the dining-room and pets outside only.

OWNER Mrs Ann Foley OPEN 1 March– 1 November
ROOMS 4 family (all en suite) TERMS B&B IR £15.00 p.p.; reductions for children; single supplement IR £4.00; evening meal IR £13.00

Robinstown Farmhouse

New Ross, Co Wexford
Tel: (051) 28337

This 250-year-old farmhouse, set in 20 acres, makes a perfect base in which to explore the many places of interest close by. The house dates from the seventeenth century and has been the family home since it was built. The grounds are lovely and there is a peaceful and friendly atmosphere. The lounge is spacious and very comfortable, and there is an alcove with an interesting wooden ceiling and an antique chaise-longue and chair. Light snacks are available. There are plans to have some bedrooms with en suite facilities. Locally there are lovely walks and fishing. Mrs O'Keefe is pleased to recommend local eating establishments. No smoking in the bedrooms. Located 4 miles (6 km) south of Rosslare off the Wexford road at Ballinaboola.

OWNER Mrs G O'Keefe OPEN 1 April–1 October
ROOMS 2 double/twin/family TERMS B&B IR £13.00 p.p.; reductions for children; single supplement available

St Mary's

Waterford Road, New Ross, Co Wexford
Tel: (051) 21662

A detached bungalow owned by Kay Walsh on the edge of town. The bedrooms are clean, all with fitted wardrobes and tea-makers. There are no en suite rooms, but all the rooms have sinks and there are two bathrooms exclusively for guests' use. There's a lounge with TV and a fireplace. Kay Walsh offers basic, clean accommodation close to town, in a warm and comfortable atmosphere. Breakfast is served to non-residents, and the Kennedy Homestead is a 10-minute drive away. No smoking in the dining-room. No pets.

OWNER Mrs Kay Walsh OPEN 1 May–1 September
ROOMS 2 double, 1 twin, 1 family TERMS B&B IR £12.00 p.p.; reductions for children; single supplement IR £2.00

ROSSLARE

Ballybro Lodge

Rosslare, Co Wexford
Tel: (053) 32333

The Doyles bought the land surrounding Ballybro Lodge, which once was an old stone quarry, while they were living in England. They filled in enough of the quarry to build the house, and now the garden gets bigger every year as they fill in more. The house, which is down a quiet country lane, is very accessible to Rosslare, about 2¹/₂ miles (4 km) away. All except one of the bedrooms have both a double and single bed and all have tiny shower rooms and tea- and coffee-making facilities. There is also a public bathroom. The lounge/dining-room is long and narrow and overlooks the garden and small stream which borders the property. There is also a games room with table tennis and a snooker table. Pets outside only. The house is signposted off the main Rosslare to Wexford road.

OWNER Mrs L Doyle   OPEN All year, except Christmas
ROOMS 5 double/twin/family (all en suite)   TERMS B&B IR from £15.50 p.p.; reductions for children; single supplement IR £5.00

Kilrane House

Kilrane, Rosslare Harbour, Co Wexford
Tel: (053) 33135

Kilrane House is an attractive nineteenth-century farmhouse close to the ferry and on the main Kilrane village road. There's an elegant period lounge with log fires, which together with the dining-room has retained its attractive ceiling cornices. The 2 family rooms are exceptionally large and all rooms are now en suite. There is a play area in the garden for children. The house is clean and fresh looking and the Whitehead family are most accommodating. Although evening meals are no longer provided, the house is opposite a restaurant and close to hotels. Access and Visa cards accepted.

OWNERS Siobhan and Peter Whitehead   OPEN All year
ROOMS 2 double/twin/family (all en suite)   TERMS B&B IR £15.00 p.p.; reductions for children; single supplement IR £6.00

Laurel Lodge

Rosslare Harbour, Co Wexford
Tel: (053) 33291

An attractive, low, modern house down a quiet country lane in the village of Kilrane, just a couple of kilometres from

Rosslare Harbour. The rooms are clean and comfortable and all are en suite. There is a guest lounge; the dining-room, where breakfast only is served, overlooks a small patio at the back of the house. Smoking only in the lounge and pets by arrangement only. Laurel Lodge is signposted off the main Rosslare to Wexford road.

OWNERS Mary McDonald   OPEN 1 March–1 December
ROOMS 3 double, 1 twin, 1 family (all en suite)
TERMS B&B IR £13.00 p.p.; reductions for children; single supplement IR £2.00

Old Orchard Lodge

Kilrane, Rosslare Harbour, Co Wexford
Tel: (053) 33468

Old Orchard House is a 2-year-old red-brick house, just 1¹/₂ miles (2¹/₂ km) from Rosslare, 50 yards off the main road down a quiet country lane, in the village of Kilrane. The property, which is enclosed by walls, was originally the orchard to Kilrane House next door. The house is clean and comfortable, and Aileen Ironside is a friendly lady who welcomes families. There are plans to add a conservatory and a wing for the family. No smoking in the bedrooms and no pets.

OWNERS Aileen Ironside   OPEN 1 March–mid November
ROOMS 1 double, 2 twin, 1 single, 1 family (3 en suite)
TERMS B&B IR £12.00–£14.00 p.p.; reductions for children; single supplement IR £3.00–£4.00

WEXFORD

Ardruadh

Spawell Road, Wexford, Co Wexford
Tel: (053) 23914

Ardruadh, meaning "high red house", is an elegant Gothic-style residence built in 1892, set in ³/₄ acre of landscaped gardens. Peter and Nora Corish are a friendly couple and guests are assured of genuine old-fashioned hospitality. The house is full of character, with the original pitch pine and wrought-iron staircase. The beautifully appointed bedrooms are individually furnished and decorated, and all have clock radios, TVS, hairdryers and tea- and coffee-making facilities. The front bedroom overlooks the River Slaney and is often

used as a bridal suite. There are several antique furnishings
about, including an ornate Italian 3-piece suite in the
spacious lounge. Peter and Nora have been here just over 3
years and have done a splendid job in restoring the house to
its original splendour. Five minutes' walk to the town centre
and to the bus and train station. No smoking in the dining-
room. No pets. Visa and Mastercard accepted.

OWNERS Peter and Nora Corish   OPEN All year, except Christmas
ROOMS 3 double, 1 twin, 1 family (all en suite)
TERMS B&B IR £16.00 p.p.; reductions for children

Chez Nous

New Line Road, Wexford, Co Wexford
Tel: (053) 24104

Chez Nous, meaning "our house", offers one of the warmest
welcomes in Ireland. Situated on the edge of town, the
rooms are small but adequate, all with tea- and coffee-
makers. One room is suitable for wheelchair access, ap-
proved by the National Rehabilitation Board. Michael and
Florence Hyland are down-to-earth, informal folk who really
enjoy what they do. This is very much a family-run affair,
with Florence cooking breakfast, served by Michael, who
has a great sense of humour. The TV lounge is tiny but cosy,
and beyond is the small dining-room and patio. All drinking

water has been purified. No smoking in the dining-room
and no pets. Visa and Access cards accepted. One mile (1¹/₂
km) from the Quay.

OWNER Mrs Florence Hyland   OPEN 1 April–1 December
ROOMS 2 double, 1 twin, 1 family (all en suite)
TERMS B&B IR £13.00 p.p.; reductions for children; single
supplement IR £5.00

Clonard House

Clonard Great, Wexford, Co Wexford
Tel: (053) 42141

John and Kathleen Hayes and their family own and run this
Georgian farmhouse. The 120-acre dairy farm is set in
idyllic surroundings with a clear view of Wexford Harbour.
Clonard House was completely renovated in 1986, but
many of the original fixtures remain, such as cornices,
ceiling rose and the dining-room fireplace. Since then the
house has been redecorated, maintaining its already high
standard. The spacious rooms are extremely attractive, with
traditional and antique furnishings. The well-appointed
lounge is the perfect spot to relax in after a busy day
sightseeing. This is a lovely, peaceful house with a lot of
character and a stairway to nowhere. Evening meals by
prearrangement. There is a wine licence. No smoking in the
bedrooms and no pets. A half-mile off the Ring Road,
signposted on the N25. Visa and Access cards accepted.

OWNERS John and Kathleen Hayes   OPEN Easter–mid November
ROOMS 4 double, 1 twin, 4 family (all en suite)
TERMS B&B IR £15.00 p.p.; reductions for children; single
supplement IR £4.00; evening meal IR £12.00

Killiane Castle

Drinagh, Wexford, Co Wexford
Tel: (053) 48885/58898

An eighteenth-century house attached to the tower of a
fourteenth-century castle on a dairy farm, down a quiet
country lane. Killiane Castle is very handy for the Rosslare
ferry, which is only 10 minutes away, and early breakfasts
are provided. The house has been attractively decorated and
furnished, in particular the dining-room. The bedrooms on
the first floor are large and those on the second floor

considerably smaller. There is a hard tennis court and 4 self-catering apartments at the back of the house. No smoking in the dining-room and pets outside only.

OWNERS Jack and Kathleen Mernagh   OPEN 1 March–mid November   ROOMS 7 double/twin, 1 single (all en suite) TERMS B&B IR £14.00-£16.00 p.p.; reductions for children; single supplement IR £3.00; evening meal IR £12.00

Newbay Country House

Wexford, Co Wexford
Tel: (053) 42779, Fax: (053) 46318

Newbay Country House is a family-run house where the emphasis is on good food, a warm welcome and comfort in a relaxed, tranquil atmosphere. The house was built in 1822 and incorporates in its outbuildings a fourteenth-century castle and a seventeenth-century farmhouse. The house is set in 30 acres of park garden and woodland. Open peat and log fires welcome guests and the house has stripped pine furniture, which Paul Drum restores. Mientje Drum makes the patchwork covers for the four-poster beds, made by Paul, all with duvets. The bow-ended drawing-room and elegant dining-room have kept their long sash windows and original shutters. Paul's collection of top-hats, solar topis and plumed helmets is on the top of a carved Austrian tall-boy in the drawing-room. A still-working symphonium stands in the hall. There is a pond with wild ducks, moorhens and a peacock. Paul and Mientje are both excellent cooks, and you will be well cared for at Newbay House. Early reservations highly recommended. The house has a wine licence. No pets. Visa and Access cards accepted.

OWNERS Paul and Mientje Drum   OPEN All year, except Christmas ROOMS 6 double (all en suite)   TERMS B&B IR £28.00 p.p; reductions for children; single supplement IR £8.00; evening meal IR £22.00

The West and North West

County Clare

Two hundred castles and 2,300 stone forts going back to pre-Celtic times testify to County Clare's turbulent past. Although Shannon airport lies on the southern border, most of the county is underpopulated by tourists. The scenery varies from the barren terrain of the Barony of Burren, which in spring is covered with a profusion of northern and southern plants, and the scenic lakes and hills of Slieve Bernagh, wonderful walking country, to the towering Cliffs of Moher. Water plays an important role, the sea bordering the west, and the Shannon Estuary the south and east.

The Franciscan Ennis Friary, noted for its sculptures and decorated tombs, is one of the principal sights of the county capital, Ennis, which is situated on a bend of the River Fergus.

A bridge crosses the Shannon at Killaloe. Nearby is the twelfth-century cathedral built on the site of an earlier church. It has a magnificent door and the views from the top of the square tower are splendid. Across the Shannon lies Bunratty Castle, well known now for its medieval banquets. It dates from 1460 and was at one time occupied by Admiral Penn, the father of William Penn, founder of Pennsylvania. A Folk Park is to be found in the castle grounds with examples of houses from the Shannon area.

The island of Iniscealtra on Lough Derg can be reached by boat from the attractive village of Mountshannon. There are five old churches, a round tower, saints' graveyard, hermit's cell and a holy well.

Moohaun Fort, one of the largest Iron Age hill forts in Europe, is to be found at Newmarket on Fergus. Knappogue Castle, another venue for medieval banquets, and Quinn Abbey are close to Craggaunowen.

Of special interest to both botanists and historians is the Burren. Once densely populated, this savagely rocky area is rich in prehistoric and historic monuments. Look closely at its limestone and discover a wealth of exquisite, delicate plant life thriving in a myriad of tiny crevices. The Burren Display Centre explains the fauna and flora of the 200 square miles of the Burren and its remains of ancient civilisation. The ruined Leamaneh Castle is near Kilfenora, which is on the edge of the Burren. Between Kilfenora and Ballyvaughan is Ballykinvarraga, one of Ireland's finest stone forts, and south east of Ballyvaughan is Aillwee Cave, which dates back to 2 million BC.

The road from Lisdoonvarna, Ireland's foremost spa

town, leads to the impressive Cliffs of Moher, which stretch for nearly 5 miles (7^1/$_2$ km). Liscannor is famous for the Holy Well of St Brigid, which is an important place of pilgrimage.

Lahinch, a small seaside resort, is best known for its champion golf course and to the south is Spanish Point, where many ships of the Spanish Armada were wrecked.

Around the village of Quilty seaweed can be seen drying on the stone walls for kelp-making. The coast south of Kilkee is every bit as spectacular as the Cliffs of Moher, with caverns and strange rock formations.

BUNRATTY

Bunratty Hillside

Clonmoney North, Bunratty, Co Clare
Tel: (061) 364330

A pleasant, warm and relaxing family home 4 miles (6 km) from Bunratty Castle. There are 6 comfortable bedrooms, a lounge with TV and a separate dining-room. Breakfasts only are served, but the famous pub Durty Nelly's, serving lunch and evening meals, is only 1 mile (1^1/$_2$ km) away. The McCabes are a friendly family, the atmosphere is warm and welcoming, and a hot drink is offered in the morning or evening at no extra charge. The Medieval Banquet at nearby Bunratty Castle can be pre-booked upon request. Local activities include golf and horseback-riding. No pets. Four miles (6 km) to Shannon airport. Turn off at Sixmilebridge (R471); signposted from there.

OWNERS Mrs Maureen McCabe   OPEN 1 January–20 December
ROOMS 2 double/twin/family   TERMS B&B IR £12.00-£14.00 p.p.; reductions for children; single supplement IR £4.00

Bunratty View

(formerly Brooklawn), Cratloe, near Bunratty, Co Clare
Tel: (061) 87352

Bunratty View, formerly known as Brooklawn, is a purpose-built bed-and-breakfast establishment. The bedrooms are large, with good-sized en suite facilities, dressing tables and hairdryers. Breakfasts are served in the bright dining-room, which has a conservatory effect due to its large windows which overlook scenic countryside. The house is exceptionally well maintained, and there are quality carpets throughout. All of the rooms are on the ground floor and one is suitable for wheel-chair access. There are views of floodlit Bunratty Castle at night, and free transportation to the castle is available. Guests may enjoy evening meals and light snacks, if prearranged. There is a guest lounge. Smoking is not permitted in the dining-room and there are 2 bedrooms reserved for non-smokers. No pets. Located only 10 minutes from Shannon airport, 600 yards off N18; take first left beyond Bunratty Castle on route to Limerick.

OWNERS Joe and Maura Brodie   OPEN All year   ROOMS 2 double, 2 twin, 3 family (all en suite)   TERMS   B&B IR £14.00 p.p.; reductions for children; single supplement IR £3.00; evening meal IR £10.00, high tea IR £8.00

Rockfield House

Hill Road, Bunratty, Co Clare

Tel: (061) 364391

Two minutes' walk from Bunratty Castle and the famous pub/restaurant Durty Nelly's, you will find Rockfield House, an attractive home in a peaceful setting overlooking the Shannon River. Margaret Garry is an accommodating host, dedicated to ensuring her guests receive a warm welcome. There is a TV lounge, where tea and coffee are served upon request. All of the bedrooms have private bathrooms and lovely warm duvets. There is a no smoking area in the house. Margaret is happy to pre-book the Bunratty Castle banquet. No pets. An easy drive from here to Shannon airport.

OWNER Mrs Margaret Garry   OPEN All year   ROOMS 2 double, 3 twin, 1 family (all en suite)   TERMS B&B IR £12.00-£14.00 p.p.; reductions for children; single supplement IR £4.00

ENNIS

Ardlea House

Clare Road, Ennis, Co Clare

Tel: (065) 20256, Fax: (065) 29794

Ella Leyden is a congenial host who has been successfully running her bed and breakfast for just over 6 years. Ardlea House is a detached corner house on the edge of town, 200 yards to all amenities. There are TVs and hairdryers in the bedrooms; electric blankets are provided upon request.

There are 3 ground-floor rooms. Excellent breakfasts, featurng home-made breads, are served in the bright and sunny dining-room. A good location for exploring the Cliffs of Moher, Bunratty Castle, and within easy driving distance to Shannon. No smoking in the dining-room or bedrooms. On the N18 main Shannon airport road. Access and Visa cards accepted.

OWNER Ella Leyden   OPEN All year, except 22 –30 December
ROOMS 2 double, 1 twin, 1 family (3 en suite)
TERMS B&B IR £12.00-£13.00 p.p.; reductions for children; single supplement IR £3.00

Carberry House

Kilrush Road, (Carferry Road), Ennis, Co Clare
Tel: (065) 24046

This house, built in 1964, stands in its own grounds on the edge of town in a quiet location. Mrs Roberts has been offering her special brand of hospitality for over 27 years, and was one of the first B&Bs in the area. The motto here is: "There are no strangers here, only friends we have not met." The bedrooms are average in size, all with orthopaedic beds and electric blankets. There are tea- and filtered coffee-making facilities in the sun-lounge. Tasty fresh-cooked breakfasts are served in the bright, sunny dining-room. Very popular with tourists and business people in the winter; advance reservations are recommended. Situated on the road to the car ferry and within easy driving distance of Shannon and Bunratty. No smoking in the bedrooms. Pets outside only. Evening meals must be prearranged. Visa accepted.

OWNER T J and Pauline Roberts   OPEN 1 February–1 December
ROOMS 1 double, 4 twin (4 en suite)   TERMS B&B IR £13.00 p.p.; reductions for children; single supplement IR £5.00; evening meal IR £12.00

Masabiella

off Quinn Road, Ennis, Co Clare
Tel: (065) 29363

The standard of maintenance and decor is exceptionally high throughout the public rooms and bedrooms of this house. The bedrooms, which are in an extension to the house, are beautifully furnished and individually decorated with warm duvets and restful colour-coordinated matching fabrics. The large, bright lounge features a carved inlaid mahogany sideboard with a fine display of Waterford crystal. There is a TV, and guests can also enjoy fireside conversation with the family. Masabiella is set in a beautiful landscaped garden surrounded by trees, with a stream running by the house. There is a hard tennis court for guest use. Pets outside only. Smoking permitted only in the lounge. From Ennis turn left at Old Ground Hotel and drive straight for 1½ miles (2½ km); signposted from there. Located one mile (1½ km) from the CIE railway station, signposted on the Quinn Road.

OWNER Mrs Monica O'Loughlin   OPEN Easter–15 October
ROOMS 1 double, 2 twin, 3 treble (4 en suite)   TERMS
B&B IR £13.00–£15.00 p.p.; reductions for children; single supplement IR £5.00

Newpark House

Tulla Road, Ennis, Co Clare
Tel: (065) 21233

A 300-year-old country residence with an old-world atmosphere, set in 85 acres of pasture and woodland. The bedrooms are a good size, all have tea-making facilities, most have pastoral views. Breakfasts and evening meals are served, with wholesome home-cooked food featuring fresh produce when the season allows. Mrs Barron is a congenial host, happy to give advice on local activities. A baby-sitting service is available. There are 2 sitting-rooms for guests and 2 dining-rooms. Pets by arrangement. Guests may bring their own wine. Take the Tulla Road from Ennis at the Roselevan Arms, turn right – Newpark House is around the corner.

OWNER Mrs Bernadette Barron   OPEN 1 March–1 November
ROOMS 6 family rooms (all en suite)   TERMS B&B IR £15.00–
£20.00 p.p.; reductions for children; single supplement IR £7.00;
evening meal IR £12.00

ENNISTYMON

Station House

Ennis Road, Ennistymon, Co Clare
Tel: (065) 71149, Fax: (065) 71709

Station House offers what must be just about the best value

in the area. Originally built in 1930 as a family home, it was extensively remodelled 5 years ago, another floor being added to accommodate additional bedrooms. All of the rooms are spacious, with standard decor. The large bedrooms have dressing-tables, tea-makers, orthopaedic beds and good-sized bathrooms with plenty of hot water. Adjacent to the east side of the house is the original stone building which was the Co Clare railway shop, made famous by the Percy French song "Are you right there Michael are you right". Perhaps the Station House has lost some of the intimacy of a small B&B, but the proprietors and staff are extremely helpful. Two miles (3 km) to Lahinch, a great area for golf and beautiful scenery. No pets. No smoking in the dining-room. Advance reservations highly recommended. Visa accepted.

OWNER Mrs Kathleen Cahill   OPEN All year, except Christmas
ROOMS 2 double/twin/family (all en suite)   TERMS B&B IR £12.50 p.p.; no reductions for children; single supplement IR £4.00

Tullamore Farmhouse

Kilshanny, via Ennistymon, Co Clare
Tel: (065) 71187

This is a working farm of 203 acres of suckler herd, situated in a picturesque location with panoramic views and a river running through the property. The house was built over 100 years ago and has been added onto and modernised over the years. The house is in good decorative order, the bedrooms are clean and comfortable. There is a tastefully furnished sun porch with magnificent views which guests may use. Guests are assured of a warm welcome by the Carroll family - a cup of tea is offered upon arrival at no extra charge. An excellent base from which to explore this area, Kilshanny is only 4 miles (6 km) away from Lahinch and the Cliffs of Moher are only a 20-minute drive away. Fishing is available in the nearby river and traditional Irish music can be heard nightly in Liscannor's famous McHugh's pub. Hairdryers are provided in the bedrooms. No pets. From Ennistymon to Lisdoonvarna, turn left at Kilshanny – the farmhouse is signposted from there.

OWNER Mrs Eileen Carroll   OPEN 1 March–1 October
ROOMS 1 double, 2 twin, 1 family (3 en suite)   TERMS B&B
IR £13.00-£13.50 p.p.; 20% reduction for children; single supplement IR £3.00

Cois Fharraige

Cregg, Lahinch, Co Clare

Tel: (065) 81580

Cois Fharraige, which means seaside, is a modest bungalow in a quiet location on the coast road. The lounge has ocean views, is comfortably furnished and has an open fire. Rosemary Donohue is a friendly lady who has been offering bed and breakfast for 4 years; breakfasts are plentiful and include home-made bread. Tea and coffee is available just about any time upon request. The house is adjacent to a pitch and putt and Lahinch Golf Course is close by. Smoking permitted in the lounge only. No pets.

OWNER Mrs Rosemary Donohue   OPEN 17 March-31 October
ROOMS 1 double, 1 twin, 1 family (2 en suite)
TERMS B&B IR £13.50 p.p.; children under 4 free; 50% reduction for children under 12; single supplement IR £3.00; special off-season rates upon request

Lehinchy House

Dough, Lahinch, Co Clare

Tel: (065) 81512

Lehinchy House is situated in a quiet, peaceful location surrounded by open rolling countryside with views in the distance on clear days of the Cliffs of Moher. This is a serene and tranquil place with some lovely walks in the area and just minutes from the golf course. The rooms are fresh, clean and comfortable, with semi-orthopaedic beds. There is a doll collection in the TV lounge, which has been added onto over the years from happy guests as far away as South Africa. Breakfast only is served but there are lots of pubs and restaurants in Lahinch with a wide choice of evening meals. Pets by arrangement. Take the hospital road halfway between Ennistymon and Lahinch, turn left at the T-junction - Lehinchy House is the first house on the right.

OWNER Dympna Armstead   OPEN All year, Christmas by arrangement   ROOMS 1 double/twin/family (all en suite)
TERMS B&B IR £13.50 p.p.; 50% reduction for children; single supplement IR £3.00; special off-season rates upon request

Nazira

School Road, Lahinch, Co Clare
Tel: (065) 81362

Nazira is a friendly, comfortable house in an elevated position with magnificent views of the bay and the beautiful, scenic countryside. As one guest commented, "It's like looking down on creation." The house was named after Mr Sarma's home in India and was for many years the family holiday home. In 1989 an extension was added, including a dining-room and lounge which overlook the bay. The well-furnished bedrooms are airy and bright. The en suite family room has one double and an adjoining twin room, ideal for 2 couples or a family. A wonderful spot for golfers, just minutes from the golf course. Mrs Sarma is a very congenial host who takes excellent care of her guests. No pets. Located approximately 850 metres off the main Lahinch/Milltown Malbray ferry road. Private car park.

OWNER Frances Sarma   OPEN 1 April–31 October
ROOMS 2 double, 1 twin, 1 family (2 en suite)
TERMS B&B IR £14.00-£15.00 p.p.; reductions for children; single supplement IR £3.00

Seafield Lodge

Ennistymon Road, Lahinch, Co Clare
Tel: (065) 81594

A double-glazed bungalow on the edge of Lahinch, 5 minutes' walk away from the town, golf courses and beaches. From the lounge and front bedrooms there are lovely countryside views and the ruin of one of the O'Brien castles. The bedrooms are clean and comfortable, all with their own bathrooms, TVs, hairdryers and electric blankets. The bungalow also overlooks a fairy fort (obscured somewhat by new construction), treated with great respect by the local farmers who are careful to farm around it. There are 3 ground-floor rooms. Breakfast is served in the pretty dining-room with lace tablecloths and fine china. Smoking in the bedrooms only. No pets. Situated on the main N67 road approaching Lahinch from Shannon.

OWNER Joseph and Ita Slattery   OPEN Easter–30 November
ROOMS 2 double/family (4 en suite)   TERMS B&B IR £14.00 p.p.; reductions for children; single supplement IR £4.00

Ore a Tava House

Lisdoonvarna, Co Clare

Tel: (065) 74086

A pleasant, modern bungalow in a quiet area, 1 mile (1½ km) from Lisdoonvarna. The bedrooms, with pretty duvets, are basic, clean and functional. All have en suite facilities, are simply furnished and 3 have TVs. The dining-room and lounge both have fireplaces. The owners live in a separate unit so residents have the run of the house. There is a patio for guests' use overlooking scenic countryside. This is an ideal base for touring the Burren, the limestone area, the Cliffs of Moher and the well-known health spa in Lisdoonvarna. There is horse-riding close by. No pets. Drive through Lisdoonvarna on Galway road 1 mile (1½ km); turn left at the pump – Ore a Tava is the third house on the left.

OWNER Mrs Helen Stack   OPEN 1 April–31 October
ROOMS 4 double, 2 twin (all en suite)   TERMS B&B IR £13.50 p.p.; reductions for children; single supplement IR £3.00; high tea IR £10.00

Tessie's

Fernhill Farmhouse, Doolin Road, Lisdoonvarna, Co Clare

Tel: (065) 74040

A comfortable 300-year-old farmhouse set in scenic countryside with distant views of the sea. Tessie Linnane, a warm and friendly lady, has been in business for over 18 years. Guests enjoy refreshments in the conservatory lounge overlooking green fields. There is a sweet little parlour with the original cornices and ceiling rose. The bedrooms all have their own bathrooms and are clean and comfortable. The dining-room has been enlarged and there is an open fire; the tables have been arranged so that guests may enjoy the view. Fernhill Farmhouse has a wonderfully informal, relaxed atmosphere, and Tessie does everything possible to ensure that guests are well taken care of. All the food is home-made and features fresh vegetables and freshly baked brown bread. This is definitely a peaceful and tranquil spot from which to explore the area; the Gateway of the Burren, beautiful sandy beaches and Lisdoonvarna Spa Wells are only a 5-minute

drive away. Traditional music can be heard nightly in
Doolin and Lisdoonvarna. Smoking not permitted in the
dining-room or bedrooms. Pets outside. Signposted off the
Doolin and Coast road.

OWNER Mrs Tessie Linnane   OPEN Easter–31 October
ROOMS 5 bedrooms: double, twin, family (4 en suite)
TERMS B&B IR£14.00 p.p.; 15% reduction for children under 10;
single supplement available; evening meal IR £12.00, high tea
IR £8.00

MILLTOWN MALBAY

Leagard House

Mullagh Road, Milltown Malbay, Co Clare

Tel: (065) 84324

Situated in its own grounds of 6 acres in a peaceful location,
this comfortable house offers a home-from-home
atmosphere. The lounge has a TV and video. The dining-
room, where breakfasts and evening meals are served, leads
out onto the verandah. Meals include a choice of starters
and desserts, all made fresh daily. There is a wine licence,
and morning coffee and afternoon tea are served.The
bedrooms are furnished with a mixture of modern and old-
fashioned furniture, and the ground floors are large enough
for wheel-chair access. This is an ideal starting point for the
Ring of Clare, and the 9-hole golf course at Spanish Point is
half a mile away. Pets outside only. Situated on the Mullagh
Road 400 yards from town.

OWNERS John and Suzanne Hannon   OPEN April–October
ROOMS 2 double/twin/family (2 en suite)   TERMS B&B IR £12.00
p.p.; 33% reduction for children under 10; single supplement
IR £3.00; evening meal IR £12.00, high tea IR £7.00

NEWMARKET ON FERGUS

Beechgrove Farmhouse

Shannon-Ennis Road, Knocknagun, Newmarket on Fergus,
Co Clare

Tel: (061) 368140

Just 3 miles (4½ km) from Shannon airport is this modern
bungalow on a 100-acre cattle and sheep farm. A tranquil
location with views of the River Shannon and rolling
farmland. Mrs Conheady is proud of the personal attention

given to guests, and nothing is too much trouble to ensure they have a comfortable and enjoyable stay at the farm. There is one ground-floor en suite bedroom, and the family room has a king-size bed plus 2 more beds. The TV lounge has a fireplace and is shared with the family. Mr Conheady used to train racehorses and there are 2 riding stables within 1 1/2 miles (2 1/2 km). There are free pony rides for the children on the farm. Evening meals consist of home-grown meat, home-baking, and when possible fresh home-grown vegetables. Smoking in the lounge only. Follow the main N18 Galway to Ennis road from Bunratty village; there are signs on the left-hand side and Beechgrove is 4 miles (6 km) from Bunratty.

OWNERS Mr and Mrs Conheady OPEN 1 March–1 November ROOMS 2 double, 1 twin, 2 family (2 en suite) TERMS B&B IR £12.00 - £13.00 p.p.; reductions for children; single supplement IR £4.00; evening meal IR £10.50, high tea IR £7.50

County Donegal

County Donegal is a large county with a spectacular variety of scenery and an indented coastline of bays, beaches, cliffs and peninsulas set against a backdrop of mountains, moors and lakes. It has many archaeological sites and much evidence of the old Irish culture and traditions. The Irish language is still the spoken language in areas north and west of Killybegs, an important fishing port.

Donegal gets its name from the fort the Vikings established – Dun na nGall – the Fort of the Foreigners. The town built by Sir Basil Brooke is on the estuary of the River Eske, a busy place and good for buying tweeds. The castle with its great square tower, once the stronghold of the O'Donnell's, was refurbished by Basil Brooke in 1610.

Bundoran is one of Ireland's best-known seaside resorts with a good golf course and famous beaches. Further north is Ballyshannon, long a centre of importance because of its river; the town winds up a steep hill above the River Erne. Rossnowlagh has a 2 1/2 mile (4 km)-long beach.

Beyond Killybegs the coastal scenery becomes wild and spectacular. Kilcar is a centre for the handwoven tweed industry, as is Ardara. The scenery at Glencolumbkille is magnificent, with its blend of hills and sea. Here the late Father MacDyer organised a cooperative movement to try to keep young people from emigrating and also established a folk museum. Portnoo and Narin are popular seaside towns for holidaymakers.

Letterkenny is the largest town in Donegal, dominated by St Eunan's Cathedral, built in the modern Gothic style between 1890 and 1900. The winding road approaching Doocharry from Fintown is known as the "corkscrew" and brings you through the Gweebarra Glen to the sea. Aranmore Island is the most populated and largest of a series of islands. It can be reached by ferry from Burtonport, an attractive, unspoilt fishing port. Gweedore, situated in spectacularly wild country, is a major holiday centre. From here there is a road of remarkable scenic beauty by loughs Nacung and Dunlewy into the Derryveagh Mountains.

Gortahork and Falcarragh are Irish-speaking and good places to climb Muckish Mountain. Dunfanaghy has a fine beach and is a good place to explore the granite promontory of Horn Head. Between Creeslough, attractively situated on Sheephaven Bay, and Carrigart is the romantic Doe Castle, almost surrounded by the sea. Rosapenna, a resort town with a good golf course, is on the way to the beautiful Rosguill Peninsula, with wonderful views of Melmore Head, Horn Head and Muckish Mountain. Milford is a pretty town from where the Fanad Peninsula with its sandy beaches can be explored. The tranquil village of Rathmullan is beautifully situated with a sandy beach and is famous for its historical associations. The road between here and Ramelton is one of the most beautiful in Ireland. Ramelton also has a lovely situation and is a planned Planter's town, begun in the early seventeenth century.

The Inishowen Peninsula, which lies between the waters of Lough Foyle and Lough Swilly, is quite different to the rest of Donegal. The centre is very hilly, Slieve Snaght at 615 metres being the highest point. From the Buncrana to Clonmany and Cardonagh road there are fine views of sea and mountains, and a road runs right to the tip of the peninsula at Malin Head. One of the best views to be had of this part of Donegal is from the Grianan of Aileach. It is 250 metres high and consists of a cashel or stone fort enclosed within three earthen banks. Cardonagh's chief glory is St Patrick's Cross dating from the seventh century, making it one of the very important Christian crosses.

Glenveagh lies in a deep gorge and is the setting for a fairytale castle and wonderful gardens which were developed by Hendry McIlhenny. The gardens and the estate are now a national park, and Mr McIlhenny has bequeathed the castle to the nation. Gartan, Kilmacrenan and Raphoe, which has a fine old cathedral, are all associated with St Columba.

Rose Wood House

Edergole, Killybegs Road, Ardara, Co Donegal
Tel: (075) 41168

Located on the edge of Ardara on the Killybegs road, Rose
Wood House was originally a bungalow and had another
storey added to it by Mr McConnell, who is a builder, in
1990. Mrs McConnell is a most friendly lady who lived for
11 years in New York. There is a very large lounge/dining-
room with an open fire and lovely views from the upper
floor over the river. Freshly baked scones are served with
breakfast. No smoking in the dining-room. On the Killybegs
road 1 mile (1½ km) from Adara. Visa and Mastercard
accepted.

OWNER Mrs Susan McConnell   OPEN 1 January–1 December
ROOMS 3 double, 2 twin, 1 single (all en suite)
TERMS B&B IR £13.00 p.p.; 25% reduction for children; single
supplement IR £5.00

Woodhill House

Ardara, Co Donegal
Tel: (075) 41112

In a wonderful position up a valley from Ardara, the house
stands on a site dating from the seventeenth century, overlooking the Donegal highlands. This historic country house
formerly belonged to the Nesbitts, Ireland's last commercial
whaling family. The present owners bought the property
about 5 years ago and are continuing to make
improvements; all the bedrooms are now en suite. The 2
front rooms are large, simply furnished, with wonderful
views. The house has a friendly and informal atmosphere
and is surrounded by 4 acres of gardens, including a walled
garden, which are available for guests' use. There is a high-
quality restaurant and licenced bar. Handmade crafts are
available for purchase. The area, famous for its Donegal
tweeds and woollen goods, also offers salmon and trout
fishing, shooting, pony trekking, golf, excellent bathing
beaches and the Sheskinmore Wildlife Reserve. Stables
available for dogs. No smoking. A quarter of a mile from the
village. All major credit cards accepted.

OWNERS John and Nancy Yeats   OPEN All year, except Christmas

ROOMS 4 double, 1 single (all en suite) TERMS B&B IR £22.00
p.p., small single IR £16.00; 50% reduction for children under 11;
single supplement IR £10.00; evening meals from IR £15.00

BALLYLIFFEN

Pollin House

Carndonagh Road, Ballyliffin, Inishowen, Co Donegal
Tel: (077) 76203

An attractive whitewashed house on the outskirts of
Ballyliffin, standing in a small front garden and with lovely
views. A friendly older couple own this house and they work
the bed and breakfast together. The front room has views to
Malin Head, and this is the preferred place for visitors to sit,
as it is always warm with its Aga-type cooker which also
heats the water. The room has a sofa and TV as well as a
table and chairs for meals. There is a small front sitting-
room with open fire, and the bedrooms are all very small.
Nearby is an 18-hole golf course, and pony trekking can be
arranged on the Isle of Doagh. Evening meals can be served
by arrangement. There are several pubs in the area featuring
Irish music and a craft shop. A pitch and putt course on the
grounds of the house is available for guests' enjoyment. No
pets.

OWNER Mrs Kathleen Grant OPEN 1 April–31 October
ROOMS 1 double, 3 family (3 en suite) TERMS B&B IR £12.00
p.p.; 33% reduction for children; single supplement IR £4.00

BALLYSHANNON

Ardpatton Farmhouse

Cavangarden, Ballyshannon, Co Donegal
Tel: (072) 51546

A comfortable, informal seventeenth-century farmhouse set
in its own grounds, with over 380 acres for beef cattle. The
kitchen used to be the local school and the house was the
local post office. The present owners have modernised the
house, with only 2 of the original bedrooms remaining. Two
more bedrooms had en suite facilities added in 1991 and all
have TVs. The bedrooms are all spacious, fresh and clean,
with views over the countryside. Mrs McCaffrey's delightful
children ably assist during the school holidays. Fires are lit
on most days in both the lounge and dining-room.
Breakfasts include freshly baked scones, cereals, juice and a

115

full cooked breakfast. Evening meals are available if prearranged; light meals including salads and sandwiches are also served. There is a tennis court, tea room and craft centre on the premises. On the N15 3 miles (4 ½ km) from Ballyshannon and 11 miles (16½ km) from Donegal. Visa accepted.

OWNER Mrs Rose McCaffrey   OPEN 1 February–31 October
ROOMS 5 double, 1 single (3 en suite)   TERMS B&B IR £12.00-£13.50 p.p.; 50% reduction for children under 12; single supplement IR £3.00; evening meal IR £12.00

Cavangarden House

Ballyshannon, Co Donegal
Tel: (072) 51365

A square, stucco-covered house standing in its own grounds, approached up a long driveway through park and farmland in lovely countryside. A Georgian house dating from 1750, it has been considerably altered. The McCaffreys are only the second family to have lived in the house. Mr McCaffrey and his brother run the 380-acre arable farm. The interior is comfortable, with a long entrance hall. The dining-room has one enormous table, seating 14 people, with an open peat fire, piano and old pictures; a warm and friendly room. The sitting-room also has an open fire and is a comfortable room. The bedrooms are large with solid, old-fashioned furniture and there is a view from all rooms. Three have TVs. Evening meals are served by arrangement at 7.30 pm and there is a wine licence. Three miles (4½ km) from Ballyshannon on the N15 main Donegal road. All major credit cards accepted.

OWNER Mrs Agnes McCaffrey   OPEN All year, except Christmas
ROOMS 2 double/twin/family (4 en suite)   TERMS B&B IR £12.50-£14.00 p.p.; 50% reduction for children; single supplement IR £4.00; evening meal IR £12.00

BUNCRANA

Kinvyra

14 St Orans Road, Buncrana, Co Donegal
Tel: (077) 61461

A 1930s large whitewashed detached house close to town. All the bedrooms are upstairs and have washbasins, are spotlessly clean, freshly decorated, with solid, old-fashioned

116

furniture. There is a small TV lounge with open fire. A cup of tea or coffee is available just about any time at no extra charge. Mrs Molly McConigly has been welcoming guests into her home for over 20 years, offering true old-fashioned hospitality. The rear of the house overlooks Snagh and Farhn hill. No pets.

OWNER Mrs Molly McConigly   OPEN All year, except Christmas
ROOMS 1 double, 2 twin, 1 family   TERMS B&B IR £14.50 p.p.; reductions for children; no single supplement

Ross na Ri House

Old Road, Ballymacarry, Buncrana, Co Donegal
Tel: (077) 61271

The house stands a couple of hundred yards from the main road to Londonderry, 200 yards from the Motor Inn, and enjoys wonderful views of Lough Swilly. Mrs McCallion makes her own jams and also bakes; as much of the food as possible is home-made. She loves meeting people and making them feel at home in her friendly house. There is a cosy little dining-room with TV and a fireplace and a small front sitting-room with TV, open fire and lovely sea views. The bedrooms are small but fresh and bright, and 2 overlook the sea. Evening meals are available by arrangement. There is no licence, but guests may bring their own wine. All the bedrooms are on the ground floor. No smoking in the bedrooms.

OWNER Mrs Anna McCallion   OPEN All year, except Christmas
week   ROOMS 2 double/family   TERMS B&B IR£12.00 p.p.; 25% reduction for children; single supplement IR£2.00

BUNDORAN

Conway House

4 Bayview Terrace, Bundoran, Co Donegal
Tel: (072) 41220

A modest Victorian property located on the south side of the main Bundoran Road. Conway House is situated close to all the amenities of this popular seaside town, including Water World. Two of the bedrooms have sea views, as does the dining-room and lounge; both have their original fireplaces which are lit on chilly days. This house certainly has an easy-going atmosphere. Mrs McGureen does all the cooking, ably assisted by her daughter Mairead, while Mr McGureen keeps busy decorating, maintaining the house and restoring antiques. There is a lot to see and do in the area and this is definitely an ideal base from which to explore the region. Horseback-riding and golf are offered within a mile. No pets.

OWNER Dorothy McGureen   OPEN Easter–31 September
ROOMS 1 double, 12 twin, 1 family (all en suite)
TERMS B&B IR £12.00–£13.50 p.p.; 50% reduction for children under 12; single supplement upon request

Strand View

East End, Bundoran, Co Donegal
Tel: (072) 41519

Strand View is an older refurbished townhouse, right in the centre of Bundoran on the main road, with safe off-street parking. It is a functional guest house, with good-sized bedrooms and a pleasant dining-room and TV lounge. There are views from the front bedrooms of the beach. No smoking is permitted in the dining-room. The house is well maintained and all the bedrooms are now en suite. Evening meals are not available, but there are plenty of restaurants and pubs close by. No pets.

OWNER Mrs Mary Delaney and family   OPEN All year, except Christmas   ROOMS 1 double, 3 twin, 1 family (all en suite)
TERMS B&B IR £13.00 p.p.; 20% reduction for children; single supplement IR £4.00

CASTLEFINN

Gortfad

Castlefinn, Co Donegal
Tel: (074) 46135

Gortfad has been the home of the Taylor family for 7 generations. The house has been built onto and adapted over the years, though the front is mainly Victorian and Edwardian. Gortfad is furnished with old-fashioned possessions, stained glass windows and is set in peaceful grounds. The rooms are large and there is a comfortable sitting-room with a log fire. Mrs Taylor is a hospitable, kind lady who has been offering her special welcome for over 25 years - little wonder that she has guests returning year after year. Home-baking, delicious scones and fruit cake are often offered with tea on arrival at no extra charge. Evening meals are available only if prearranged, and there are several good eating establishments in the area. Guests can visit the tweed weaving area of Glenties and the 10,000 hectares of the National Park at Glenveagh Castle, as well as Derek Hill's remarkable art collection at Church Hill. There are 2 golf courses within 6 miles (9 km) and salmon, trout and coarse fishing are available in the River Finn. Lifford is 5 miles (7^1/$_2$ km) away and Donegal town only 25 miles (37^1/$_2$ km). Dogs by arrangement. Located on the north side of Castlefinn, signposted off the N15.

OWNER Mrs J Taylor OPEN Easter–mid September
ROOMS 2 double, 2 twin, 1 family (2 en suite)
TERMS B&B IR £15.00 p.p.; 20% reduction for children under 12; single supplement IR £4.00

CLAR

Craward

Birch Hill, Clar, Co Donegal
Tel: (0732) 2584

A modern and immaculate bungalow in an elevated position with spectacular views of the Sligo Mountains and Lough Eske. The bedrooms are average in size and individually decorated in blue and pink. The one bedroom that is not en suite has its own bathroom – all have a radio. There is a separate dining-room and lounge which overlooks the view, and although there is a TV, guests seem to prefer to sit and chat and enjoy the beautiful scenery. This is an ideal spot for people who are looking for peace and serenity: there are some lovely walks close by, including a 12 mile (18 km)-walk around the lake. Home-cooked evening meals are served at reasonable prices; fresh fish is a speciality of the house and is provided by Mr Ward, who is a fish merchant. Guests may choose what they would like for breakfast. There are few rules here – Deborah Ward is a very congenial host who wants guests to feel relaxed and at home in her warm and friendly house. Pets by arrangement. Signposted off the Letterkenny Road, 3 miles (4^1/$_2$ km) from Donegal.

OWNER Deborah Ward OPEN 1 March–1 October
ROOMS 1 double/twin (2 en suite) TERMS B&B IR £13.00-£14.00 p.p.; 50% reduction for children; single supplement IR £1.00; evening meal IR £10.00

Culdaff House

Culdaff, Inishowen, Co Donegal
Tel: (077) 79103

This large, slightly forbidding, grey stucco building is approached up a long driveway from the edge of the attractive village of Culdaff in the extremities of Co Donegal, from which

there are lovely views of hills and sea. The sombre exterior in no way reflects the fresh and bright interior. This is very much a family home, with large rooms and high ceilings. There is a large comfortable drawing-room, with a fireplace and TV, a smaller dining-room, and the beds have old Irish linen bedspreads. The property has been in Mr Mills's family for the last 300 years. Since taking over the house 5 years ago the Mills have done a tremendous amount of remodelling and redecorating, gradually taking in bed-and-breakfast guests. There are no private bathrooms, but there are 3 bathrooms exclusively for guests' use. The motto of this informal, happy house is: "We share our home with our guests." Culdaff House was the recipient of the BHS Farmhouse of the Year award. Evening meals by prior arrangement; there is a wine licence. No smoking and no pets. On route via Carndonagh; take Beach Road in Culdaff.

OWNER Mrs Frances Mills   OPEN 1 February–30 November
ROOMS 4 double, 2 twin   TERMS B&B IR £14.00 p.p.; 20% reduction for children; single supplement IR £4.00; evening meal IR £12.00

Ard Dallan

Stranacorkra, Derrybeg, Co Donegal

Tel: (075) 31209

The house is in an elevated position just off the main road, and has lovely views. Derrybeg is in an Irish-speaking area and many people come here to study the language. The TV lounge, dining-room and one of the bedrooms all have front-facing views. All the bedrooms are on the ground floor and are small, bright and clean. No pets.

OWNER Mrs Anne Shonlin   OPEN 1 April–30 September
ROOMS 2 double, 1 twin (1 en suite)   TERMS B&B IR £12.00 p.p.; 50% reduction for children; single supplement IR £2.00

Arranmore House

Killybegs Road, Donegal, Co Donegal

Tel: (073) 21242

The Keeneys built this house in 1968. It is located up a steep hill in a quiet peaceful area with lovely views yet is only 3 minutes from town. Mrs Keeney, who comes from England, is a most friendly lady and runs a comfortable house with a pleasant atmosphere. The guest lounge has a TV and open fire. Substantial breakfasts are served in the bright dining-room. The bedrooms are quite good-sized with tiny shower rooms and most of them are on the ground floor. Smoking is not permitted in the dining-room and pets are not allowed. Take the Killybegs road from Donegal, cross over the bridge; Arranmore is the sixth house on the left, past the library.

OWNER Mrs Doreen Keeney   OPEN All year   ROOMS 3 double, 2 twin, 1 family (6 en suite)   TERMS B&B IR £14.00 p.p.; 25% reduction for children; single supplement IR £4.00

Shanveen House

Donegal Town, Co Donegal

Tel: (073) 21127

Shanveen House is an attractive house in an elevated position overlooking the Blue Stack Mountains. Three minutes' walk from town, opposite the eighteenth-century Presbyterian church. The bedrooms are spotlessly clean and all have chairs and individual wardrobes. Although there is only one en suite bedroom, another does have its own shower. There is a comfortable lounge with Victorian furnishings and a piano which guests are welcome to play. A lovely grandfather clock stands in the hallway and there is an interesting doll collection displayed in a cabinet on the landing. There's a pleasant homely atmosphere, and Mrs McGarrigle does everything possible to ensure her guests feel welcome and comfortable. No pets.

OWNER Mrs Anna McGarrigle   OPEN All year, except Christmas
ROOMS 2 double, 1 twin, 1 family (1 en suite)
TERMS B&B IR £12.50-£13.50 p.p.; 20% reduction for children; single supplement upon request

St Ernan's House Hotel

St Ernan's Island, Donegal, Co Donegal
Tel: (073) 21065, Fax: (073) 22098

Just 2 miles (3 km) south of Donegal town, St Ernan's was built in 1826 by John Hamilton, a nephew of the Duke of Wellington. Originally an island, it is now linked to the mainland by a short causeway and covers some 8 acres. It is a most elegant, lovely country house in a beautiful position, offering peace and tranquillity in wonderful surroundings. It was turned into a hotel in 1983 and has been in the O'Dowd's hands since 1987. The rooms are beautifully proportioned and very spacious, each bedroom with marvellous views of sea and countryside and equipped with telephones and TVS. À la carte meals using local produce are served in the large dining-room. The elegantly furnished drawing-room is a good place to relax in at the end of the day. There is a bar which is used by residents; non-residents are not encouraged. There are several golf courses close by and horseback-riding and fishing are available locally. Smoking is not permitted in the dining-room and pets are not allowed, nor are children under 6. The house is signposted from the main road between Donegal and Sligo. Visa and Access cards accepted.

OWNER Mr Brian O'Dowd   OPEN Easter-mid November
ROOMS 13 double/twin/single (all en suite)
TERMS B&B IR £40.00-£60.00 p.p.; 25% reduction for children; single supplement available upon request; evening meal IR £23.50

Baymount Bed and Breakfast

Downings, Co Donegal

Tel: (074) 55395

Mrs McBride was born in the small house at the bottom of the driveway. Twenty-two years ago she and her husband built their present house. At the time Mr McBride was a builder; now he is a driving-test examiner. The house stands above the narrow country road, with spectacular views over the water to the mountains. At the time the house was built the family was very large; the couple had 12 children. Some have now left home, which has provided space for Mrs McBride's bed-and-breakfast business. The TV/video lounge is a large, bright room, enjoying the same magnificent views as does the dining-room, which has separate tables as well as a TV and sitting area and sliding doors onto the terrace: a lovely place to sit in on a fine day. A hairdryer and iron are available upon request. Smoking allowed in the lounge only. No pets. The house can be found half a mile from Downing village on Atlantic Drive.

OWNER Mrs Mary McBride OPEN Easter–31 August
ROOMS 4 double, 2 twin (1 en suite) TERMS B&B IR £13.00–£14.00 p.p.; 50% reduction for children under 10; single supplement IR £7.00

DUNFANAGHY

Rosman House

Figart, Dunfanaghy, Co Donegal

Tel: (074) 36273

Standing on the edge of Dunfanaghy, Rosman House is in a wonderful position, an elevated spot with marvellous views all round. Mrs McHugh is a bright, friendly lady who formerly was a teacher in Falcarragh. Her husband looks after the 100-acre dairy and sheep farm. There have been several improvements to the property, and the spacious TV lounge is an ideal spot to relax in after a busy day. The bedrooms are of a high standard, all individually decorated in coordinated colour schemes and fitted with tea-makers and electric blankets. There are 5 ground-floor bedrooms.

Breakfast is served in the elegant dining-room on separate tables, where guests have views of Horn Head. Smoking permitted in the lounge only. Rosman House has lovely scenic walks close by and an 18-hole golf course. Located by turning right after the art gallery on the main Falcarragh road.

OWNER Mrs Roisin McHugh   OPEN All year   ROOMS 3 double, 1 family, 1 treble (all en suite)   TERMS B&B IR £13.50 p.p.; 25% reduction for children; single supplement IR £4.50

DUNGLOE

Barr a' Ghaoith

Quay Road, Dungloe, Co Donegal
Tel: (075) 21389

Barr a' Ghaoith means "Top of the Wind", an apt description as this house is in an elevated position with pleasant views. This is very much a family-run establishment with all the family joining in to help with the work. There is a separate dining-room and a very comfortable lounge with TV, video and games. The house is situated in a picturesque seaside area, only 200 metres from the sea and within walking distance of the town. The bedrooms are fresh and clean and all have tea-makers. Breakfasts include home-baked breads and preserves. Close by the visitor will enjoy angling, golf, hill walking and scenic drives; tennis courts and a leisure centre are also available. Children are welcome. Pets welcome by arrangement.

OWNER Mrs Susan Gallagher   OPEN All year, except Christmas
ROOMS 2 double, 1 twin, 1 family (2 en suite)
TERMS B&B IR £12.00-£13.00 p.p.; 50% reduction for children under 12, children under 3 free; single supplement IR £3.00

DUNKINEELY

Bruckless House

Bruckless, Dunkineely, Co Donegal
Tel: (073) 37071, Fax: (073) 37070

This attractive creeper-covered Georgian house with its traditional cobbled courtyard was built around 1750. Standing in 18 acres in a lovely position right on the coast, it is surrounded by an attractive garden with numerous plants

and a meadow with mature trees. Irish draught horse
Connemara ponies are bred here and can often be se
grazing down by the shoreline. The house has recent
completely redecorated and is comfortably furnished ... ...
oriental flavour, as the Evans family spent many years in
Hong Kong. The 2 reception rooms have log fires and views
of the bay, while the 2 front bedrooms also have lovely views
and are of a good size. Evening meals are served if
prearranged and include vegetables grown in the garden and
fresh fish, available in part from the mussel and oyster farm
in the bay. Guests may bring their own wine, as the house is
not licenced. There are 2 golf courses within easy reach. No
smoking. No pets. Take the N56 west, 12 miles (18 km) from
Donegal town on the left-hand side.

OWNERS Mr and Mrs C J Evans   OPEN 1 April–1 October
ROOMS 1 double, 2 twin, 2 single (2 en suite)
TERMS B&B IR £20.00-£25.00 p.p.; no reductions for children;
evening meal IR £16.50

FALCARRAGH

Sea View Guest House

Upper Ray, Falcarragh, Co Donegal
Tel: (074) 35552

An attractive bungalow set in 3 acres of land in an elevated
position, surrounded by open countryside and sweeping
views of the mountains and sea – on clear days Tory Island
can be seen. Guests are greeted upon arrival with a cup of
tea or coffee, and substantial breakfasts, including home-
made bread and preserves, are served in the cosy kitchen.
The lounge is bright, cheerful and comfortably furnished
and there is a TV. Evening meals are not served, but advice
on good local restaurants is given as well as information on
what to see and do in the area. Mrs McFadden is a very
helpful lady and guests are well taken care of here. This is a
wonderful spot to relax in and there are lovely walks close
by. Situated 2¹/₂ miles (4 km) from Falcarragh on the N56
(East) road. Pets outside only.

OWNER Mrs Jean McFadden   OPEN All year, except Christmas
ROOMS 2 twin, 1 single   TERMS B&B IR £11.00 p.p.; 50%
reduction for children and senior citizens; single supplement
IR £1.00

Corner House

Cashel, Glencolumbkille, Co Donegal
Tel: (073) 30021

The Corner House is right in the centre of the village and,
as its name implies, it is on a corner. Mrs Byrne, a very
pleasant lady, runs the bed and breakfast as well as the
adjoining small shop, and her husband runs the pub. From
the outside the house looks quite modest but it is surpris-
ingly big inside, with an enormous dining-room and small
upstairs TV lounge. The house is well maintained; the
bedrooms are small, but very clean. The one bedroom that
is not en suite has its own bathroom. The surroundings are
beautiful and this is a great place for walking and hill-
climbing. Sandy beaches are close by and there is good
fishing. No pets. There is a public phone.

OWNER Mrs John P Byrne   OPEN 1 April–30 September
ROOMS 2 double, 3 family (4 en suite)   TERMS B&B IR £12.50-
£14.00 p.p.; reductions for children; single supplement IR £4.00

INVER

Cloverhill House

Cranny, Inver, Co Donegal
Tel: (073) 36165

Approached up a driveway lined on each side with high yew
hedges, this attractive, long, low, whitewashed modern
building stands in an elevated position with lovely views over
the river. The house was constructed with some
imagination. There is an enormous and very pleasant open
sitting-room/dining-room with a real fire, and the bedrooms
are spacious and well furnished. Three of the bedrooms are
on the ground floor, and en suite facilities have recently
been added to one of the bedrooms. An evening meal is
available on request at 7 pm and there is a wine licence. Pets
are not permitted. Seven miles (10^1/$_2$ km) from Donegal
town on the Killybegs road.

OWNER William Coyle   OPEN All year, except Christmas
ROOMS 2 double, 3 twin, 1 single (1 en suite)
TERMS B&B IR £14.50–£18.00 p.p.; 10% reduction for children;
no supplement in single room; high tea from IR £12.00

Hollyhaven

Kerrykeel, Co Donegal
Tel: (074) 50064

Hollyhaven has wonderful views over sea and mountains, and although out in the country it is only a 4-minute walk from the village. The small, whitewashed bungalow stands in an attractive front garden on a quiet country road. Mrs Dougherty is a most friendly lady who greets her guests with a cup of tea or coffee whenever possible at no extra charge. Evening meals are served at 7 pm if ordered in advance. There is no licence, but guests are welcome to bring their own wine. All the bedrooms are on the ground floor and all are very small, spotlessly clean and simply furnished. The dining-room has one table and lovely views and there is a TV lounge. No pets.

OWNER Mrs Rose Dougherty   OPEN Easter–31 October
ROOMS 2 double, 1 twin, 1 single (2 en suite)
TERMS B&B IR £11.50-£13.50 p.p.; 25% reduction for children; single supplement IR £2.00; evening meal IR£11.00

KILCAR

Rockville House

Roxborough, Kilcar, Co Donegal
Tel: (073) 39107

Midway between Killybegs and Glencolumbkille, this small, modern house stands in a slightly elevated position with marvellous views of the sea at Slieve League, where the cliffs at Bunglas, the highest marine cliffs in Europe, are 3 miles (4¹/₂ km) away. This is a popular destination with tourists from many parts of the world. Maureen Hughes has lots of energy and is responsible for organising walking tours in the Kilcar area. Teelin, an Irish-speaking area, lies just below and attracts people wishing to learn Irish. The house is about a mile (1¹/₂ km) from the nearest beach and from Carrick village. The family room has wonderful views, as does the lounge, which has a dining table at one end and sliding doors onto the patio. The bedrooms are small but very bright and prettily and simply decorated. All have TVs, tea- and coffee-makers and electric blankets and are located on the ground floor. Four-course meals are served on request between 7 and 9 pm, and breakfasts are served on pottery plates specially made in Sligo. There is no licence, but guests are welcome to bring their own wine. No pets. Take the Carrick road from Killybegs, then the Coast road outside Killcar to Carrick.

OWNER Maureen Hughes   OPEN All year   ROOMS 1 double/twin/family (2 en suite)   TERMS B&B IR £12.50-£13.50 p.p.; 33% reduction for children; single supplement IR £4.00; evening meal IR £11.50

KILLYBEGS

Bannagh House

Fintra Road, Killybegs, Co Donegal
Tel: (073) 31108

Bannagh House may be recognised by the ambulance that stands occasionally in the driveway (when off duty), as Mr Melly is an ambulance driver. Mrs Melly takes care of the bed-and-breakfast business and her 5 children. This modern house stands in an elevated position in a small front garden on the edge of Killybegs, with wonderful views over the harbour, town and hills both near and distant. Killybegs is a big fishing port, and the harbour always seems to be full of enormous fishing boats; consequently it is an excellent place for fresh fish. Melly's Café does excellent fish and chips in vast portions. There is a TV lounge and dining-room overlooking the bay. All the bedrooms are on the ground floor. No pets. An ideal location for touring the Donegal area. Located by driving through Killybegs; Bannagh House is the first bungalow on the left on Glencolmcille Road.

OWNER Mrs Phyllis Melly   OPEN 1 April–31 October
ROOMS 4 double, 1 twin, 1 family (all en suite)
TERMS B&B IR £13.00 p.p.; 20% reduction for children under 10; single supplement IR £4.00

LAGHY

Hillcrest

Ballyshannon Road, Laghy, Co Donegal
Tel: (073) 21837

Three-and-a-half miles (5 km) from Donegal, just off the Ballyshannon Road, Hillcrest offers a warm, friendly

welcome. All the bedrooms, which are on the small side,
have pretty front-facing views and are located on the ground
floor. Each bedroom has tea-making facilities. The small TV
lounge has a piano and comfortable chairs, and the dining-
room has a pleasant view. The modern bungalow stands on
the side of a hill and is set in an attractive front garden. No
smoking is permitted in the dining-room and pets are not
allowed.

OWNER Mrs Sheila Gatins   OPEN 1 April–31 October
ROOMS 1 double, 3 family (2 en suite)   TERMS B&B IR £12.00-
£13.50 p.p.; 25% reduction for children; single supplement
IR £3.00

LETTERKENNY

Hillcrest House

Lurgybrack, Letterkenny, Co Donegal
Tel: (074) 22300, Fax: (074) 25137

Spotlessly clean and with a warm welcome, Hillcrest House
is on the main Sligo road, just a mile from Letterkenny, so it
is potentially noisy. However, there is a great view over the
water, town and mountains. The Maguires are a friendly
couple with 5 children and they serve guests with cakes and
tea when they arrive. The rooms, although a little small, are
comfortable and there are 4 ground-floor bedrooms. No
smoking is permitted in the dining-room, a pleasant room
with separate tables. There is a small TV lounge. Hillcrest
House is RAC acclaimed. Pets outside. This is an ideal
location for touring. Situated on N56 to Sligo, 1 mile (1½
km) from the roundabout on Derry Road. All major credit
cards accepted.

OWNERS Larry and Margaret Maguire   OPEN All year, except
Christmas ROOMS 1 double, 2 twin, 3 family (5 en suite)
TERMS B&B IR £13.00 p.p.; 33% reduction for children; single
supplement IR £4.00

White Gables

Dromore, Derry Road, Letterkenny, Co Donegal
Tel: (074) 22583

White Gables is a spacious house in an elevated position
overlooking the river and town; the house is sandwiched
between a new dual carriageway and the former main road.

Double-glazed windows in the house keep traffic noise to a minimum. There is a lovely view from the breakfast room/ lounge, which has a small sitting area and one table for breakfast facing the windows. The small bedrooms are clean and simply furnished; 2 are on the ground floor. There is quite an attractive rear garden. No pets. The house is on the Derry Road about 2 miles (3 km) outside Letterkenny.

OWNER Mr and Mrs J McConnellogue   OPEN All year, except Christmas   ROOMS double/twin/family (4 en suite)
TERMS B&B IR £13.00 p.p.; 30% reduction for children; single supplement IR £3.00

LIFFORD

The Hall Greene

Porthall, Lifford, Co Donegal

Tel: (074) 41318

A neatly kept, whitewashed farmhouse dating from 1611 and standing back from the road looking into Co Tyrone and the Sperrin Mountains. Salmon fishing is available on the river at the bottom of the garden. Licences can be obtained in Lifford. This is a wonderful place for children – it is off the road, has large rooms, and on the farm there are lambs, goats and a donkey. Mrs McKean, a very friendly lady, has 4 children of her own, so children are especially welcome. The house is a comfortable family home with a large TV lounge and open fire in an old fireplace. The bedrooms have tea-making facilities and hairdryers. The large dining-room has 2 tables, and there is one family room which is very spacious, with massive pieces of old furniture. Evening meals are served at any convenient time if arranged in advance. There is no licence, but guests are welcome to bring their own wine or beer. The 150-acre farm has sheep, cattle, pigs and cereals. Non-smokers preferred. No smoking in the dining-room. The house is signposted 1½ miles (2½ km) from Lifford on the N14.

OWNERS Mervyn and Jean McKean   OPEN All year, Christmas by arrangement   ROOMS 1 double, 3 family (1 en suite)
TERMS B&B IR £12.00 p.p.; 50% reduction for children under 12; evening meal IR £11.00, high tea IR £7.00

The Haw Lodge

The Haw, Lifford, Co Donegal
Tel: (074) 41397

A small farmhouse on the main road, about a mile (1½ km) from Lifford in the direction of Sligo. The rooms have been redecorated in pretty wallpaper and matching fabrics. The dining-room at the back of the house was the original farmhouse kitchen, this part dating from over 100 years ago. There is a small front garden. Haw Lodge has one ground-floor bedroom with a toilet and washbasin close by and an ideal family suite, consisting of 2 self-contained en suite bedrooms. All the beds have electric blankets and orthopaedic beds. A cot is available. The cosy lounge has a TV and fireplace. Evening meals or high teas can be served by arrangement at 6.30 pm. Salmon and trout fishing are available in the River Finn, which flows through the farm. Golf, walking, bird-watching and a fully equipped leisure centre are close by. This is a friendly house, with a home-away-from-home atmosphere. No smoking. Pets outside. Off the main Lifford to Sligo road (N15). Visa and Access cards accepted.

OWNER Eileen Patterson OPEN 1 March-1 November
ROOMS 3 double, 3 twin, 1 family (3 en suite)
TERMS B&B IR £12.00-£13.50 p.p.; 50% reduction for children; single supplement IR £4.00; evening meal IR £11.00

MALIN HEAD

Barraicin

Malin Head, Inishowen Peninsula, Co Donegal
Tel: (077) 70184

Barraicin takes its name from the field on which it was built by the Boyles 21 years ago and means "the square toecap". Just 3½ miles (5 km) from Malin Head Point, it is in a superb position about half a mile from the sea and with lovely sea views. The small, cosy dining-room, where guests share 2 tables, overlooks the pretty garden which has an old pump. The large, bright lounge has an open fire and sea views. The Doyles are a very pleasant older couple who started doing bed and breakfast 12 years ago. The bedrooms are clean and bright; all are equipped with washbasins. Tea-and coffee-making facilities and a hairdryer are available upon request. Evening meals or high teas can be served by arrangement after 7 pm and include vegetables from the garden and home-made breads and jams and marmalades. Pets are not permitted. There is no licence, but guests are welcome to bring their own. Six miles (9 km) from Malin village, opposite public telephone in Malin Head.

OWNER Mrs M Doyle   OPEN Easter-31 October   ROOMS 1 double/ twin/family   TERMS B&B IR £12.00 p.p.; 25% reduction for children; single supplement IR £3.00; evening meal IR £12.00, high tea IR £8.00

MOUNTCHARLES

Star of the Sea

Station Road, Mountcharles, Co Donegal
Tel: (073) 35094

This bed and breakfast is in a lovely position, with views of the Sligo Mountains and the sea. It is signposted from Mountcharles. The Breslins are a very friendly couple with a young son and two older boys. Most of the rooms are small but comfortable and fresh and bright. The beach is nearby, and fishing trips can be arranged. There is a TV lounge and small dining-room. Mrs Bresling no longer serves evening meals but is happy to recommend local eating establishments. Smoking is not permitted in the dining-room. The bedrooms are all on the ground floor.

OWNER Mrs Olga Breslin   OPEN 31 March–31 October
ROOMS 2 double, 1 family, 1 single (2 en suite)
TERMS B&B IR £12.00-£15.00 p.p.; reductions for children; single supplement IR £3.00

RAMELTON

Ardeen

Ramelton, Co Donegal
Tel: (074) 51243

An attractive, small country house on the edge of Ramelton, standing in a most pleasant lawned front garden with views of the River Lennon. The rooms are good-sized and prettily decorated and the front ones have lovely views. There's a TV lounge and dining-room with one big table, and outside a hard tennis court at the back of the house. The house at one time belonged to a private nurse of King George V and latterly to 2 doctors. The Campbells bought the house about 14 years ago. Mr Campbell is now retired from running a local shop and Mrs Campbell, who has 3 children, concentrates on the bed-and-breakfast business. Smoking is not permitted in the dining-room.

OWNER Mrs Anne Campbell   OPEN Easter–31 October
ROOMS 2 double, 1 twin, 1 family (1 en suite)
TERMS B&B IR £14.00-£15.00 p.p.; reductions for children; single supplement IR £3.00

Gleann Oir

Ards, Ramelton, Co Donegal
Tel: (074) 51187

A modest, modern house located in a hilly area with spectacular views all around of farmland and hills, situated about 3 miles (4^1/$_2$ km) from Ramelton and signposted off the Letterkenny road. It is a quiet, peaceful, comfortable family home, simply furnished. Mrs Crawford has 7 children of her own and children are especially welcome here. The 35-acre farm is quite an attraction, with sheep, 2 milking cows and arable land. There is a comfortable sitting-room with TV and open fire, a small rear dining-room, and an additional family room is now available. Evening meals are served to suit guests if arranged in advance. There is no licence, but guests are welcome to bring their own wine. There are 2 ground-floor rooms and all rooms have a hairdryer. Located off the N56 at Ellistrin or the R245 at Ramelton.

OWNER Mrs Rosemary Crawford   OPEN 1 March-31 October
ROOMS 2 double/family (3 en suite)   TERMS B&B IR £13.00 p.p.; 50% reduction for children; single supplement IR £2.00; evening meal IR£10.00

The Manse

Ramelton, Co Donegal
Tel: (074) 51047

The appearance of the house today is Georgian, a most attractive ivy-covered house standing in lovely gardens with views down to the river. The original house dated from 1690 and was a planter's cottage, 3 storeys high, one room on top of the other, and was added onto. The drawing-room is regency, with a bowed end and open fireplace, a most

133

attractively shaped room. Mrs Scott, who is quite a character, moved into the house 30 years ago, and everything has
been left as the family house it was, with photographs,
ornaments and even a rocking horse on the upstairs landing.
It's consequently somewhat faded and old fashioned, but
this lends to its charm. Visitors find the bathroom, with its
original fittings, quite intriguing. The bathtub has the old
shower, with enormous head and vast brass taps which allow
the water to come from three different directions, from
above, the sides and below. The study/library has a piano,
open fire and comfortable chairs, and the dining-room is at
the rear of the house in the part added in 1900. Mrs Scott
encourages her guests to have the run of the house, and
consequently most visitors forsake the more formal rooms
for what is known as the "warm" old kitchen, which is now
her own sitting-room. It is a delightfully lived-in, warm
room with an old Aga stove and table and chairs. The
functional kitchen is known as the "cold" kitchen and is in
the room behind. Mrs Scott really enjoys her guests and
prefers a few at a time so she has a chance of talking to them
and filling them in on the area and old anecdotes. A
downstairs cloakroom and wc were installed recently.
Smoking is permitted in the study/library only. No pets.
Seven miles (10^1/$_2$ km) north of Letterkenny on the shore of
Lough Swilly, direct road from Dublin.

OWNER Mrs Florence Scott   OPEN Easter to mid-September
ROOMS 1 double, 2 twin, 1 single   TERMS B&B IR £16.00 p.p.;
reductions for children negotiable; no single supplement

County Galway

Galway contains the widely renowned area of Connemara,
which stretches northwards from Galway city up to Killary
Harbour and is bordered on the east by beautiful Lough
Corrib, which boasts an island for every day of the year.

Galway, the "city of the tribes", and the nearby popular
resort of Salt Hill, which overlooks the famous Galway Bay,
have lovely beaches, a promenade for walking, lots of
restaurants; an ideal holiday spot.

Wild Connemara has inspired song and poetry. Today
Galway, Connemara and the west of Ireland are a haven for
ancient customs and culture. You will hear lilting and
evocative Irish music in the pubs and probably the Irish
language being spoken as well. Travel offshore even deeper
into Ireland's traditional way of life, with trips to Inishbofin,

Co Clare, Achill and the Aran Islands.

There's plenty to see and do in the west of Ireland: pony trekking, dramatically located golf courses, angling (which is well catered for, with abundant salmon and trout in clean waters).

If you are interested in sixteenth-century castles, visit the ruins of Ardamullivan Castle 5 miles (7^1/$_2$ km) south of Gort, an O'Shaughnessy stronghold. Fiddaun Castle, 5 miles (7^1/$_2$ km) south-south west of Gort, is another of their strongholds.

Clarinbridge is a popular place in September when it hosts the Oyster Festival. Portumna, a market town, is at the head of Lough Derg. For the more adventurous, a climb up the Slieve Auchty Mountains is well worth the view.

Two castles worth seeing include Derryhivenny Castle, 3 miles (4^1/$_2$ km) north east of Portumna. Built in 1653, it is well preserved, as is Pallas Castle, 6 miles (9 km) from Portumna on the Loughrea Road.

Ballinasloe is well known for the October Horse Fair which lasts for eight days, and includes carnival events and show-jumping exhibitions.

ANNAGHDOWN

Corrib View Farm

Annaghdown, Co Galway

Tel: (091) 91114

A charming old farmhouse near Lough Corrib, approximately 4 miles (6 km) off the Galway-Headford-Castlebar N84 road. Good old-fashioned hospitality is offered here, with the emphasis on a warm welcome and good food featuring home-baking and local fresh produce. The rooms are clean and comfortable and all the bedrooms have tea- and coffee-making facilities. The family room has en suite facilities, and there are 2 additional bathrooms exclusively for guests. Corrib View has a separate dining-room and TV lounge – smoking is permitted only in the lounge. Evening meals must be prearranged, and guests are welcome to bring their own wine. Pets outside. This is a convenient base for touring Connemara and the West. Trips to the Arran Islands can be arranged. Galway city is 8 miles (12 km) away and the National Historic Ruins at Annaghdown Pier are a short drive away. Signposted at Cloonboo Cross near Regan's Bar.

OWNER The Scott family   OPEN May–September   ROOMS 2
double, 1 twin, 1 family, 1 single (family room is en suite)
TERMS B&B IR£14.50 p.p.; reductions for children; single supplement IR£4.50; evening meal IR£15.00

CASHEL

Cashel House

Cashel, Co Galway

Tel: (095) 31001, Fax: (095) 31077

Cashel House, formerly one of Connemara's most gracious homes, stands at the head of Cashel Bay in a tranquil and secluded setting, a 40-acre estate of flowering shrubs and woodland walks. It has quickly gained an international reputation for good food and comfort in a quiet, relaxing atmosphere; carefully cooked fresh garden and sea produce are its specialities, and there are open turf fires. In 1969 the late General and Madame de Gaulle spent 2 weeks of their Irish holiday here. The house is furnished with fine antiques and other treasures. The charming, recently upgraded bedrooms are beautifully appointed and all have direct dial telephones, TVs and hairdryers. Beaches, golf, and sea fishing are available in the vicinity. There is a hard tennis court, tiny private beach and horse-riding facilities. No pets. Situated on the main Galway/Clifden road, the N59; turn left at Recess. All major credit cards accepted.

OWNERS Dermot and Kay McEvilly   OPEN All year   ROOMS 32
rooms: double/twin/family (all en suite)   TERMS IR£48.00-IR£54.00 p.p.; reductions for children upn request; evening meal from IR£25.00

CLARINBRIDGE

Spring Lawn

Stradballey, Clarinbridge, Co Galway

Tel: (091) 96045

An attractive house set in 2½ acres in the heart of oyster country. There is a wooded area behind the house where guests may walk down to the sea. The bedrooms are good-sized, clean, freshly decorated and with modern, comfortable furnishings. There is a sitting-room for guests and a separate dining-room. Maura McNamara has been in business for over 7 years and takes a personal interest in her guests. Breakfast only is served, but there are 3 restaurants close by. Located three quarters of a mile off the N18. No smoking. No pets.

OWNER Mrs Maura McNamara   OPEN 1 March–30 November
ROOMS 1 double/twin/family (all en suite)   TERMS B&B IR£13.00
p.p.; reductions for children; single supplement IR£4.00; evening
meal IR£11.00, high tea IR£8.00

CLIFDEN

Ardmore House

Sky Road, Clifden, Co Galway

Tel: (095) 21221

Ardmore House is a luxury farmhouse set in beautiful scenic
countryside overlooking the sea. It is warm and inviting,
Kathy Mullen is a delightful and pleasant host, and guests
are assured of true Irish hospitality. The bedrooms are
immaculate, individually decorated, with comfortable beds.
There's a well-furnished TV lounge with open fires. Evening
meals with home-style cooking are served, if prearranged,
and seafood is a speciality. Lake and deep-sea angling, pony
trekking and beautiful walks, sandy beaches and golf are all
available in the area. No pets. No smoking. Situated 4 miles
(6 km) west of Clifden (50 miles/75 km west of Galway).

OWNER Kathy Mullen   OPEN 1 March–1 November   ROOMS 6
double/twin/family (all en suite)   TERMS B&B IR£14.00 p.p.;
reductions for children; single supplement IR£4.00; evening meal
IR£13.00

Cregg House

Goulane, Clifden, Co Galway

Tel: (095) 21326

An immaculate dormer bungalow in an elevated position
standing in is own grounds of one acre. The house has a
spectacular view of Roundstone Bog and the mountains
beyond. The bedrooms are prettily and individually decorated in pink, blue, green and peach, with tasteful matching
fabrics; all are en suite but one, which has its own bathroom.
The O'Donnells have been offering their special brand of
hospitality for over 9 years and guests feel very much at
home here. There is a TV lounge with turf fires. Breakfasts
are excellent and include fresh fruits, home-made yoghurt
and soda bread. An ideal base from which to tour Conne-

mara, there is a fishing river less than 5 minutes away; golf and horseback-riding are also available. Pets by arrangement. Ideally situated 2 miles (3 km) from Clifden on the main Galway N59 road.

OWNER Mary and Hugh O'Donnell   OPEN Easter–31 October
ROOMS 2 double/family/twin (5 en suite)   TERMS B&B IR£13.50
p.p.; reductions for children; single supplement IR£2.00

Mallmore House

Off Ballyconneely Road, Clifden, Co Galway
Tel: (095) 21460

A lovely Georgian house with a friendly and warm atmosphere set in 35 acres within walking distance of the sea. The house overlooks the bay and most of the bedrooms have lovely views. Mr and Mrs Hardman have been in business for 12 years and during that time have been renovating the house, cleverly combining the old-world charm with modern conveniences. All of the bedrooms are on the ground floor and are spacious and comfortable. There is a comfortable well-furnished lounge with TV and open peat fireplace. Guests are assured of personal service: Kathleen Hardman is a considerate and helpful host. Excellent breakfasts are served in the separate dining-room and there are several places to eat in the area. No smoking in the dining-room. Situated approximately 1¹/₃ miles (2 km) from Clifden.

OWNER Mrs Kathleen Hardman   OPEN 1 March–1 November
ROOMS 2 double, 3 twin, 1 family (all en suite)   TERMS B&B
IR£13.50 p.p.; reductions for sharing; single supplement IR£4.00

CLONBUR

Ballycline House

Clonbur, Co Galway
Tel: (092) 46150

Ballycline House is situated on the road between the pictur-esque villages of Cong and Clonbur, the Gateway to Conne-mara. The house overlooks the famous fishing lake of Lough Mask with its own private grounds of gardens and lawns surrounded by beautiful woodlands. The oldest part of the house belonged to the Guinness family; the house and land were purchased by the family in 1940 and in 1992 an

138

addition was added. Mr and Mrs Lamb have created a
warm and inviting atmosphere – the rooms are bright and
clean and the bedrooms all have hairdryers. There is a cosy
sitting-room with open fire and a conservatory to relax in
with tea- and coffee-makers provided, as well as an adjacent
billiard room. There are wonderful forest walks: guided
walks from Ballykine House can be arranged, as well as
walks to the summit of magnificent Benlevi. The immediate
area is a fisherman's paradise. Evening meals are served if
prearranged and there is a wine licence. Pets in outside
accommodation. Situated off the Cong/Clonbur road.

OWNER Ann Lambe   OPEN 1 April–1 November   ROOMS 1
double/twin/family (all en suite)   TERMS B&B IR£13.00 p.p.;
reductions for children; single supplement IR£2.00; evening meal
IR£13.50, high tea IR£8.50

CORRANDULLA

Cregg Castle

Corrandulla, Co Galway

Tel: (091) 91434

Cregg Castle, the last castle to be built west of Shannon, sits
in a peaceful and secluded spot on 165 acres of wildlife
reserve. This is a very lived-in and informal property and
there are no strict rules here: guests may make tea or coffee
at any hour of the day free of charge or walk in the woods
and spot the wildlife. Breakfast, which includes free-range
eggs and home-made bread, is served in the Great Hall with
its huge log fire until noon. The emphasis here is on relaxation, and guests are encouraged to get to know each other
and enjoy conversation which often goes on late into the
night. Irish music is played here and guests are able to enjoy
an evening of music and fun. This is an ideal spot for those
who want to learn and be involved in Irish music; they have
an opportunity to learn at their own pace from musical
director John Hoban, a renowned musician and singer who
has had many years experience teaching in Ireland. Owners
Pat and Ann Marie are both experienced musicians.

This is a unique property with many original items, such
as the huge locks and security bars, the foot scraper with the
rampant black car of the Blake crest, and shutters on the big
windows. The Blake crest is also on the fireplace with its
black marble, which is believed to have come from the
Menlo quarries. Outside in the courtyard is a Queen Ann

bell tower, in the inner yard is the original forge and the remains of an oven for firing pottery. There is also a beautiful spring well which supplies Cregg Castle with natural spring water. No rooms have private baths, but guests don't seem to mind; after all, it is not often that one has an opportunity to stay in such an interesting building at such modest prices. Cregg Castle's welcome is aptly described on the front of their brochure, "Hail Guest, we ask not what thou art; if friend we greet thee hand and heart; if stranger, such no longer be, our friendly faith shall conquer thee." Cregg Castle is a place that exudes Ireland's history and culture. There is a wine licence. Stables outside for pets.

OWNER The Broderick family   OPEN 1 March–1 November ROOMS 12 double   TERMS B&B IR£18.50-£20.00 p.p.; reductions for children; no single supplement; evening meal IR£12.00 p.p.

KYLEMORE

Kylemore House

Kylemore, Co Galway
Tel: (095) 41143

Kylemore House was built in 1785 by Lord Ardelaum and stands in 7 acres of woodlands. The house overlooks the lake and there are also 3 private lakes attached to the house that are noted for salmon and sea trout. The house has a delightful family atmosphere; guests can relax and feel at home here, the rooms are spacious, and the enormous sitting-room is full of antiques and is adjacent to a comfortable TV lounge. Kylemore House is noted for its excellent food both English and continental. Nancy Naughton, the owner, offers a warm and friendly welcome in this secluded property, and guests are assured of a peaceful and tranquil holiday. Kylemore Abbey, a school run by the Benedictine Nuns, is close by with an interesting craft shop on the premises. There is a wine licence. No pets. Located 2 miles (3 km) from Kylemore on the N59.

OWNER Nancy Naughton   OPEN 1 April–1 October   ROOMS 2 double/single/family (4 en suite)   TERMS B&B IR£15.50 p.p.; reductions for children; single supplement IR£3.00; evening meal IR£14.50

Delphi Lodge

Leenane, Co Galway,
Tel: (095) 42213, Fax: (095) 42212

Delphi Lodge is one of the finest sporting lodges in Ireland. Beautifully restored in 1988, this magnificent 1830s country house has a rich history. Set in 1,000 acres with 3 loughs in a stunning lakeside location and surrounded by ancient woodlands and towering mountains, the lodge is the ultimate Connemara retreat. The house has antique pine furniture and the bedrooms have lovely views. Originally the sporting estate of the Marquis of Sligo, Delphi is now the home of Jane and Peter Mantle; Jane is a Cordon Bleu cook who particularly specialises in local seafood. The lodge has a strong emphasis on salmon and sea-trout fishing and Delphi is one of the finest game fisheries in Ireland. The fishing season runs from spring to the middle of October. Outside the fishing season the lodge is popular with shooting parties, ramblers and golfers. Horse-riding and hunting can also be arranged. Superb uncrowded beaches are within 20 minutes' drive, and the lodge is conveniently placed for visiting Westport and all the sites of Connemara. A huge snooker room and a magnificent fishing library are open to guests. Evening meals are served at a superb old oak dining-room table and the wine cellar is extensive. Not suitable for children. French spoken. No pets. There are 4 charming country cottages available for self catering.

OWNER Jane and Peter Mantle   OPEN 1 January–1 October
ROOMS 5 double 2 single (with baths)   TERMS B&B IR£44.00-£75.00 p.p.; evening meal à la carte

Glen Valley House and Stables

Leenane, Co Galway
Tel: (095) 42269

Glen Valley House is down a rather bumpy private road in a remote location amidst lovely countryside. This large, modest farmhouse, nestled in the foothills of the Lettershanbally Mountain, has spacious rooms, is clean and comfortable and is simply furnished. There is a small, cosy sitting-room with TV and turf fires. This is an ideal base for those who enjoy hill walking; pony trekking is available on the farm which is run by Mr O'Neill. Substantial breakfasts and evening meals, if prearranged, are served in the farmhouse dining-room. Pets outside only. Situated 1¹/₂ miles (2¹/₂ km) off the N59 down a private road, signposted on the N59, 5 miles (7¹/₂ km) from Leenane.

OWNER Joseph and Josephine O'Neill   OPEN Easter–31 October
ROOMS 1 double/twin/family   TERMS B&B IR£12.50 p.p.;
reductions for children; single supplement IR£3.00; evening meal IR£13.00

MOYCULLEN

Moycullen House

Moycullen, Co Galway
Tel: (091) 85566

Moycullen House lies down a narrow, quiet road on one of the highest points in the area overlooking Lough Corrib. This large house was designed in the arts-and-crafts style and has great oak doors with the original iron locks and latches. It was built in the 1900s by Lord Campbell, a Scot who came to the West for sporting holidays. The house is set in 30 acres of rhododendrons and azaleas, and there is a pure spring which still provides the house with water. When Moycullen was first built it included a servants' wing and to this day bell pushes still exist in the sitting-room, dining-room and 4 of the bedrooms. The bedrooms are large, all have their own bathrooms, are tastefully decorated, well furnished and most have period fireplaces. There is a lovely sitting-room with an old stone fireplace. Philip and Marie are charming hosts who can organise coarse, trout and salmon fishing as well as boats on Lough Corrib. For golfers there are two 18-hole golf courses within a 30-minute drive. Excellent freshly prepared evening meals are served if prearranged. This is a delightful, tranquil and peaceful spot from which to explore this scenic area. Smoking is not permitted in the bedrooms. No pets. Take the N59 from Galway to Moycullen village. Turn left in the village centre onto Spiddal Road. Moycullen House is 1 mile (1¹/₂ km) on the left. All major credit cards accepted.

OWNER Philip and Marie Casburn   OPEN 1 March–1 November
ROOMS 5 double/twin (all en suite)   TERMS B&B IR£25.00 p.p.;
reductions for children; single supplement IR£10.00; evening meal IR£16.00

Corrib Wave House

Oughterard, Connemara, Co Galway

Tel: (091) 82147, Fax: (091) 82736

Corrib Wave House is a lakeside farmhouse in picturesque surroundings overlooking Lough Corrib. The bedrooms are modest and clean, most of them with views of the lake. There is a separate lounge with an open fire and a dining-room where breakfasts and evening meals are served, if prearranged, which include fresh home-baking. This is an ideal spot for people who like the outdoors, with lovely walks close by, and salmon, trout and coarse fishing. Boats/ engines for hire, gillies arranged. Swimming, canoeing and sailing on the lake. There is an 18-hole golf course within a mile (1 1/2 km) and the house is conveniently located near Galway and Connemara. Smoking is not permitted in the dining-room. No pets. Located off the N59 road, one mile (1 1/2 km) east of Oughterard.

OWNERS Maria and Michael Healy   OPEN 1 April–15 October
ROOMS 2 double/twin/family (all en suite)   TERMS B&B IR£13.50 p.p.; reductions for children; single supplement IR£5.00; evening meal IR£12.50

SALT HILL

Carraig Beag

1 Burren View Heights, Knocknacarra Road, Salt Hill, Galway, Co Galway

Tel: (091) 21696

Carraig Beag is a luxurious red-brick house just off the promenade, with views of the bay. The bedrooms are a good size, furnished with every comfort in mind, and all have their own bathrooms and hairdryers. There are attractive rich wood doors and a handsome staircase. Breakfasts are served on separate tables in the elegant dining-room, which has a beautiful crystal chandelier and marble fireplace. There is a lounge with TV where guests can relax after a busy day. An added bonus are the owners, Mr and Mrs Lydon, who are a most accommodating and helpful couple. Catherine and her husband often take walks along the promenade in the evening; guests may join them, but beware, you may find them hard to keep up with! Located one block from the beach and close to all amenities. Smoking is not permitted in the bedrooms. Pets outside. Situated in Salt Hill, past the golf course, second road on the right.

OWNER Catherine Lydon   OPEN All year, except Christmas
ROOMS 2 double, 2 twin, 1 family (all en suite)
TERMS B&B IR£14.50 p.p.; reductions for children; single supplement IR£4.50

The Connaught

Barna Road, Salt Hill, Galway, Co Galway
Tel: (091) 25865

An attractive residence set back off the road in a quiet position. The house has recently been redecorated and is impeccably maintained. The bedrooms are pleasantly furnished with comfortable beds, all of which have electric blankets. There is a pleasant dining-room and well-furnished lounge, which has rich carpeting throughout. An extremely cordial and helpful couple, the Keaveneys do everything they can to ensure their guests are comfortable and well taken care of: there is a warm and friendly atmosphere here, and the Connaught would be an ideal base from which to explore this lovely region. No smoking. No pets. To locate the Connaught, drive past the promenade along the sea-front, continue approximately for 1 mile (1½ km), turn left at the T-junction – the house is on the right-hand side, the last house in the lay-by.

OWNER Mrs Colette Keaveney   OPEN 17 March–31 October
ROOMS 2 double, 1 twin, 3 family (5 en suite)   TERMS B&B IR£12.50-£14.50 p.p.; reductions for children; single supplement IR£4.00

Dun Roamin

30 Beach Court, Gratton Road, Salt Hill, Galway,
Co Galway
Tel: (091) 62570

The Bogan family named their attractive modern red-brick house after their decision to stay put and enjoy all that Galway has to offer. The house has a warm and welcoming atmosphere, the rooms are clean and all the beds have duvets. Each bedroom has tea- and coffee-making facilities and hairdryers are available. There's a cosy guest lounge and a separate dining-room where freshly prepared breakfasts of cereals, fruit and savouries are served. Located less than 2 minutes from the beach, restaurants and other amenities. Jo Bogan is a helpful and considerate host. Guests are welcomed with a hot drink upon arrival, and evening tea is served upon request at no extra charge. No pets.

OWNER Mrs Jo Bogan   OPEN 1 February–1 December, except Christmas   ROOMS 1 double, 3 twin (all en suite)   TERMS B&B IR£13.50 p.p.; reductions for children; single supplement IR£5.00

Mandalay

10 Gentian Hill, Salt Hill, Galway, Co Galway
Tel: (091) 24177

This beautiful new Georgian-style house is in a superb location overlooking the bay and the Aran Islands. Mr and Mrs Darby, who built the house, are from Rhode Island in the US. Mandalay is furnished and decorated to extremely high standards: there are rich wood furnishings and several antiques. The rooms are spacious, 2 have balconies, all have views and their own bathrooms. The entry hall and the kitchen have Liscannor stone floors from the Burren of Co Clare. The elegant lounge has a TV and piano and there are lots of plants and exquisite dried-flower arrangements throughout the house. Excellent breakfasts are served in the bright dining-room at separate tables. For nature lovers there are some nice walks close by and a bird sanctuary can be seen in front of the house. For guests wanting luxury at modest prices, Mandalay is certainly an excellent choice. The house is open all year, including the Christmas holiday period. No pets. Smoking is not permitted in the dining-room or bedrooms. Situated in lower Salt Hill – past the Spinnaker pub, signposted on the road. Visa, Access and Mastercard accepted.

OWNER Georgianna Darby   OPEN All year, including Christmas ROOMS 1 double, 2 twin, 2 family (all en suite)   TERMS B&B IR£14.00 p.p.; reductions for children; single supplement IR£3.00

Seaview

Beach Court, Gratton Road, Salt Hill, Galway, Co Galway
Tel: (091) 62109

A detached, attractive white house across from the bay. The front bedrooms overlook the sea; they are all colour-coordi-

nated and 2 have orthopaedic beds, satellite TVs, hairdryers
and tea- and coffee-making facilities. There is a balcony for
guests' use and a small TV lounge. The house is 5 minutes'
walk away from the town centre and directly across the road
from the beach. Private parking is available. No smoking in
the dining-room. Pets by arrangement. Situated between
Salt Hill and Galway, just off Stratton Road overlooking
Galway Bay. All major credit cards accepted.

OWNER Mrs Bready Tracey   OPEN All year, except Christmas
ROOMS 3 double, 1 twin, 1 family (4 en suite)   TERMS B&B
IR£16.00 p.p.; reductions for children; single supplement IR£4.00

SPIDDLE

Cala 'n Uisce

Green Hill, Spiddle, Co Galway
Tel: (091) 83324

Cala 'n Uisce means little harbour and is in a picturesque
setting facing the bay. The house was designed by owner
Paraic Feeney and has leaded windows, a red-brick exterior
and is exceptionally well maintained. There are 3 ground-
floor bedrooms, attractively decorated with colour-coordinated matching fabrics. Many interesting paintings are hung
throughout the house depicting local scenes painted by Mrs
Feeney and other family members. There is a comfortable
lounge with a TV and turf fire which leads out onto a patio.
The dining-room overlooks the bay where a tasty breakfast
is served on linen table-cloths and pretty china. Paraic
Feeney's father was a cousin of John Ford's, who directed
The Quiet Man. This is an Irish-speaking area and the
Feeney family speaks Irish. Cala 'n Uisce is a most comfortable and peaceful place; the house stands in an acre of
landscaped gardens and there are beautiful bog areas and
sea walks close by. No smoking in the bedrooms. No pets.
Situated 1½ miles (2½ km) west of Spiddle village.

OWNER Mrs Moya Feeney   OPEN 1 March–30 November
ROOMS 3 double, 1 twin, 2 family (5 en suite)   TERMS B&B
IR£12.50-£14.50 p.p.; reductions for children; single supplement
IR£5.00 during high season only

County Limerick

Bordered on the north by the expanses of the Shannon,
Limerick is a peaceful farming county with its fair share of

146

relics from the past.

The origins of the city of Limerick go back to the days of the Vikings. Always a principal fording point for the Shannon River, it has played an important part in Irish history, particularly during the 1690s. Old English Town and the old Irish part of the city across the river are the most interesting parts of the city to explore, particularly around St John's Square with its Georgian architecture. The most noteworthy sights to visit are the Granary, a restored eighteenth-century warehouse, which houses the tourist office as well as restaurants, shops and an exhibition gallery. King John's Castle, with its massive rounded tower, St Mary's Cathedral, dating from 1172, and the Hunt Collection at the National Institute for Higher Education can also be visited.

Adare has some splendid ruins to see, the finest one being the Franciscan Friary. Others include the Trinitarian Abbey, the Augustinian Abbey and St Nicholas Church. It is a most attractive town, with pretty thatched cottages and lovely views of Desmond Castle and Adare Manor on the river.

It is thought the "limerick" may well have come from Croom, which was the meeting place of eighteenth-century Gaelic poets who wrote extremely witty verse.

LIMERICK

Cloneen Guest House

Ennis Road, Limerick, Co Limerick
Tel: (061) 454461, Fax: (061) 310588

Built around the turn of the century, Cloneen Guest House is conveniently located on Ennis Road, which is close to the city centre. The house is set back off the road and has double glazing. There is private parking. The bedrooms, all freshly decorated, are good-sized, spotlessly clean and some have old-fashioned furniture. All bedrooms have TVs. The lounge has the original fireplace.

Breakfast is served on blue willow china in the pleasant dining-room. Each guest receives a Guest Privilege card offering discounts to various places of interest and alternative visiting hours. The direct bus to Shannon airport stops very close to the house. Incoming phone calls accepted for guests. No pets. No smoking in the dining-room. On the main route to Shannon airport and 10 minutes to Limerick city centre. Most major credit cards accepted.

OWNERS Robert and Bridget Power   OPEN All year, except Christmas Day   ROOMS 2 double, 2 twin, 1 single, 1 family (4 en suite)   TERMS B&B IR£14.00-£18.00 p.p.; reductions for children; single supplement IR£4.00-£7.00

Trebor

Ennis Road, Limerick, Co Limerick
Tel: (061) 454632

Trebor, named after the owner's son Robert, spelt backwards, is a comfortable turn-of-the-century townhouse. The bedrooms are spotless, tastefully decorated with colour-coordinated wallpapers and fabrics. An additional room has en suite facilities, making a total of 3, and there are 2 additional bathrooms exclusively for guests. Breakfasts include freshly squeezed orange juice, muesli or porridge, home-made breads, followed by a cooked breakfast. Popular with cyclists: a small group from America return every year. Drying facilities are available. There is a lounge with TV. Evening meals, vegetarian and special diets are catered for if prearranged. Smoking is not permitted in the dining-room. Pets by arrangement. Located on the main Ennis road past Jury's Hotel.

OWNER Mrs Joan McSweeney   OPEN All year, except Christmas week   ROOMS 1 double, 2 twin, 2 family (3 en suite)   TERMS B&B IR£12.50-£14.00 p.p.; reductions for children; single supplement IR£5.00; evening meal IR£11.00, high tea IR£9.00

Trelawne House

Ennis Road, Limerick, Co Limerick
Tel: (061) 54063, Fax: (061) 54491

A 100-year-old house standing in its own grounds in a peaceful location, 5 minutes' walk away from the town centre. The house has been modernised over the years and is spacious and bright. The family room is exceptionally large, as is the comfortable lounge. There is also a quiet sitting area for residents who want to sit and read. Mrs Boylan has been in business for over 24 years, originally buying the house specifically for bed and breakfast. During that time she has made friends from all over the world and has lots of repeat guests. There is one double en suite room on the ground floor and 3 additional bathrooms exclusively for guests' use. The 2 family rooms have an option for en suite facilities. Evening meals are not served, but there are plenty of places to eat in the area. There is a public phone. Pets are permitted if proper sleeping facilities are available. No smoking in the dining-room. Located on the main Ennis-Shannon-Galway road, just beyond Jury's Hotel, outside of Limerick.

OWNER Mrs Bernadette Boylan   OPEN All year, except Christmas
ROOMS 4 double, 2 family or twin (4 en suite)   TERMS B&B
IR£12.50-£14.00 p.p.; reductions for children; single supplement
IR£4.00

NEWCASTLE WEST

Limetree Lodge

Killarney Road, Newcastle West, Co Limerick
Tel: (069) 62366, Fax: (069) 62662

Limetree Lodge is a modernised Georgian house standing in its own beautifully landscaped garden. The house is spacious, well maintained and immaculate. Tastefully decorated, the bedrooms are also comfortably furnished, individually decorated with matching fabrics and lots of wardrobe space. All the bedrooms have TVs and hairdryers. There are heated towel racks in the bathroom. Guests have the choice of being served breakfast in the conservatory, with linen napkins and pretty flower arrangements. Tea and delicious home-baked cakes or scones and jam are offered upon arrival and in the evening. If you are looking for a little luxury, with a host offering lots of personal service at reasonable prices, Limetree Lodge is the answer. However, many others have already discovered it, so reserve early. No pets. One-and-a-half miles (2¹/₂ km) to Newcastle West on the N12 half way between Shannon airport and Killarney.

OWNER Mrs Peggy Geary   OPEN All year, except Christmas
ROOMS 2 double, 1 twin, 1 family (3 en suite)   TERMS B&B
IR£12.00-£13.00 p.p.; reductions for children; single supplement
IR£3.00; evening meal IR£10.00, high tea IR£7.00

149

County Mayo

County Mayo is a maritime county with the Atlantic Ocean making deep inroads into its coastline on the west and on the north. The sea influences the shaping of its beauty, whether it is the long, narrow fjord of Killary Harbour or the island-studded Clew Bay. Castlebar is the county town of Mayo and a good centre for touring. The most interesting building in the town is that occupied by the art centre and the education centre. It was formerly a chapel, the stone of which was laid by John Wesley in 1785.

Westport is a gem of a town. The architect is not known, although some locals believe it to be a French architect left behind from Humbert's expedition in 1798. The main feature is the Octagon, a fine piece of planning. In the centre stands a Doric pillar on an octagonal granite base on which the statue of George Glendenning once stood. Innisturk Island can be visited from Roonah Point. It is an exceptionally attractive island with a lovely harbour; there is a glorious beach on the south side.

Killary Harbour is a striking example of what is called a fjord, after the Norwegian model. Its 5½ mile (8 km) length cuts deep into the surrounding mountains.

At Knock there is the Knock Folk Museum, which pays tribute to our forefathers. The collections and exhibitions on show help us to understand what life was like for our ancestors.

ACHILL ISLAND

Aquila

Sraheens, Achill Sound, Achill Island, Co Mayo
Tel: (098) 45163

This cosy, clean, modern bungalow is situated in an elevated position, with magnificent views of Achill Sound and the Corraun Mountains. The bedrooms are well appointed, prettily decorated with comfortable beds. One very popular room is the converted attic en suite room. It is most attractive, with its sloping ceilings, but it is not suitable for everyone, as the approach is by a very narrow staircase. There are 4 rooms on the ground floor with wheelchair access. There is a comfortable sitting-room and lounge with TV/video and an open turf fire. All types of outdoor activities are available: fishing, swimming, mountain climbing, surfing, sailing and sub-aqua diving. Cots are available. Pets in outside garage only. The house is located near 3 Blue Flag beaches. Well signposted off the L141 Achill Sound road.

OWNER Mrs Kay Sweeney   OPEN Easter–31 October   ROOMS 3 double, 1 twin, 1 family (4 en suite)   TERMS B&B IR£14.00-£21.50 p.p.; reductions for children; single supplement IR£3.00

BALLINA

Ashley House

Ardoughan, Crossmolina Road, Ballina, Co Mayo

Tel: (096) 22799

An attractive Georgian-style dormer bungalow situated off the main road and set in a beautifully landscaped garden,• three quarters of a mile from Ballina, established as a bed and breakfast over 9 years ago. The well-appointed bed-rooms all have tea-makers and are on the ground floor. Carmel Murray is a friendly lady with a good sense of humour. The dormer was converted several years ago into private quarters for the family. Mr Murray is very handy and works hard to maintain the high standards. The owner's son is an enthusiastic fisherman and can advise guests on the best local fishing spots. Carmel is into set-dancing and, if guests are interested, could easily be persuaded to give guests a lesson and/or a demonstration. No smoking in the dining-room. Self-catering unit available. No pets. All major credit cards accepted.

OWNER Mrs Carmel Murray   OPEN 1 March–1 November ROOMS 3 double, 1 twin, 1 family (3 en suite)   TERMS B&B IR£12.00-£13.00 p.p.; 33% reduction for children; single supplement negotiable; high tea IR£8.00

Belvedere House

Foxford Road, Ballina, Co Mayo

Tel: (096) 22004

A spacious, modern, two-storey house standing in its own grounds, a 10-minute walk from the town centre. The bedrooms are of a good size, attractively decorated, clean, and all have orthopaedic beds. There is a very large dining-room and lounge, with TV and fireplaces. The owners are attentive and work hard to maintain the high standards. Ursula, the daughter, helps out during the holidays and is an excellent gymnast, as evidenced by the fine display of medals. Breakfast only is served, but there are many fine eating establishments in the area. A popular place with fishing enthusiasts, Ballina is situated on the lower reaches of the River Moy and directly between Lough Conn/Cullen and Killala Bay. Bicycles for hire locally. For guests who would like a day trip to Dublin there is a good local bus service. Pets by arrangement. Situated off the N57 Dublin/ Foxford road.

OWNER Mary Reilly   OPEN All year, except Christmas
ROOMS 2 double/twin/family (4 en suite)
TERMS B&B IR£12.00-£24.00 p.p.; 25% reduction for children; single supplement IR£6.00

Coolabah House

Culleens, Killala Road, Ballina, Co Mayo
Tel: (096) 70343

Coolabah House derived its name from an Australian tree. The family lived at Coolabah for 3 years and the name and the design of the house are pleasant reminders of the time spent there. The house is set in its own grounds, and there are some lovely walks nearby. Mrs McGreever is an extremely artistic lady, as evidenced by the high standards of style and design of the interior. The large bedrooms are very comfortable, individually decorated, with quality furnishings and some with satin bed covers. All bedrooms have tea- and coffee-making facilities, as well as hairdryers and irons. Coolabah is immaculate throughout and there is a peaceful and restful atmosphere. Breakfasts only are served; vegetarians catered for. Smoking is not permitted in the dining-room. No pets. Situated 1¹/₂ miles (2¹/₂ km) to town centre, signposted off the Killala road.

OWNER Mrs Margaret McGreever   OPEN 1 May–30 September
ROOMS 2 double/twin/family (3 en suite)   TERMS B&B IR£12.50-£14.00 p.p.; 20% reduction for children; single supplement negotiable; high tea IR£8.00

Hillcrest House

Main Street, Bangor Erris, Ballina, Co Mayo
Tel: (097) 83494

A modern, cosy bungalow located in the centre of the village
very close to the Owenmore River. Mr and Mrs Cosgrove
are a very congenial couple; Mr Cosgrove was born in the
village. The restaurant, which is part of the house, is very
popular with the locals. Mrs Cosgrove, who does all the
cooking, has built up an excellent reputation for providing
good food. The bedrooms are comfortable; hot water bottles
and hairdryers are provided. There's a TV lounge with video.
This is a popular spot with fishermen, with river and lake
fishing close by. No pets. No smoking in the bedrooms.
Bangor Erris is 25 miles (37½ km) from Ballina on the N59.

OWNER Evelyn Cosgrove   OPEN All year, except Christmas
ROOMS 3 twin, 1 family (1 en suite)   TERMS B&B IR£12.00-
£24.00 p.p.; reductions for children; single supplement IR£3.00;

BALLYCASTLE

Hilltop House

Ballycastle, Co Mayo
Tel: (096) 43089

A modest bungalow on a dry stock farm with panoramic
views of the countryside, the sea and Downpatrick Head.
Anne O'Donnell is a congenial lady who extends a warm
welcome to visitors. A cup of tea and some of her delicious
home-made cake is offered on arrival. The lounge is comfortable and overlooks the glorious view. There is a video
and TV where guests can watch the Ceide Field Project video
and learn about the oldest enclosed farmland in Europe, or,
indeed, the world. Older than the pyramids, the enclosure
and neolithic tombs are preserved by a blanket of bog. The
project is 5 miles (7½ km) west of Ballycastle, where an
interpretative centre is to open in 1993. Home-cooked
evening meals are available, if prearranged. Pets outside
only. No smoking in the dining-room. Take the Ballycastle
road from Ballina; the farm is well signposted.

OWNER Anne O'Donnell   OPEN All year, except Christmas
ROOMS 2 double, 1 twin,   TERMS B&B IR£13.00 p.p.; 50%
reduction for children; single supplement IR£3.00; evening meal
IR£12.00

Kilmurray House

Castlehill, Crossmolina, Co Mayo
Tel: (096) 31227

Kilmurray House is a large, attractive, two-storey farmhouse
on 55 acres of dry-stock farming, beautifully situated under
Nephin Mountain. It is hard to believe that the house was a
ruin before Joe and Madge Moffatt lovingly restored the
interior, cleverly combining modern conveniences in a
traditional setting. The original oak staircase and wooden
doors have been retained, as has the fireplace in the lounge
made by a local craftsman. Recipient of two awards: Farmhouse of the Year and BHS and Bord Fáilte Farmhouse
award. The bedrooms are large, with matching fabrics, and
are tastefully decorated and comfortably furnished. A turf
fire burns brightly in the TV lounge on chilly days. An ideal
base from which to explore this scenic area and a fisherman's delight, with the farm's own boats for guests on
Lough Conn for salmon and trout fishing. Excellent farmhouse evening meals are served if prearranged and guests are
welcome to bring their own wine. Very enjoyable Irish
evenings a quarter of a mile away, as well as Irish dancing
from the family. Historic Heritage Museum for tracing
ancentry 1^1/$_2$ miles (2^1/$_2$ km) away. Baby-sitting available.
No smoking in the dining-room. Pets outside by arrangement. Three miles (4^1/$_2$ km) from Crossmolina on Castlebar
road.

OWNERS Joe and Madge Moffatt   OPEN 1 March–1 November
ROOMS 1 double, 2 twin, 2 family, 1 single (4 en suite)
TERMS B&B IR£14.00 p.p.; 50% reduction for children; single
supplement IR£4.00; evening meal IR£13.00

KILLALA

Avondale House

Pier Road, Killala, Co Mayo
Tel: (096) 32229

Located in a glorious position on the sea-front and 150
yards from the pier, this attractive bungalow is highly
recommended for its hospitality. Three of the bedrooms are

on the ground floor; the other 2 are reached by a spiral staircase. There are no en suite rooms, but 2 bathrooms are exclusively for guests' use. Mr and Mrs Caplice are a charming couple and are very knowledgeable about this historical area. The lounge, which is large and comfortable, is on the ground floor. The original granary can be seen from the house, and Killala Cathedral has the original organ built by Thomas Telford in 1838. An ideal location for exploring the Ceide Fields, the oldest enclosed farmland in the world, said to be older than the pyramids. Excellent breakfasts and evening meals, if prearranged, are served in the cosy dining-room. Pets welcome.

OWNERS Mrs P Caplice OPEN All year, except Christmas ROOMS 2 double, 2 twin, 1 family TERMS B&B IR£12.00 p.p.; 25% reduction for children; single supplement IR£2.00; evening meal IR£10.00

LOUISBURGH

Rivervilla

Shraugh, Louisburgh, Co Mayo
Tel: (098) 66246

Rivervilla is a bungalow situated in a peaceful and secluded setting along the banks of the Runrowen River on a 25-acre sheep farm. Salmon and trout fishing are available, as well as lovely riverside walks. A real home-from-home atmosphere pervades here; all meals are freshly prepared and home-baked breads and desserts are a feature. Guests are welcome to join the O'Malleys for a wonderful Irish Christmas holiday, rates upon request. The bedrooms are tastefully decorated, some have glorious views of the Shreffy Mountain and of Croagh Patrick. Of special interest is the Great Famine and Granvaile Interpretative Centre. There is a TV lounge. All the bedrooms have tea-makers and for the 2 bedrooms that are not en suite there are 2 accompanying bathrooms. Guests may bring their own wine. Dogs are welcome – outside sheds available. Located 1 mile (1½ km) from the village off the 3335 Westport/Louisburgh road.

OWNERS Mary O'Malley OPEN 1 April–1 January, except Christmas ROOMS 1 double, 1 twin, 2 single, 1 family (2 en suite) TERMS B&B IR£13.00 p.p.; 50% reduction for children under 12; 2 single rooms available with no supplement

Loch Morchan Farm

Kilbride, Newport, Co Mayo
Tel: (098) 41221

This is a working farm of sheep and cattle situated in a quiet location a quarter of a mile off the N56, with good views all round, just 10 minutes from Clew Bay. The house is fresh and bright, the bedrooms average in size with comfortable beds. One of the nicest things about Loch Morchan Farm is Mrs Chambers herself, a delightful lady who is a most caring and attentive host; the bed and breakfast was established over 15 years ago, with many guests returning for the special hospitality found here. There is an antique marble wash-stand in the hallway. Evening meals are available by prior arrangement and there are several good eating establishments close by. Loch Morchan has a TV lounge and separate dining-room. The area is excellent for sea, river and lake fishing, with special group rates for fishing groups. An 18-hole golf course is close by. Smoking is not permitted in the dining-room. No pets.

OWNERS Mrs C Chambers   OPEN 1 May–30 September
ROOMS 1 double, 2 twin, 1 family (1 en suite)
TERMS B&B IR£12.00 p.p.; 25% reduction for children; single supplement IR£2.00

WESTPORT

Altamont House

Ballinrobe Road, Westport, Co Mayo
Tel: (098) 25226

Altamont House is a pre-Famine wistaria-covered farm-house built in the 1800s, situated within a 5-minute walk of the town centre. This is a most pleasant and welcoming house. Established as the first guest house in the area, it has built up an excellent reputation for offering good service at reasonable prices. The spotless bedrooms are prettily decorated and the rooms to the rear of the house overlook the lovely gardens, as does the lounge, which has an open fire. The gardens are a popular spot with guests and have been host to several weddings. Breakfasts are served in the attractive dining-room, which is decorated in red; silver service is used and, when possible, there are fresh flowers on the table. A new addition to the property is a sun lounge and patio. Evening meals can be had at several good pubs and restaurants close by. No pets.

OWNER Mrs Rita Sheridan   OPEN 1 February–1 November
ROOMS 2 double, 3 twin, 3 family (2 en suite)   TERMS B&B
IR£13.50 p.p.; 33% reduction for children; single supplement
IR£5.00

Cedar Lodge

Kings Hill, Newport Road, Westport, Co Mayo
Tel: (098) 25417

A pleasant family home in a quiet residential area, 1½ miles (2 ½ km) from the town and approximately a 6-minute walk. The bedrooms are most attractive and there is a comfortable family suite all in pine. The 2 bedrooms that are not en suite have an additional 2 bathrooms exclusively for guests. The TV lounge has wood block polished flooring and very comfortable chairs to relax in. Breakfast only is served in the bright dining-room, but there are several eating establishments in town. Non smokers preferred. Pets are not permitted. Easily located on the Newport road N56, first turn to the left after passing the tennis court in the town centre.

OWNERS Maureen Flynn   OPEN All year, except Christmas
ROOMS 1 double, 1 twin, 2 family (2 en suite)
TERMS B&B IR£13.00-£15.00 p.p.; 25% reduction for children;
single supplement IR£3.00

Coral Reef

Lecanvey, Westport, Co Mayo
Tel: (098) 64814

Coral Reef is an attractive house standing in its own grounds. Located across the road from the beach, it has magnificent views of Clew Bay and is in the shadow of Croagh Patrick, where the pilgrimage climb takes place in July. This is a superb location with lovely walks close by. An added bonus is the wonderful, welcoming atmosphere created by the friendly owners. The house is well furnished, 3 of the bedrooms are on the ground floor and 2 are reached by a spiral staircase. Anne Colgan is a good cook, evening meals are available if prearranged, all breads, cakes and desserts are home-made. A specialty of the house is the home-made health bread, the recipe of which has been taken to many parts of the world by satisfied guests. There is a cosy guest lounge with TV. Located 8 miles (12 km) west of Westport.

OWNERS Anne Colgan   OPEN Easter–31 October   ROOMS 2 double, 2 twin, 1 family (2 en suite)   TERMS B&B IR£12.50 p.p.; 50% reduction for children under 12; single supplement IR£2.50

Moher House

Liscarney, Westport, Co Mayo
Tel: (098) 26360

Marion O'Malley is a delightful lady who knows just how to make her guests feel at home, and a cup of tea and some of her delicious home-made scones are offered upon arrival. The bedrooms are clean, with pretty duvets; there are electric blankets and hot water bottles upon request. En suite facilities were added to a bedroom in 1991. Hairdryers provided upon request. Excellent breakfasts and evening meals are served, using the best cuts of meat provided by Mr O'Malley, a butcher. There is a pleasant sitting-room with TV. This is an ideal spot for walking; there are 4 designated walks in the area, and for the more adventurous, Croagh Patrick Mountain, with its magnificent view of 365 islands. Mrs O'Malley climbs the mountain once a year on the last Sunday in July. Washing and drying facilities are available. Siobhán, aged 13, plays the tin whistle and can easily be persuaded to play for guests. Fishing available in Moher Lake across the road from the house. No pets. Five miles (7½ km) from Westport on the main Clifden-Westport road (N59).

OWNER Marian O'Malley   OPEN All year, except Christmas ROOMS 2 double, 1 twin, 1 family (2 en suite)   TERMS B&B IR£12.00-£14.00 p.p.; reductions for children; single supplement IR£4.50; evening meal IR£12.00

Riverbank House

Rosbeg, Westport Quay, Co Mayo
Tel: (098) 25719

An inviting, spacious country house with attractive black shutters, flower baskets and window boxes, situated in a peaceful spot adjacant to a river, one mile (1½ km) from

Westport. The rooms are a good size, with modern furnishings, and are clean and comfortable. There's a relaxing guest lounge with TV and open fires. Kay O'Malley is pleased to help guests plan activities or day trips. Home-cooked breakfasts are served in the sunny dining-room; vegetarians catered for upon request. Local amenities include shooting at the Tirawley Game Reserve, bathing, boating, trout and salmon fishing, and golf. Smoking permitted in the lounge only. No pets.

OWNER Mrs Kay O'Malley   OPEN 15 March–1 November
ROOMS 4 double, 3 twin, 1 family (4 en suite)   TERMS B&B IR£12.50-£14.50 p.p.; 33% reduction for children; single supplement IR£4.50

Seapoint House

Kilmeena, Westport, Co Mayo
Tel: (098) 41254

Seapoint House is situated in a beautiful, unspoilt setting overlooking an inlet of Clew Bay. Most of the rooms have views of the sea and mountains. There is a very large lounge with a fireplace and a tastefully decorated dining-room with matching ceiling light and curtains leading out onto a sun porch. Evening meals are served, if prearranged, featuring fresh farm food, home-baking, fresh vegetables, home-made soups and local fish and meat. The bedrooms are spotlessly clean and functional. Self catering is available and there is a pony for children to ride. Non smokers preferred. Fishing, sailing, walking and an 18-golf course are available nearby. Baby-sitting can usually be arranged. Situated midway between Newport and Westport, approximately 5 miles (7½ km) from Westport.

OWNER The O'Malley family   OPEN 1 March–31 October
ROOMS 2 double/ twin/family (all en suite)   TERMS B&B IR£15.00 p.p.; 20% reduction for children; single supplement upon request; evening meal IR£12.50

County Sligo

County Sligo is located in one of the most beautiful and least explored regions of Ireland, surrounded by rugged mountains and rolling hills. The landscape is a patchwork of picturesque lakes, lush forests and sparkling rivers, its coastline dotted with peaceful coves.

Sligo's seaside resorts stretch along the coast from Innishcrone to Mullaghmore, with sandy beaches, fishing, golfing, beautiful walks and horse-riding – there is so much to do in this uncrowded corner of Ireland.

Explore the Gleniff Horseshoe, the Ladies Brae, visit Lissadell House and, for the more adventurous, climb to the summit of Queen Maeve's Cairn. Tour the loughs – Arrow, Gill, Easky, Gara, Glencar, Templehouse, Talt, and feast your eyes on Sligo's beauty.

Yeats, the poet, is buried at Drumcliffe. He called Sligo "The Land of Hearts Desire", and after you have visited, you will too.

BALLYMOTE

Temple House

Ballymote, Co Sligo

Tel: (071) 83329, Fax: (071) 83808

Approached through an impressive gateway bordered by white iron railings, the drive meanders through parkland to this massive Georgian mansion. Set in 1,000 acres of farm and woodland, the estate has been in the Perceval family since 1665, the present house being redesigned and refurnished in 1864. The entrance to the house is through a portico to a large square entrance hall with tiled floor and

shooting gear to a second larger hall, off of which is an enormous dining-room and 3 sitting-rooms, all with open fires. The larger room has lovely views over the garden to the lake and a ruined castle, built by the Knights Templar in 1200. The bedrooms are enormous, furnished with antiques and family portraits and with original bathroom fittings, curtains, carpet, etc; consequently some are faded and worn, but this all lends charm and atmosphere to the house. All but one are en suite, which has its own bathroom.

The Percevals are a very friendly couple. Mrs Perceval does all the cooking and Mr Perceval runs the farm, which is stocked with sheep, Kerry cattle, pigs and poultry, providing the kitchen with meat, bacon, eggs, vegetables and fruit. The vegetables and fruit are grown organically in a walled garden and the surplus are sold locally. Almost everything is home-grown and home-made, including yoghurt, jams and even their own flour. Evening meals are served at 7.30 pm if ordered in advance. The house has a wine licence and guests may bring their own spirits. Temple House is within easy reach of beautiful beaches, mountains, trout lakes and golf courses. The house is signposted from the main Galway to Sligo road – N17, 9 miles (13½ km) south of Sligo. Smoking is not encouraged in the dining-room. No pets. Visa, Access and Mastercard accepted.

OWNER Mrs D Perceval   OPEN 1 April–30 November   ROOMS 2 double, 2 twin, 1 single (4 en suite)   TERMS B&B IR£30.00 p.p.; reductions for children; single supplement IR£4.00; evening meal IR£16.00

CLIFFONEY

Dun Emer

Cliffoney, Co Sligo

Tel: (071) 66197

Dun Emer is a modern two-storey house. The rooms are clean and comfortable, 3 have showers only, and there is a ground-floor room with a bathroom on the same floor. Three of the bedrooms have lovely views of the sea and of Classie Bawn, Lord Mountbatten's castle, and the Donegal Mountains. Freshly prepared home-cooked meals are available, if prearranged. There is a guest lounge with TV for guests' use. Mary McCann has been in the catering trade for over 24 years and enjoys dealing with the public, offering lots of personal service to her guests. On the main N15 road. No pets.

OWNER Mrs Mary McCann   OPEN Easter–31 October   ROOMS 1 double, 2 twin, 2 family (3 with showers)   TERMS B&B IR£13.00 p.p.; reductions for children; single supplement IR£2.00; evening meal IR£10.00

161

Villa Rosa

Bunduff, Cliffoney, Co Sligo
Tel: (071) 66173

A small family home with wonderful views of the Donegal Mountains and sea, standing on the main road between Donegal and Sligo. Breakfast and home-cooked evening meals are served in the dining-room, which has a sitting area, a piano and stairs to the TV lounge – a large room with marvellous views of the sunsets. Mrs McLoughlin has been doing B&B for 21 years and is a most friendly, cheerful, welcoming lady. The bedrooms are very small and simply furnished and the house has a good, homely atmosphere. Evening meals can be provided between 6 and 8.30 pm if arranged in advance and there is a wine licence. Smoking is not permitted. All the bedrooms are on the ground floor. No pets. On the N15 to Donegal. American Express and Visa cards accepted.

OWNER John & Beatrice McLoughlin   OPEN 1 April–30 September   ROOMS 2 double/family/twin (2 en suite)   TERMS B&B IR£13.50 p.p.; no reductions for children; single supplement IR£2.50; evening meal IR£14.00

COLLOONEY

Union Farm

Collooney, Co Sligo
Tel: (071) 67136

This 300-year-old house, painted pale blue, stands in a very neat front garden in quiet, peaceful countryside, about a mile (1½ km)off the main road and with lovely views. The house is part of a 50-acre cattle farm and is well kept, with a comfortable TV lounge and attractive dining-room. Low doorways and thick walls abound, and the bedrooms are small and simply furnished. Evening meals or high tea are served at 7 pm if arranged in advance and there is a wine licence. No smoking permitted in the dining-room. One mile (1½ km) east of the N4 at Collooney. Pets by arrangement.

OWNERS Des and Tess Lang   OPEN 1 March–15 October   ROOMS 1 double, 2 twin, 1 family, 1 single (2 en suite)   TERMS B&B IR£13.50 p.p.; reductions for children; single supplement IR£2.00; evening meal IR£13.00, high tea from IR£5.00

Benbulben Farm

Drumcliff, Co Sligo

Tel: (071) 63211

A large modern farmhouse set amidst lovely mature gardens on 90 acres of sheep farming with unparalleled views of Benbulben Mountain and 100 square miles of beautiful Yeats country. This is very much a family home, and Mr and Mrs Hennigan are very congenial people, offering a welcome tray of tea or coffee upon arrival. The rooms are spotlessly clean and simply furnished with fitted wardrobes and firm beds. Evening meals are available, featuring fresh farm produce and home-style cooking. A lovely area for walking (there is a nature walk on the farm), fishing and hang-gliding. Sligo also has some fine examples of early megalithic tombs. There is no licence, but guests may bring their own wine. There is a TV lounge. Visa accepted. Located approximately 3 miles (4¹/₂ km) north of Drumcliff off the N15. Signposted.

OWNER Ann Hennigan   OPEN 1 April–31 September   ROOMS 2 twin, 3 family, 1 single (2 en suite)   TERMS B&B IR£12.00-£15.00 p.p.; reductions for children; single supplement IR£3.00; light evening meal IR£5.00, evening meal £11.00

Urlar House

Drumcliff, Co Sligo

Tel: (071) 63110

Urlar House is a Georgian house in a quiet location off a private drive off the N15, 1 mile (1¹/₂ km) north of Drumcliff. This spacious house with its comfortable lounge has the original marble fireplace and 2 archways with the original Wedgewood figure design. The bedrooms vary in size; there is a family suite consisting of a twin and double room with en suite facilities, ideal for friends or a family travelling together. Excellent breakfasts are served family-style on a large antique table and consist of a choice of yoghurts, stuffed pancakes, fishcakes, omelets, full Irish breakfast, and home-baked breads. Mrs Healy is a proud recipient of the northwest region Agri-Tourism award. Excellent home-cooked evening meals are also available if prearranged. There is an enclosed sun porch for the children to play

games in, which leads out to the garden. Pets by arrangement. Six miles (9 km) north of Sligo.

OWNERS Mrs Healy   OPEN 1 March–1 November   ROOMS 2
double, 2 twin, 1 family, (2 en suite)   TERMS B&B IR£13.50-
£15.50 p.p.; reductions for children; single supplement IR£3.50;
evening meal IR£12.50

INISHCRONE

Ceol na Mara

Main Street, Inishcrone, Co Sligo
Tel: (096) 36351

Ceol na Mara, which means "Music of the Sea", is a 120-
year-old house; because of its renovations it looks quite new,
with its modern windows and stucco façade. The house was
recently redecorated in a tasteful, homely style and 2 new
bedrooms added, with views of the beach. The O'Regans
are both teachers and the house was owned by Mr
O'Regan's parents. They took over the house when they
married and have carried out a lot of renovations. The house
stands in the middle of Inishcrone, one side on the main
street, the other with sea views. There is a large lounge with
an open fire, which is lit on chilly evenings, and the large
dining-room has sea views at one end. All twin-bedded
rooms have double beds, so they can also be used as family
rooms. The rooms are quite good-sized and simply furnished. The championship course at Inishcrone (meaning
"hamlet by the river") draws many golfers. Evening meals
are served on request and there is a wine licence. Two
bedrooms are on the ground floor. Pets are not allowed. The
beach at Inishcrone has been awarded the Blue Flag and is
one of the finest in Ireland. On T40 off L150 8 miles (12 km)
west of Ballina. Visa and Mastercard accepted.

OWNER Mairéad O'Regan   OPEN 1 March–31 October
ROOMS 1 double, 3 twin, 4 family (all en suite)
TERMS B&B IR£15.00 p.p.; reductions for children; single supple-
ment IR£2.00; evening meal IR£12.00

RIVERSTOWN

Coopershill

Riverstown, Co Sligo
Tel: (071) 65108

Approached through parks, woods and farmland, a long drive winds it way up to this wonderful Georgian mansion which has splendid views over woods, hills and the River Arrow which runs through the property. It was built in 1774 and 7 generations of the O'Haras have lived in it since then. Peacocks strut on the front lawn and the building has recently been cleaned up to reveal the pristine stone work. The present O'Haras have lived in the house for the last 6 years and are gradually restoring it to an extremely high standard of comfort, without in any way detracting from the ambience of the period. In fact, much of the furniture is what was originally there. Family portraits adorn the walls, the rooms are big enough to make massive pieces of furniture look insignificant, and the dining-room has enormous sideboards covered with gleaming family silver. Mr O'Hara farms the 500-acre estate with his brother, and Mrs O'Hara takes care of the guests and does all the cooking. There is a large, comfortable drawing-room with a log fire and 5 of the bedrooms have four-poster or canopy beds. Boats and gillies can be arranged for fishing on Lough Arrow and boating, trout and coarse fishing are available on the River Arrow. Evening meals, if arranged in advance, are served at 8.30 pm and a light lunch can also be provided. There is a wine licence. Hairdryers and tea- and coffee-making facilities are in all bedrooms. Guests are encouraged to smoke in the drawing-room and lounge only. Pets outside only. Signposted from the Drumfin crossroads, 11 miles (16^{1}/$_{2}$ km) south west of Sligo on route N4 to Dublin. All major credit cards accepted.

OWNERS Brian and Linda O'Hara   OPEN   16 March–31 October
ROOMS 6 double, 1 twin (6 en suite)   TERMS B&B IR£40.00-£42.50 p.p.

Ross House

Ross, Riverstown, Co Sligo
Tel: (071) 65140

A 100-year-old house in attractive farmland surroundings, standing in a small, slightly overgrown, pretty front garden, the farmyard stretching to the back of the house. It is well signposted from the main Dublin road into Sligo on the N4 and is located 3 miles (4^{1}/$_{2}$ km) from Drumfin and approached down narrow lanes. Mrs Hill-Wilkinson is a very friendly lady who loves baking and she is most happy for guests to come into the kitchen and see how it is done. Home-cooked evening meals are available on request at 7 to 7.30 pm and a cup of tea is provided later in the evening. It is a simple family home, and guests have use of a TV lounge with peat fire and a dining-room. One bedroom is small, the other 3 are of average size; all have tea-making facilities and hairdryers. This is a wonderful place for children; there is a donkey, hay-making, and cows on a mixed 120-acre farm. Many come for the fishing on Lough Arrow, and fishermen are able to hire boats, tackle and engines from the Hill-Wilkinsons. Smoking is not allowed in the dining-room. Sligo has many ancient monuments at Carrowmore, Carrowkeel, Creevykeel and Deerpark, some dating back 3,000 years. There are many beautiful beaches close by. Pets by arrangement.

OWNERS Oriel and Nicholas Hill-Wilkinson OPEN 1 March–
1 November   ROOMS 1 double, 2 family   TERMS B&B IR£14.00
p.p.; reductions for children; single supplement IR£2.00; light
meals availble, evening meals from IR£12.00

ROSCOMMON

Munsboro House

Sligo Road, Roscommon, Co Sligo
Tel: (903) 25611

Munsboro House is a lovely Georgian house situated 300 yards off the main road in a peaceful and tranquil setting. The Dolan family run an intensive sheep-rearing, cattle and tillage farm on the 150 acres surrounding the house. Munsboro House is now known as the Munsboro Equestrian Centre, which specialises in horse-riding and activity holidays; qualified instruction is provided in all cases, though the emphasis for all is on fun and enjoyment. The rooms are spacious, and you will find a warm welcome in this comfortable house with its open fires, whether you are there to relax or to partake in any of the activities. Excellent evening meals are available and are prepared from fresh local produce, served in the lovely dining-room. The Dolans are justly proud of their BHS Farmhouse of the Year award. For those looking to escape the chaos of modern life, Munsboro House is an excellent choice. Lovely forest walks in Moate Park 1½ miles (2½ km) away. Wine licence. No pets.

OWNER Mrs Delia Dolan   OPEN 1 April–1 September   ROOMS 2 double/twin   TERMS B&B IR£14.00 p.p.; reductions for children; single supplement off season only; evening meal from IR£11.00

SLIGO

Arus na Greine

Pearse Road, Sligo, Co Sligo
Tel: (071) 69280

An immaculately kept, delightful, small townhouse, just a couple of minutes' walk from the town centre. There are fresh flowers everywhere and Mrs Flavin is a most friendly lady. A small walled garden with patio leads off the very pleasant and comfortable TV lounge, and the dining-room has front bowed windows. The bedrooms are very attractive, although a little small, with shower rooms. Guests are advised to leave their car at the B&B and stroll into town. No pets. Located opposite Monoghan's shop, near the second set of traffic lights at the town end of Pearse Road. (Main entrance to town centre from Dublin road – N4).

OWNER Mrs Deirdre Flavin   OPEN 1 April–31 October   ROOMS 1 double, 2 twin, (all en suite)   TERMS IR£13.50 p.p.; reductions for children; single supplement IR£3.50

Aisling

Cairns Hill, Sligo, Co Sligo
Tel: (071) 60704

Aisling, which means Irish dream, is an immaculate bungalow standing in its own grounds in an elevated position on the south side of Sligo. The bedrooms are average in size and comfortably furnished; all are on the ground floor. Des and Nan Faul are a down-to-earth, congenial couple who share the work. Nan cooks breakfast, which is flexible (there is a varied choice), Des enjoys chatting to guests and helping them plan daily activities. Breakfast only is served, but there are plenty of good restaurants close by. Aisling has a comfortable lounge with a TV and coal fire. Not suitable for children. No pets. Smoking not permitted in the bedrooms. Situated 300 metres off Pearse Road (the Dublin/Galway road N4).

OWNER Des and Nan Faul   OPEN All year, except Christmas ROOMS 6 double/twin/family (3 en suite)   TERMS B&B IR£13.00-£15.00 p.p.; single supplement IR£5.00-£7.00

167

Hillside

Kilsellagh, Enniskillen Road, Sligo, Co Sligo
Tel: (071) 42808

An attractive, small, cream-washed farmhouse standing just off the main Sligo to Enniskillen road, with a pretty front garden and lovely views. The house is about 200-years old and was originally a one-storey building. It belonged to Mrs Stuart's grandfather and she has been doing bed and breakfast for over 25 years. The house is well kept and cosy, with small, freshly decorated bedrooms (en suite facilities were

added to a bedroom in 1991), a dining-room and small TV lounge with open fire. Tea and coffee are available on request and evening meals are served if booked in advance at 6.30 to 7 pm, featuring fresh vegetables and meat from the farm. There is a pony and donkey for children under the supervision of parents. Smoking is not encouraged in the dining-room or bedrooms. There is one downstairs bedroom. There is no licence, but guests may bring their own wine to a meal. Pets by arrangement. Convenient to sandy beaches, golf, horse-riding, fishing and mountain climbing. Off the N16 Enniskillen road, 3 miles (4½ km) from Sligo.

OWNER Mrs Elma Stuart   OPEN 1 April–31 October   ROOMS 2 family/twin (2 en suite)   TERMS B&B IR£13.00 p.p.; reductions for children; single supplement IR£3.50; evening meal IR£12.50

Lisadorn

Lisnalurg, Donegal Road, Sligo, Co Sligo
Tel: (071) 43417

A spacious, modern two-storey house just off the main road in the heart of Yeats country. Lisadorn is set back off the main road in a large, beautifully maintained garden with colourful flowers, manicured lawn and lovely views. No expense has been spared in making this a top-class bed and breakfast. The rooms are spacious and the decor and furniture of a high standard. All the twin-bedded rooms have double beds, so they can also be used as family rooms. Each room has a TV and electric blankets. The dining-room, where breakfast only is served, is attractively furnished with separate tables and good views; the TV lounge has an open fire. Tea and coffee are available when required at no extra charge. Pets by arrangment. Lisadorn is an ideal base from which to explore the north-west region. On the Donegal road, N15.

OWNER Mrs Lily Diamond   OPEN All year, except Christmas
ROOMS 2 twin, 1 triple, 3 family (all en suite)   TERMS B&B
IR£14.50 p.p.; reductions for children; single supplement IR£5.00

Lissadell

Pearse Road, Sligo, Co Sligo
Tel: (071) 61937

An attractive, whitewashed, creeper-clad house with red front door, standing just back from the main road close to the centre of town. The Caddens moved here approximately 3 years ago and have more or less done up the whole house, putting in bathrooms, etc. Mrs Cadden is a friendly lady, and this is a pleasant, spacious house. The bedrooms are quite good-sized as are the TV lounge and dining-room: a warm and comfortable house in the heart of Yeats country. There is a large rear garden. Smoking is not permitted in the dining-room. No pets. Situated 4 minutes' walk from the town centre.

OWNER Mrs Mary Cadden   OPEN All year, except Christmas
ROOMS 2 double/twin (all en suite)   TERMS B&B IR£13.50 p.p.;
reductions for children; single supplement IR£2.50

Sea Park House

Rosses Point Road, Sligo, Co Sligo

Tel: (071) 45556

The Fullertons built this modern bungalow about 12 years
ago and later extended it. It is a low, one-storey whitewashed building just off the main road in Rosses Point and
has pleasant views of sea and mountains. The bedrooms are
small and spotlessly clean, and guests have use of a
hairdryer, iron and telephone. Breakfast only is served in the
bright dining-room and there is a TV lounge. Smoking is not
permitted in the dining-room and pets are not allowed.
Situated on the main Sligo to Rosses Point road on the left-
hand side, 3 miles (4¹/₂ km) out of town and overlooking
the sea.

OWNER Mr Ismay Fullerton   OPEN 1 March–31 October
ROOMS 3 double, 1 twin, 2 family (4 en suite)   TERMS B&B
IR£12.50-£13.00 p.p.; reductions for children; single supplement
IR£5.00

Tree Tops

Cleveragh Road, Sligo, Co Sligo

Tel: (071) 60160/62301

Tree Tops is a spacious, modern, attractive house in a secluded location, set in a pretty garden with a fishpond and
within a 10-minute walk to town. The immaculate
bedrooms are large, prettily decorated and all have
hairdryers. The house is well maintained and tastefully
furnished; there is also a collection of prints and paintings.
Substantial, wholesome breakfasts are served in the dining-
room/lounge, which has a TV and wicker furniture. Smoking
in moderation in bedrooms only. There are some lovely
walks and views close by. No pets. One hundred miles (150
km) off the N4, signposted on the right as you enter Sligo.
Access, Visa and Mastercard accepted.

OWNERS Ronan and Doreen MacEvilly   OPEN All year, except
Christmas   ROOMS 6 double/twin (4 en suite)   TERMS B&B
IR£13.00-£14.00 p.p.

Glen Lodge

Culleenamore, near Strandhill, Co Sligo

Tel: (071) 68387, Fax: (071) 68391

A most attractive ivy-clad Georgian house, the oldest part dating from 1790. The house takes its name from the Glen – a strange cleft on the south face of Knocknarea which runs within the borders of the estate. It is in a most lovely position towards the end of a narrow road, right on the coast, with wonderful views of Ballisodare Bay and the Ox Mountains and set in 4 acres of gardens of trees, shrubs and lawns. Owned originally by the Cockburns and later by the Jamesons of Irish whiskey fame, it has for the last couple of years belonged to Toby (English) and Anneli (Swedish) Wear. Although it had already been converted into a restaurant and house offering accommodation, the Wears have done a lot to it. The rooms are spacious and well proportioned with original fireplaces, and some bedrooms have four-poster beds. There are flowers everywhere, and the house has been most tastefully and comfortably decorated and furnished.

The restaurant, where W B Yeats and his uncle George used to dine, is open to non-residents and there are 2 chefs. Herbs, fruit and vegetables are all organically grown on the premises. In their first season (1989) the Wears won the Regional Finalists Galtee Breakfast award. Packed lunches and afternoon teas are also available for residents and breakfast is served in the attractive, bright breakfast room. All bedrooms have TVs and telephones. The premises are licensed. A 12-seater cross-country vehicle is available for collecting people at railway stations or airports; it may also be used to take people fishing or to explore remote areas. No pets. Follow the signs from Sligo. All major credit cards accepted.

OWNERS Toby and Anneli Wear   OPEN 1 March–31 October
ROOMS 3 double/twin (all en suite)   TERMS B&B IR£32.00-£50.00 p.p.; single supplement IR£10.00; evening meal from IR£19.00

Cruckawn House

Ballymote Road, Tobercurry, Co Sligo
Tel: (071) 85188

Mrs Walsh, who is director of the North West Regional
Tourism Organisation and an expert on all local attractions,
makes this a special place to stay. An extremely outgoing,
friendly lady, she likes her guests to feel that they are at
home. Cruckawn House is very much a family home. The
house stands back a little from the road on the edge of town
and overlooks the golf course; there are clubs and caddies
for hire and the green fees are moderate. The bedrooms are
small, with hairdryers and TVs on request. There is a comfortable TV lounge which leads into a dining-room. Excellent
home-cooked meals are served if arranged in advance.
Separating the dining-room from a small sun-lounge are
sliding glass doors with the family crests of the 2 families
engraved in the middle of each door. Tobercurry is quite a
lively place with traditional Irish music every Thursday, June
through to September. There is a wine licence. Dog kennels
are provided. Local amenities include salmon and trout
fishing, game shooting, mountain climbing, horse-riding and
pony trekking. Located 300 metres off N17 on the Galway to
Sligo road, signposted on main N17 and in centre of town.
Visa accepted.

OWNERS Jo and Maeve Walsh   OPEN All year, except Christmas
ROOMS 1 double, 2 twin, 2 family (4 en suite)   TERMS B&B
IR£15.00 p.p.; reductions for children; single supplement
IR£5.00; evening meal IR£12.00

Pine Grove

Ballina Road, Tobercurry, Co Sligo
Tel: (071) 85235

A square, whitewashed house standing in a somewhat
overgrown but pretty small front garden just on the edge of
town on the Ballina Road. Mrs Kelly caters for non-residents for lunch as well as evening meals, which are served in
a large dining-room with a piano at the back of the house,
overlooking the back patio. Here guests can sit on fine days.
The house is furnished very simply, with rather old-fashioned furniture. The lounge with open fire and TV is some-

what crowded with dark furniture, but there are comfortable chairs. There is no licence, but guests are welcome to bring their own. All the beds have electric blankets and an iron and hairdryer are available. Pets by arrangment. Located a quarter of a mile off N17 on Ballina Road.

OWNER Mrs Teresa Kelly   OPEN All year, except Christmas
ROOMS 1 double, 3 twin, 1 family (all en suite)
TERMS B&B IR£14.50 p.p.; reductions for children; evening meal IR£5.00

The Midlands

County Carlow

One of the smallest counties in Ireland, Carlow lies just below Wicklow and is in an area of rich farmland.

The county town, Carlow, has had an eventful history, including being captured by Cromwell in 1650. Now it manufactures beet sugar and has quite a few sights worth looking at, including the ruins of the Norman Castle, a Gothic Revival Catholic Church, the Carlow Museum and the fine courthouse with a Doric portico fashioned after the Parthenon.

There is a ruined twelfth-century church at Killeshin, with a fine Romanesque doorway, and fourteenth-century Ballymoon Castle which has apparently never been occupied.

BAGENALSTOWN

Lorum Old Rectory

Kilgreaney, Bagenalstown, Co Carlow
Tel: (0503) 75282

Dating from the eighteenth century, Lorum Old Rectory is set in 18 acres, nestling beneath the Blackstairs Mountains. It is surrounded by open countryside with views as far as Tipperary. There are plenty of animals about, including goats, horses, dogs, a peacock and Jacob sheep. One of the double rooms is en suite and there are plans to put bathrooms in the remaining 3 rooms. The bedrooms are spacious, furnished with antiques and all have their original fireplaces. There is a comfortable, informal atmosphere here, and Don and Bobbie Smith are a friendly couple. Five-course, imaginative evening meals are available, with home-grown organic vegetables. There is a wine licence and a tiny snug bar with a fireplace and chaise-longue. Smoking in public rooms only. Visa and Access cards accepted.

OWNERS Don and Bobbie Smith   OPEN All year, except Christmas   ROOMS 4 double (2 en suite)   TERMS B&B IR£20.00 p.p.; reductions for children; single supplement IR£3.00; evening meal IR£15.00

Lisnavagh

Rathvilly, Co Carlow
Tel: (0503) 61104

Approached up a great wide driveway, past farm buildings and bordered by rhododendrons, Lisnavagh is a splendid Victorian Gothic country house built in 1848. Since then it has belonged to the Rathdonnells and was redesigned in 1952, mostly by demolishing about half the building. It is hard to imagine that what now is a most attractive library was formerly the kitchen: beautifully carved bookshelves encase the room, interspersed with family portraits, a stone fireplace and comfortable chairs and sofas. There is one enormous four-poster room with an old-fashioned en suite bathroom. The other bedrooms are smaller, but still of a good size, with private bathrooms. The house is set in 1,000 acres of farm and woodlands and is surrounded by expansive lawns beyond which are lovely views. The outdoor heated swimming pool is set in its own beautiful walled garden; there is a grass tennis court and clay pigeon shooting can be arranged. Golf, riding, squash, hunting, shooting and fishing are all available with notice.

OWNER Lord Rathdonnell   OPEN All year, except Christmas
ROOMS: 2 four-posters, 2 twin, 1 single (3 en suite)   TERMS B&B IR£42.00 p.p.; evening meal IR£18.00

County Kildare

County Kildare is famous for horse breeding and training, which take place on the Curragh, a great plain leading into a boggy area, the Bog of Allen. Many horse-race meetings are held here, including the Irish Sweep Derby, the Irish 2,000 Guineas, the Irish Oaks and the Irish St Leger. The town of Kildare is the centre for horse breeding and has a well-preserved Church of Ireland cathedral and round tower.

At Robertstown the eighteenth-century buildings along the Grand Canal have been restored to look as they did when this was a great water thoroughfare. Here it is possible to visit Europe's largest falconry. Two of Ireland's greatest Georgian country houses, Carton and Castletown, are located at Celbridge. A music festival takes place in June at Castletown, as does one of the hunt balls held during the Dublin Horse Show week.

The very pretty village of Leixlip has many associations with the Guinness family; the twelfth-century Norman castle belongs to Desmond Guinness.

Remains of a Franciscan Abbey can be seen at Castledermot, and Athy has many historic sights worth exploring, including the sixteenth-century Woodstock Castle just out of town. Moone High Cross, one of Ireland's most beautiful high crosses, is at Moone Abbey, 8 miles (12 km) from Athy.

BARBERSTOWN

Windgate Lodge

Barberstown, Maynooth, Co Kildare

Tel: (01) 6273415

An attractive red-brick two-storey house set back off the road in an acre of landscaped gardens. The house is in good decorative order and there are 2 bedrooms on the ground floor, one of which has its own bathroom This is an ideal location from which to reach either the Dublin airport or Dublin city; there is a train station at Maynooth 2 miles (3 km) away where cars can be left, as well as a frequent bus service to Dublin. Owner Mrs Pat Ryan is most pleasant, always eager to offer assistance to guests, and she serves a good home-cooked freshly prepared breakfast. There is a separate dining-room and TV lounge. Easy access to Naas and the south. Dublin airport approximately 40 minutes' drive away. Pets by arrangement. There is a self-catering unit available. Situated on the R406 Maynooth to Straffan road.

OWNER Mrs Pat Ryan   OPEN All year, except Christmas Day
ROOMS 1 double, 2 twin, 1 family (2 en suite)   TERMS B&B
IR£15.00 p.p.; reductions for children; single supplement IR£3.00

CASTLEDERMOT

Kilkea Lodge Farm

Castledermot, Co Kildare

Tel: (0503) 45112

A comfortable family house set in rolling parkland with a pleasant, rural aspect; it is approached down a long driveway off the Castledermot Road, about half a mile from Kilkea

Castle. Kilkea Lodge, which has belonged to the Greene family since 1740, has a relaxed, informal atmosphere and friendly owners. Marion Greene runs the riding centre, offering a variety of instructional and fun holidays, and Godfrey runs the 260-acre farm. There is one enormous bedroom, converted from an old barn, with its own entrance, 4 beds, a small loft and a sitting-area in the middle: ideal for families or small groups. There is a comfortable drawing-room with fireplace and piano and traditional home-cooked evening meals are served in the dining-room at the large table. No smoking in bedrooms. Pets outside only by arrangement.

OWNER Godfrey and Marion Greene OPEN All year, except Christmas and January ROOMS 2 double, 1 twin, 1 single (all en suite) TERMS B&B IR£21.50-£25.00 p.p.; reductions for children; evening meal IR£15.00-£18.00

DUNLAVIN

Grangebeg

Dunlavin, Co Kildare
Tel: (045) 51367

Grangebeg probably dates from the first half of the eighteenth century and when acquired by Aine McGrane's father in the 1940s was twice as big as it is today. Although half the house was pulled down in the 1950s, today it has a neat, square and complete look to it with a front porch and classical lines. Grangebeg stands in a park-like setting on a quiet country lane, about $1^1/2$ miles ($2^1/2$ km) from Dunlavin. Aine McGrane was born here, and now that her 6 children have moved away or gone to school she has plenty of room for guests. The eldest daughter runs the riding centre, with stables at the back of the house. The house is decorated in an individual style with flamboyant wallpapers and matching curtains and chair covers. There's a formal dining-room, a smaller dining-room off the kitchen, a pleasant drawing-room with open fire and a smaller TV room. This is a delightful, friendly place and very handy for the Punchestown Races. Grangebeg can be found off the Naas to Kilkenny road.

OWNER Aine McGrane OPEN All year, except Christmas ROOMS 2 double, 2 twin, 3 single (2 en suite) TERMS B&B IR£15.00-£30.00 p.p.; evening meal IR£12.00-£15.00

Freemont

Tully Road, Kildare, Co Kildare
Tel: (045) 21604

Freemont is a modern bungalow in a private setting, 3 minutes' walk to the town centre and the twelfth-century cathedral. The bedrooms, all on the ground floor, are spotlessly clean, with modern furnishings and shower units. The bathrooms, hall and dining-room have been completely refurbished. The comfortable TV lounge has a lovely Leitrim stone fireplace, and the bright dining-room has a beautiful unit displaying a fine collection of Waterford, Galway and Cavan crystal. Mrs O'Connell is a considerate host who enjoys meeting people, and she extends a warm welcome to everyone. Breakfasts only are served, but there are several restaurants and pubs within walking distance. A short drive or a 15-minute walk to the Irish Stud and the Japanese Gardens. No smoking in the bedrooms. Private parking. Signposted from the town centre.

OWNER Mrs Frieda O'Connell   OPEN All year, except December
ROOMS 2 double, 1 twin (all with shower units)   TERMS B&B
IR£13.00 p.p.; reductions for children; single supplement IR£4.00

Mount Ruadhan

Old Road, Kildare, Co Kildare
Tel: (045) 21637

Mount Ruadhan is easily located, as it is signposted at the only traffic light in Kildare. The house is situated 1 mile (1½ km) from town in peaceful surroundings and set in a pretty garden. The decor is bright, with red the predominant colour. All the bedrooms are on the ground floor. The owners have their quarters upstairs, but are on hand to answer questions or make a pot of tea. There is good fishing 2 miles (3 km) away at a relatively unknown spot. Information on this is gladly given to interested fishermen. Breakfasts only are served, but there are several venues for good food in town. Smoking in TV room only

OWNER Mrs Eileen Corcoran   OPEN 1 March–1 October
ROOMS 1double/twin/family (1 en suite)   TERMS B&B IR£15.00-
IR£18.00 p.p.; reductions for children; single supplement IR£4.00

Rossa House

Dublin Road, Kildare, Co Kildare
Tel: (045) 21210

A Georgian-style townhouse standing in its own grounds, 10 minutes' walk from town. The house is bright with an open-style floor plan. The bedrooms are adequately furnished, spotlessly clean, all with hairdryers, tea-making facilities and electric blankets. There's a very spacious, comfortable lounge with a TV and a pleasant dining-room where break-fasts only are served. The house has recently been redeco-rated both inside and outside and one room has had an en suite bathroom added. Prior to retirement the O'Donovans owned a pub for 25 years. The house they bought was really too big, and as they missed their contact with people, decided it was perfect for a bed and breakfast. Not suitable for babies or small children. No pets. A short drive to the Irish Stud and the Japanese Gardens. The house is located on the main Dublin to Cork road.

OWNER Joanna O'Donovan   OPEN 1 April–1 September   ROOMS 2 double/twin, (2 en suite)   TERMS B&B IR£13.00-£17.00 p.p.; reductions for children

County Kilkenny

Kilkenny, the county town, is one of the oldest and most interesting towns in Ireland. It comes alive at the end of August during the Kilkenny Festival, which is one of Ire-land's foremost cultural festivals. Kilkenny Castle stands in the centre, dominating the town, and just opposite is the Kilkenny Design Centre Workshops, which can be visited. The cathedral stands on the site of a monastery built by St Canice in the sixth century and from which the city took its name. The Kilkenny Archaeological Society houses its collection in a most interesting Tudor merchant's house, Rothe House; the City Hall, built in 1761, was formerly the Tolsel, or Toll House. Some well-known writers, including Swift, Berkeley and Congreve, were educated at Kilkenny College, a fine Georgian building.

   The County Kilkenny countryside is pretty and compact, and places of interest to visit include the attractive town of Thomastown, near to which is Dysart Castle, former home of George Berkeley after whom the city and university in

California, Berkeley, is named. Near to Callan on the King's River is Kells, a fortified, turreted and walled collection of early ecclesiastical buildings, and near Urlingford are the ruins of four castles.

CASTLECOMER

Wandesforde House

Moneenroe, Castlecomer, Co Kilkenny

Tel: (056) 42441

Wandesforde House was built in 1824 by Lady Ann Ormonde as a school for the children of the Castlecomer estate. When the Flemings bought it in 1989 it was almost a ruin. They have cleverly united the whole building by enclosing the front porch behind glass and putting in a new front door; at the back of the house is a lovely conservatory which leads onto a sunny patio. The 2 enormous school rooms with high ceilings to each side of the house have been converted into a sitting-room/restaurant for guests and into the family living quarters. The central area, where the teacher lived, has been altered to accommodate the bedrooms, which are comfortable and attractively decorated. David is a trained chef, and interesting meals are available to residents and non-residents. The Flemings have horses, and guests are welcome to bring their own. Packed lunches are available. There is a wine licence and pets are accepted by arrangement only. Located 10 miles (15 km) from Kilkenny on the main Dublin road. All major credit cards accepted.

OWNER David and Phil Fleming   OPEN All year, except Christmas
ROOMS 2 double, 3 twin, 1 single (all en suite)   TERMS B&B
IR£15.00-£16.50 p.p.; evening meals à la carte

FRESHFORD

Kilrush House

Freshford, Co Kilkenny

Tel: (056) 32236

An interesting family house built in 1820 with large rooms containing many of the original furnishings. Kilrush House stands in lawns, gardens and parkland, surrounded by its 250-acre farm which supports sheep and a few thorough-bred National Hunt mares. The St George family have lived at Kilrush for 3 centuries and until the present house was built they inhabited the old Tower House, which in spite of its age still stands. One of the features of the house is the graceful cupola that is set high above the hall, the circular landing on the first floor accentuating its lines. Home-cooked meals including vegetables, lamb and free-range pork from the farm are served in the enormous dining-room, which has the furniture originally made for the house and the old, somewhat faded wallpaper dating from around 1820. The welcome and enthusiasm of the delightful owners more than compensates for some of the more old-fashioned amenities and casual lifestyle. There is a hard tennis court; hunting holidays can be arranged during the winter. Pets by arrangement. Kilrush can be found on the road to Cashel 2 miles (3 km) from Freshford.

OWNER Richard and Sally St George   OPEN All year, except Christmas   ROOMS 4 double (3 en suite)   TERMS B&B IR£20.00-£28.00 p.p.; reductions for children; evening meal IR£16.00

KILKENNY

Blanchville House

Dunbell, Maddoxtown, Kilkenny, Co Kilkenny
Tel: (056) 27197

Blanchville House is an elegant Georgian residence standing in its own grounds, approached by a tree- and shrub-lined private drive. It is beautifully furnished with antiques and has large comfortable bedrooms, all of which are now en suite and have tea- and coffee-making facilities. The spacious drawing-room, with the original wallpaper and service bells, has a TV, grand piano and open fireplace. All the rooms overlook the lovely green countryside. Evening meals, if booked in advance, are served in the atmospheric dining-room and are tastefully prepared with home-grown produce; vegetarian and special diets catered for. A wonderful retreat to return to after a day's sightseeing. Local amenities include golf, tennis, horse-riding, hunting, fishing and flying at the Kilkenny Air Club. A 10-minute drive from Kilkenny, off the N10 Kilkenny/Dublin road right at Barlow Ford, approximately 3 miles (4½ km) from this point. If in doubt call for directions. All major credit cards accepted.

OWNERS Tim and Monica Phelan OPEN 1 March–1 October ROOMS 2 double/twin/family (all en suite)   TERMS B&B IR£20.00 p.p.; reductions for children; single supplement IR£4.00; evening meal IR£15.00

Burwood Bed and Breakfast

Waterford Road, Kilkenny, Co Kilkenny
Tel: (056) 62266

A modern bungalow with old-fashioned hospitality set back off the main road, with a small, pretty front garden. The bedrooms, all on the ground floor, are immaculate and individually decorated with pastel-flowered wallpapers. There's a comfortable TV lounge for guests. Joan Flanagan is a most accommodating host, and a cup of tea or coffee is offered upon arrival and in the evening. She is proud of the personal attention given to each guest, making them feel relaxed and welcome. The house is close to all amenities and local restaurants. No smoking. Dogs welcome. Located on the Waterford road 1 mile (1½ km) from the medieval city of Kilkenny.

OWNER Joan Flanagan OPEN 1 June–1 September ROOMS 1 double/twin/family (1 en suite) TERMS B&B IR£11.50 p.p.; reductions for children; single supplement IR£3.50

Dunromin

Dublin Road, Kilkenny, Co Kilkenny
Tel: (056) 61387

The standard of maintenance is exceptionally high throughout the public rooms and bedrooms of this house, situated in a quiet location on the edge of town. There are views of the countryside at the back of the house and a golf course lies to the front. The bedrooms are spacious, with a mixture of traditional mahogany and wicker furnishings, and are immaculate. Guests enjoy the secluded, landscaped garden with furniture for guests' use, and there is a wonderful, friendly atmosphere. Mr Rothwell plays the accordian and he enjoys entertaining guests; Dunromin is well known for its informality and great musical evenings. Tea or coffee are offered on arrival, and breakfasts include home-baked breads and home-made preserves. No smoking in the dining-room. No pets. The house is located on the main Dublin to Carlow road, a 5-minute walk from the bus and railway station. Visa and Mastercard accepted.

OWNER Mrs Valerie Rothwell OPEN All year ROOMS 1 double/twin/single/family (3 en suite) TERMS B&B IR£13.00 p.p.; reductions for children; no single supplement

Shillogher House

Callan Road, Kilkenny, Co Kilkenny
Tel: (056) 63249

A large modern brick house built by the owners and standing in its own grounds on the outskirts of Kilkenny on the Callan road; only a few minutes' walk to the centre. The Kennedys are very welcoming people, and the house has a friendly atmosphere. The rooms are immaculately clean and decorated with pretty wallpapers and curtains. Tea and coffee are available in the hall and there is a TV lounge off the breakfast room. The menu gives guests an excellent choice for breakfast. No smoking in the bedrooms and no pets allowed. Visa and Access cards accepted.

OWNER Aileen Kennedy   OPEN All year, except Christmas
ROOMS 4 double/twin/family   TERMS B&B IR£12.50-£20.00 p.p.;
reductions for children

STONYFORD

The Old Rectory

Ennisnag, Stonyford, Co Kilkenny
Tel: (056) 28351; Fax: same

Dating from 1618, this solid square building is located in a wonderful position – standing in its own lush grounds, it borders 2 small rivers: the King's River and the Mill Race River. Both have salmon and trout and guests are welcome to fish. The Old Rectory was bought by the Wenner family some 6 years ago and was virtually rebuilt with a distinct Germanic flavour. There are exposed wooden floors throughout the house; the bedrooms have a lot of pine finishes and feature Germanic furniture and pictures. The Wenners are friendly, welcoming people who grow organically as much produce on their 26 acres as possible. Vegetables, sausages, smoked ham, butter and prize-winning cheese can be tasted at breakfast, which is of the continental variety. The house has a sauna and sunbed and Mount Juliet golf course is 3 miles (4½ km) away. Pets by arrangement.

OWNER Klaus Wenner   OPEN All year   ROOMS 4 double/twin
TERMS B&B IR£14.00-£16.00 p.p.; reductions for children

Abbey House

Jerpoint Abbey, Thomastown, Co Kilkenny
Tel: (056) 24166

Abbey House is an attractive building located opposite
Jerpoint Abbey. The house may have been built as early as
1540 and a mill dates here from the twelfth century. Ruins
of the old mill lie behind the house, which Helen
Blanchfield would love to restore. The house itself was in a
very bad condition when the Blanchfields bought it in 1988,
and only one original wall is left after doing the work. Helen
is an amusing, chatty lady with a lot of energy. She runs not
only the bed and breakfast but also provides lunches, teas,
evening meals and snacks for non-residents. The house is
spacious with a drawing-room and simply furnished bedrooms; the pleasant dining-room has small tables. Abbey
House is located on the Dublin to Waterford road. Visa,
Access and Eurocard accepted.

OWNER Mrs Helen Blanchfield   OPEN All year   ROOMS 6 double
(all en suite)   TERMS B&B IR£16.00-£19.00 p.p.; reductions for
children; evening meal IR£12.75, also à la carte

County Leitrim

Experience the charming beauty of County Leitrim, with its
distinctive hill formations and lovely lakes. This long,
narrow county is divided in two by Lough Allen, one of the
many lakes of the Shannon River. The county is a very
popular place for anglers and the main topic of conversation
everywhere seems to be fishing.

Dromahair is a pretty village, located about 8 miles (12
km) from Manorhamilton. The road from here is scenically
superb, with views of Lough Gill and beautiful wooded
countryside.

Fenagh, which is located in the hills, has the ruins of a
Gothic church – all that remains of the monastery St
Columba, founded as a school of divinity. You can fish to
your heart's content in this area, which is full of lakes,
beautiful scenery and wildlife.

Carrick-on-Shannon is the centre of river cruising on the
Shannon. There is a large marina, several cruising compa-
nies and lots of restaurants and pubs, which during the
season have traditional Irish music.

BALLINAMORE

Glenview

Aughoo, Ballinamore, Co Leitrim

Tel: (078) 44157

Glenview is a most attractive farmhouse situated on the outskirts of Ballinamore, beside the Woodford River, part of the Ballinamore-Ballyconnel Canal and the Shannon-Erne Link – a delightful rural setting. There are large extensive gardens here, as well as a donkey and cart and a pony for children's enjoyment; a games room and pool table are available for guests' use. The house is efficiently run; bedrooms are tastefully furnished and there is a very large lounge with a marble fireplace and an antique chaise-longue. There are many lakes close by and guests are advised on the best places to fish. A tackle shed, cold room and bait service are provided. Owner Theresa Kennedy has been very successful with her bed and breakfast during the past 11 years and is the proud recipient of the BHS Agri-Tourism award. Glenview has its own gourmet licenced restaurant; guests should reserve in advance for evening meals. No pets. Self-catering available. Visa accepted.

OWNERS Brian and Theresa Kennedy   OPEN All year, except Christmas   ROOMS 1 double, 5 twin (4 en suite)   TERMS B&B IR £15.00-£26.50 p.p.; reductions for children; single supplement IR £3.00

CARRICK-ON-SHANNON

Ard-na-Greine House

St Mary's Close, Carrick-on-Shannon, Co Leitrim

Tel: (078) 20311

A modern three-storey house in a quiet cul-de-sac, within easy walking distance of the River Shannon and town centre. Helen Dee is a friendly, outgoing lady who thoroughly enjoys her guests and is happy to offer advice with local sightseeing. The well-furnished rooms are bright and spotlessly clean, and freshly prepared breakfasts are served in the cosy dining-room overlooking the woods. Traditional home-cooked evening meals are available if prearranged; vegetarians catered for. There are 2 comfortable lounges where a cup of tea or coffee is served in the evening. Helen Dee is proud to have American Senator McGovern as a regular guest. Located off the main road in a cul-de-sac, opposite the Bush Hotel. Visa accepted.

OWNER Helen Dee OPEN All year ROOMS 2 double, 3 twin, 1 family (4 en suite) TERMS B&B IR£11.00-£12.50 p.p.; reductions for children; single supplement available; evening meal IR£9.50

Corbally Lodge

Dublin Road, near Carrick-on-Shannon, Co Leitrim

Tel: (078) 20228

A country-style house with an informal, friendly atmosphere approx 1½ miles (2½ km) from Carrick-on-Shannon. The bedrooms are fresh and clean and 2 are on the ground floor. There are antique furnishings and an attractive guest lounge with TV and turf fires. Mrs Rowley is a very friendly lady who takes excellent care of her guests. Breakfasts and evening meals, with wholesome foods and fresh-baked breads, are served in the bright dining-room. The River Shannon is close by; there are 41 free lakes, with golf, swimming and local boat hire available. From Dublin take the N4 to Mullingar; the house is 1½ miles (2½ km) on the left-hand side.

OWNER Mrs Valerie Rowley OPEN All year ROOMS 1 double, 3 twin (3 en suite) TERMS B&B IR£13.00 p.p.; reductions for children; single supplement IR£3.00; evening meal IR£11.00

County Longford

The most central county of Ireland, Longford lies in the basin of the Shannon, and the landscape is consequently low and flat, interspersed with small streams and lakes dotted with islands. Longford has strong associations with writers, particularly Oliver Goldsmith, Padriac Colum, Maria Edgeworth and Leo Casey, and is a popular place for coarse fishermen.

The town of Longford is spaciously laid out with wide streets, a Renaissance-style court house and nineteenth-century St Mel's Cathedral, which is built of grey limestone with impressive towers.

Close to Newtonforbes is beautiful Castle Forbes, a fine seventeenth-century castellated mansion. St Patrick is said to have founded a church at the old village of Ardagh in a pretty wooded setting, the ruins of which can still be seen.

LONGFORD

Sancian House

Dublin Road, Longford, Co Longford
Tel: (043) 46187

A warm and informal atmosphere pervades Sancian. The rooms are simply furnished, spotlessly clean, fitted with piped colour TVs and clock radios. There is a separate dining-room and sitting-room. The house is set back off the road, the front garden is full of roses and there are colourful window boxes. Martha O'Kane is an outgoing, friendly lady who is very knowledgeable about family heritage and is willing to assist guests wishing to trace their ancestry. An 18-hole golf course is located across the street, and it is a 5 mile (7½ km)-drive to Ardagh, Ireland's tidiest village. Pets by arrangement. Located on the edge of town on the east side of the Dublin road (N4).

OWNER Martha O'Kane   OPEN All year, except Christmas
ROOMS 2 double, 1 twin, 2 single (3 en suite)   TERMS B&B
IR£14.00-£15.00 p.p.; reductions for children; no single supplement

Counties Offaly and Laois

These two counties lie in the central part of Ireland and are scenically flat and boggy, with the River Shannon forming the western border.

Clonmacnoise is an important name in Irish history. St Ciaran founded a monastery here in AD 548 which became one of Ireland's best-known religious centres. A pilgrimage is held here each September on the feast of St Ciaran.

There is an attractive castle at Clononey, and Anthony Trollope first started writing novels whilst living at Banagher, a pretty little village on the canal. At Birr the gardens of the castle are open to the public, and at Portarlington, built on the canal, the gardens of the old townhouses run down to the river instead of to the street.

Minnocks Farm Guesthouse

Clonkelly, Birr, Co Offaly

Tel: (0509) 20591

This attractive Georgian-style house with its colonnades, Georgian doors and windows, and ceiling rose and cornices was cleverly converted from a farmhouse in 1991. There are 2 bedrooms on the ground floor – all have new firm beds, are individually decorated in soft pastel shades and have matching fabrics and curtains beautifully made by a local woman. This comfortable and peaceful house is set on a 100-acre dairy farm. Breakfasts are sumptuous and include freshly made scones, potato bread, eggs, bacon, and fresh milk and cream from the farm. Five-course evening meals are available if prearranged. Veronica Minnock is a most gracious host, and although she has only been in business for 18 months has already been awarded the Golden Thoughts Tourist award, an accolade for "service above and beyond the call of duty". A cup of tea is offered upon arrival; in fact, at Minnocks Farm the kettle is rarely off the boil. There is a sitting-room with a TV. Located on the N62 Birr to Roscrae road, 3 miles (4¹/₂ km) from Birr, convenient to Birr Castle and the Clonmacnoise and West Offaly Railway.

OWNER Noel and Veronica Minnock   OPEN All year, except Christmas   ROOMS 2 double, 2 twin, 3 family (all en suite)   TERMS B&B IR£14.00 p.p.; 20% reduction for children under 12; single supplement IR£4.00

TULLAMORE

Pine Lodge

Ross Road, Screggan, Tullamore, Co Offaly

Tel: (0506) 51927

Pine Lodge is a very civilised house in an elevated position, set in 2 acres of lawned gardens with outstanding views of the surrounding countryside. This is an exceptionally well-maintained house with extremely high standards. All but one of the well-appointed bedrooms have pine furnishings. There is a sitting-room with TV and a separate dining-room, where excellent breakfasts are served on separate pine tables. Claudia Krygel is from Germany and prides herself on the wholesome food served. Breakfast consists of smoked salmon, eggs, pancakes, as well as the traditional fare. Little wonder that Claudia was the recipient of the National Winner of Irish Breakfast award. Imaginative evening meals are also served (advance notice required). Vegetarian and special diets are catered for. Wine licence. There are some lovely countryside walks and golf and fishing are close by. Not suitable for children under 12. No pets. Smoking in designated areas only. Take the A52 to Birr, turn off 3 miles (4¹/₂ km) from Tullamore to the left, signposted after 1 mile (1¹/₂ km) on the left.

OWNER Claudia Krygel   OPEN 1 April–1 September   ROOMS 1 double, 2 twin, 1 single (all en suite)   TERMS B&B IR£18.00 p.p.; no reductions for children; single supplement IR£4.00; evening meal IR£15.50

DONAGHMORE

Castletown House

Donaghmore, Co Laois
Tel: (0505) 46415

Castletown House is an early nineteenth-century farmhouse set in scenic surroundings on a 200-acre beef and sheep farm, on which the ruins of a Norman castle remain (approached through open fields full of grazing sheep). The house was completely renovated in 1979 at which time the 30-inch thick outer walls were raised by 18 inches. This must be one of the best-value accommodations in Ireland: the bedrooms are of a good size and there are several interesting pieces of antique furniture about. Fresh farmhouse breakfasts and evening meals with home-baking are served in the dining-room which has a marble fireplace; there is a sitting-room with TV. Guests enjoy gathering in the farm kitchen for a cup of tea and chatting to the friendly owners. A wonderful spot to stay a while and enjoy the many things to see and do in the area, including the Italian Heywood Gardens and the Agricultural Museum in the old Donaghmore Warehouse. Guests interested in ancestry tracing can be assisted by Moira Phelan. The house leads down to the River Erkina where fishing is allowed. Pets outside. No smoking in the bedrooms. Visa and Access cards accepted.

OWNER Moira Phelan   OPEN 1 February–1 October, or by arrangement   ROOMS 2 double, 1 twin, 1 family (all en suite)   TERMS B&B IR£12.50 p.p.; 25% reduction for children under 12; no single supplement; evening meal IR£12.50

County Roscommon

County Roscommon is an inland county 40 miles (60 km) in length. The River Shannon is the boundary in the north to Shannonbridge in the south. The River Shannon is the boundary in the east and the River Suck is the boundary in most of the west. Two-thirds of the county is bounded by water. In the north are the largest lakes: Lough Key, Lough Gara and Lough Boderg, with the great Lough Ree in the east. The limestone foundation of the whole county and the numerous lakes make it a fisherman's paradise.

Large areas of arable land are to be found in the centre of the county, and the principal occupation of the people is raising cattle and sheep.

Roscommon is a land of abbeys and castles, where you can visit Clonalis House, Castlerea, once the home of 2 of Ireland's high kings in the twelfth century; Strokestown Park House with its records of famine-ridden Ireland; prehistoric Rathcroghan; St John's Interpretative Centre; medieval Boyle; and picturesque Lough Key with its forest park.

For those interested in contemporary art, the Glebe House Gallery is situated midway between Boyle and Carrick-on-Shannon at Crossna, Knockvicar.

CARRICK-ON-SHANNON

Avondale

Roosky, Carrick-on-Shannon, Co Roscommon
Tel: (078) 38095

An attractive modern two-storey house standing in its own grounds, 500 yards from the River Shannon. This is very much a family-run establishment, with a relaxing homely atmosphere. The owners were initially in the hotel trade but missed the personal contact with guests and decided to run a B&B; they were successful from the beginning and soon added on 2 additional bedrooms. The bedroms are clean and comfortable, with orthopaedic beds. There is a TV lounge with turf fires. Excellent home-cooking for breakfasts and evening meals, if prearranged, is served. Avondale is an ideal base for anglers – there is a tackle room with fridges and drying facilities. Bait is available locally and boat hire can be arranged on request. Roosky is an excellent base for touring, midway beween Longford and Carrick-on-Shannon; Lough Rinn House and Gardens are just 6 miles (9 km) away. No pets. Signposted on the N4 at Carrick-on-

Shannon, half a kilometre over the bridge. All major credit cards accepted.

OWNER Carmel and John Davis   OPEN All year, except Christmas   ROOMS 1 double, 1 twin, 2 family (3 en suite)   TERMS B&B IR£12.50-£13.50 p.p.; reductions for children; single supplement IR£3.00

Glencarne House

Carrick-on-Shannon, Co Roscommon
Tel: (079) 67013

This charming Georgian house is located in scenic country-side with lovely views of fields and grazing sheep. A very warm welcome awaits you at Glencarne House; Mrs Harrington has received several awards, including the Galtee Breakfast award and the Agri-Tourism National award. The house is warm and peaceful, the bedrooms have every comfort, including armchairs, hot water bottles and electric blankets; some have antique brass beds. There is a comfortable guest lounge with a marble fireplace, which along with the dining-room has a blazing fire on chilly days. Mrs Harrington is an excellent cook; evening meals are all prepared fresh daily: the desserts feature some of the best pastry in Ireland. There is a golf course within half a mile and boating, fishing and shooting are available locally. Pets outside by arrangement. Situated 4¹/₂ miles (6¹/₂ km) from Carrick-on-Shannon, midway between Boyle and Carrick-on-Shannon on the N4.

OWNER The Harrington family   OPEN 1 March–1 November   ROOMS 1 double, 2 single, 2 family (3 en suite)   TERMS B&B IR£16.00-£27.00 p.p.; 25% reductions for children under 12; single supplement IR£4.50

County Tipperary

Located right in the centre of the southern part of Ireland, Tipperary is a beautiful county of rich farmland. From the top of Slievenamon, which means "mountain of the fairy women of Femin", there is a splendid view. To the north you can see the Rock of Cashel, a steep outcrop of limestone topped by impressive ruins – a truly spectacular sight, particularly during the summer when it is floodlit at night. From early times the rock was a fortress and seat of chieftains and later it became an important religious site. Today you can see the vast ruins of the Irish Gothic cathedral, which dates from the thirteenth century, the massive tower of the Castle, the cross of St Patrick, the massive base of which is said to be the coronation stone of the Munster kings, and Cormac's Chapel, a very interesting building dating back to 1130.

The Cashel Palace Hotel is a very fine Queen Anne-style house, formerly the residence of the archbishops of the Church of Ireland, located in the busy town of Cashel. A fine collection of sixteenth- and seventeenth-century books can be found in the Diocesan Library in the precincts of the St John the Baptist Cathedral, and there's a good craft shop where one can buy Shanagarry tweed. Situated between Thurles and Cashel, Holycross Abbey was built in 1110 to house a part of the True Cross and later became a popular place of pilgrimage.

Cahir, a most pleasant town on the River Suir, has a beautifully restored fifteenth-century castle on an island in the river and now houses the tourist office. Tipperary, famous for the song "It's a long way to Tipperary", is a great farming centre. The mountains between Nenagh and Toomyvara were the home of Ned of the Hill, the local Robin Hood, and at Nenagh is Nenagh Round, all that is left of an old castle built in 1200.

Kilcooly Abbey, the Abbey of the Holy Cross and the attractive old church at Fethard are all worth seeing. At Ahenny are two elaborately carved eighth-century stone crosses, and at Carrick-on-Suir is a very fine example of a Tudor mansion which can be visited by request.

BALLINDERRY

Gurthalougha House

Ballinderry, near Nenagh, Co Tipperary

Tel: (067) 22080

Gurthalougha House is approached through a peaceful avenue that winds for a mile (1½ km) through 150 acres of mature forest. Built in the nineteenth century, the house is situated on the banks of the River Shannon; in the distance can be seen the mountains of Clare and Galway. This is an informal and relaxed house, with huge log fireplaces and antique furnishings. The bedrooms are large, have wooden floors and comfortable beds, and one has a balcony over-looking the lake. Breakfast goes on until noon and is available in bed or in front of the fire in the dining-room. Michael Wilkinson, your host, enjoys cooking, keeping to a small menu – all foods are prepared with fresh, wholesome ingredients. There are lovely woodland walks with a great variety of wildlife: red squirrels, badgers, otters and kingfishers. Boats and windsurfers are available at no extra charge, with swimming from the jetty and croquet on the lawn. There is a wine licence. French is spoken. There are 4 golf courses, pony trekking and a sailing school close by. No pipes or cigars in the dining-room. Pets by arrangement.

OWNER Bessie and Michael Wilkinson   OPEN All year, except Christmas and February   ROOMS 3 double, 4 twin, 1 family (all en suite)   TERMS B&B IR£32.00-£36.00 p.p.; 33% reduction for children under 10; no single supplement

BANSHA

Bansha Castle

Bansha, Co Tipperary

Tel: (062) 54187

Built in the 1830s, Bansha Castle is a large country house with a square tower at one end and a round tower at the other. It stands in the centre of the village, with an attractive walled garden to the rear of the house, and is surrounded by 45 acres of land which are let out. Bansha Castle has been in the family for 40 years and 5 years ago Teresa and John moved in and started updating it, with some work still to do. This is a pleasant house, restfully decorated and featuring comfortable rooms. The dining-room is an attractive oval-shaped room, where delicious, attractively served breakfasts are accompanied by a welcoming open fire on chillier mornings. Evening meals, which are prepared where possible with local, organically grown produce, must be booked in advance. The Russells arrange a special programme over Christmas. No pets.

OWNER Teresa and John Russell   OPEN All year   ROOMS 3 double, 1 twin, 2 family (3 en suite)   TERMS B&B IR£16.00-£19.00 p.p.; reductions for children; single supplement IR£4.00; evening meal IR£14.00

Bansha House

Bansha, Co Tipperary
Tel: (062) 54194/54245

Bansha House is 200 yards from the village of Bansha on the main road from Shannon to Waterford. It is a lovely Georgian residence approached by an avenue of beech trees set in 100 acres of land. The house is tastefully decorated with some lovely antique furnishings dotted about. Two of the bedrooms are on the ground floor. There is a delightful lounge with a log fire which leads onto the gardens. A relaxed and comfortable atmosphere pervades, and guests can often be found in the kitchen with Mary, chatting about what to see and do in the area. John and Mary breed and train racehorses, and riding is available on an hourly basis. Cooking is of a very high standard, with home-made breads, tarts and pies. Glorious scenic tours can be taken from here. This is a superb house for guests wanting some peace and tranquillity. Some smoking restrictions and no pets. A self-catering cottage is also available.

OWNERS John and Mary Marnane   OPEN All year, except Christmas   ROOMS 4 double, 2 twin, 1 single (4 en suite)   TERMS B&B IR£13.00-£16.00 p.p.; reductions for children; single supplement IR£2.00; evening meal IR£12.00

Lismacue House

Bansha, Co Tipperary
Tel: (062) 54106, Fax: (062) 54126

Lismacue House has been in Kate Nicholson's family since it was built in 1813, a classic, beautifully proportioned Irish country house set in its own extensive grounds at the foot of the magnificent Galtee Mountains. The approach to the house is via one of the most impressive lime tree avenues in Ireland. The spacious drawing-room and dining-room have their original wallpaper. Breakfasts and evening meals are served in the imposing dining-room. The number of bedrooms has been reduced to 5, as the coach house is being used for other purposes. All rooms have telephones, hairdryers and trouser presses. Traditional log fires burn in the warm and welcoming reception rooms. Special interest holidays are available, including pony trekking for adults and children and, during November to February, hosted hunting holidays; also trout fishing on the estate's own river. There are 3 golf courses and tennis close by, not to forget the Rock of Cashel and Cahire Castle. Lismacue has a wine licence. No pets.

OWNERS Mrs Katharine Nicholson   OPEN All year, except Christmas   ROOMS 3 double, 2 twin (2 en suite)   TERMS B&B IR£25.00-£33.00 p.p.; reductions for children; single supplement IR£7.00; evening meal from IR£18.50

CAHIR

Ashling Guest House

Dublin Road, Cahir, Co Tipperary

Tel: (052) 41601

Ashling guest house is a pink-washed low building on the main Dublin road about 1 mile (1½ km) outside Cahir, with lovely views from the front of the house. Breda FitzGerald is a very friendly, chatty lady who keeps an immaculately clean and tidy house. The rooms are on the small side but comfortably furnished, and there is a large sitting-room off the dining-room. The house stands in beautifully kept gardens. No pets. No smoking.

OWNERS Breda and Michael FitzGerald   OPEN All year   ROOMS 5 rooms (3 en suite)   TERMS B&B IR£13.00-£18.00 p.p.; reductions for children

CASHEL

Ardmayle House

Cashel, Co Tipperary

Tel: (0504) 42399, Fax: (0504) 42420

A spacious, creeper-covered, unpretentious farmhouse surrounded by a 200-acre working farm. The bedrooms, furnished with old-fashioned and antique furniture, are large and comfortable. The open log fire in the dining-room is the ideal setting for making friends and enjoying a cup of tea and some delicious home-made scones. Guests are welcome to explore the dairy farm; sheep and horses are also kept. Annette is a warm, kindly host who is anxious for guests to experience the best of rural living. They are welcome to fish on the private stretch of the River Suir which runs through the property. Golf, forest walks and horse-riding can all be arranged locally. Approximately 4

miles (6 km) from Cashel on the L185 road. Evening meals
by advance arrangement.

OWNER Annette V Hunt   OPEN 1 April–mid October   ROOMS 1
double, 1 twin, 4 family (2 en suite)   TERMS B&B IR£13.50-
£15.00 p.p.; reductions for children; single supplement IR£4.50;
evening meal IR£12.50

Knock-St-Lour

Cashel, Co Tipperary

Tel: (062) 61172

A circular driveway leads to this large, square, modern
whitewashed house with its stone-pillared porch. Knock-St-
Lour lies just off the Cork to Cashel road, 1½ miles (2½
km) from Cashel, and is surrounded by 32 acres of beef and
tillage farming. The drawing-room is very formal, but the TV
lounge has comfortable chairs, a piano and a fireplace. The
rooms on the whole are large and comfortable and the house
enjoys views of the Rock of Cashel. Evening meals are
available by arrangement. There is no wine licence. No
smoking in dining-room and no pets.

OWNER Eileen O'Brien   OPEN 1 April–1 October   ROOMS 2
double/twin/family (4 en suite)   TERMS B&B IR£12.50-£14.50
p.p.; reductions for children; single supplement IR£3.00; evening
meal IR£13.00

Maryville

Bank Place, Cashel, Co Tipperary

Tel: (062) 61098

This is a popular property, situated in the town centre. An
extension was added 7 years ago to accommodate more
guests, but early reservations are still necessary. The rooms
are basic, but clean and functional, and there is a small TV
lounge. The back bedrooms have a lovely view of the Rock
of Cashel, floodlit at night. There is a pretty, secluded
garden with furniture for guests' use and adjoining the
garden, the remains of a thirteenth-century Dominican
abbey. This is a photographer's delight. Mary and Pat
Duane are helpful people, and in the lounge there is information on what to see and do. There is music, dance and
song every week night at Bru Boru, 2 minutes' walk away.
No smoking in public areas and no pets. Visa, Access and
Eurocard accepted.

OWNER Mary and Pat Duane   OPEN All year, except Christmas
ROOMS 2 double, 2 twin, 4 family (3 en suite)   TERMS B&B
IR£13.00-£16.00 p.p.; reductions for children; single supplement
IR£5.00

Rahard Lodge

Cashel, Co Tipperary

Tel: (062) 61052

A long, low, whitewashed house built by the owners 25 years
ago and offering wonderful views across to the castle and the
countryside beyond. The house is set back from the road by a
field of grazing sheep and is surrounded by its 130-acre beef
and sheep farm, the farmyard located to the back of the house.
The most attractive garden, which won 2 prizes in 1991,
stretches to one side of the house. Moira Foley is a most
friendly lady who has been in the business for 23 years; consequently she receives a lot of repeat guests. Meals are all home-
cooked and any kind of evening meal can be produced, from a
simple soup and salad to a full meal; organically grown produce is used where possible. The house is clean and comfortable with small, simply furnished bedrooms and a large lounge
with a fireplace. Visa accepted.

OWNER Moira Foley   OPEN 1 March–1 December   ROOMS 1 twin,
5 family (4 en suite)   TERMS B&B IR£13.00-£14.00 p.p.; reductions for children; single supplement IR£4.00; evening meal from
IR£13.00

Ros-Guill House

Dualla Road, Cashel, Co Tipperary

Tel: (062) 61507

This small, neat-looking house was built by the owners 24
years ago, and Mrs Moloney has been running a bed and
breakfast here for 22 years. Ros-Guill House is well protected from the road by evergreen trees and has a small
enclosed front garden. The rooms are on the small side but
immaculately clean, and the dining-room has views of the
castle and the Galtee Mountains. Mrs Moloney, who is a
most friendly lady, has won 2 garden awards as well as the
1987 Galtee Regional Breakfast award. Ros-Guill House is
on the Dualla Road, three quarters of a mile from Cashel.

OWNER Evelyn Moloney   OPEN 1 April–1 December   ROOMS 2
double, 1 twin, 1 family (3 en suite)   TERMS B&B IR£12.50-
£15.00 p.p.; reductions for children; single supplement IR£6.00

CLONMEL

St Lomans

Cahir Road, Clonmel, Co Tipperary

Tel: (052) 22916

A small modern house just off the main Cahir Road on the edge of Clonmel. The location is a bit noisy, so one room at the back of the house may be preferred. The bedrooms are very small but bright and very clean. The sitting-room leads into the dining-room, which overlooks the back of the house. Evening meals are available if arranged in advance and tea and coffee are served at night. No pets. Smoking only in the lounge.

OWNER Mrs Terri O'Callaghan   OPEN All year   ROOMS 2 double, 1 twin, 1 family (2 en suite)   TERMS B&B IR£12.00-£14.00 p.p.; reductions for children; evening meal IR£10.00

MULLINAHONE

Killaghy Castle

Mullinahone, Co Tipperary

Tel: (052) 53112

Killaghy Castle, a Georgian house attached to a ruined Norman tower, is approached through an impressive entrance. The castle is part of a 250-acre working farm and has views to the Slievenamon Mountains, views that are better still if one climbs to the top of the old tower. The walled garden to the side of the house is a lovely place to sit in on sunny days. The Sherwoods are a friendly couple who bought the property some 12 years ago and did up the whole house. The 4 bedrooms are in the front part of the house, 3 of which are very large; downstairs is a large central hallway with the drawing-room and dining-room to each side. The castle can be found on the edge of Mullinahone.

OWNER Mrs R E Sherwood   OPEN 1 April–1 October   ROOMS 1 twin, 3 family (2 en suite)   TERMS B&B IR£15.00-£16.50 p.p.; reductions for children; single supplement IR£4.00; evening meal IR£12.50

Riverrun House

Terryglass, Nenagh, Co Tipperary
Tel: (067) 22125/22187

An attractive house standing in its own grounds of 1¹/₂ acres, situated in Terryglass – the recipient of the famous Tidy Village award. Tom and Lucy Sanders are an enthusiastic couple, fairly new to the B&B business, having opened in the autumn of 1991. Three of the bedrooms, all of which are good-sized, are located on the ground floor, tastefully decorated in pretty pastel floral colours with matching fabrics and furnished in pine. Two have pretty lake views. This is a most comfortable house with lots of character, full of interesting antiques, including a gentlemen's washstand. Tom Sanders runs his pottery and craft shop in an old converted church in the village. A pleasant 5-minute stroll away is the busy harbour set on the north-east shore of Lough Derg, largest of the lakes on the Shannon system. Riverrun House has a hard tennis court, bicycles for guests' use and fishing boats and engines for hire. Excellent breakfasts are served, including freshly squeezed orange juice, home-baked soda bread, yoghurts, as well as traditional fare. Vegetarian breakfasts available upon request. Visa, Access and Mastercard accepted.

OWNER Tom and Lucy Sanders   OPEN All year, except Christmas   ROOMS 2 double, 2 twin, 1 family (all en suite)   TERMS B&B IR£20.00-£25.00 p.p.; reductions for children; single supplement available

Willmount House

Ballingarry, Thurles, Co Tipperary
Tel: (052) 54108

Formerly Pittman's summer home (of shorthand fame), this country house was built in 1814. Located in a rural setting at the foot of Slievenamon, Willmount House is surrounded by pleasant lawned gardens and entered under an arched bell tower and through a courtyard. The house extends around 3 sides of the courtyard; the comfortable drawing-room with open fire and dining-room with separate tables take up one side and overlook the garden. The bedrooms are spacious and plainly decorated and furnished. There is a games room with ping pong, pool and darts and an outdoor heated swimming pool. Riding and hunting can be arranged and dogs are welcome. The house has a wine licence. It is advisable to get directions, but the house is signposted from the Dublin to Cork road at the Urlingford sign.

OWNER Rhona Bastow   OPEN All year, except Christmas   ROOMS 5 double (1 en suite)   TERMS B&B IR£15.00-£20.00 p.p.; reductions for children; evening meal IR£12.00-£15.00

TIPPERARY

Arra View

Emly Road, Tipperary, Co Tipperary
Tel: (062) 51879

Arra View has been established for over 24 years. Anne Cronin is a most accommodating host who is dedicated to ensuring her guests feel welcome. The bedrooms, although a little small, are clean and adequate. There is an en suite family room on the ground floor; all except one room have their own bathrooms. There's a pleasant lounge with a TV and piano which guests are welcome to play. Evening meals are available; vegetarian or special diets are catered for if prearranged. The house is located in a scenic area overlooking the Galtee Mountains, a 10-minute walk to town about half a kilometre away on the N36 Killarney road. No smoking in the dining-room and pets outside only.

OWNER Anne Cronin   OPEN 1 April–1 November   ROOMS 3 twin, 1 family (3 en suite)   TERMS B&B IR£12.50 p.p.; reductions for children; single supplement IR£4.00; evening meal IR£13.00

Barronstown House

Emly Road, Tipperary, Co Tipperary
Tel: (062) 55130

Easy-going Mr and Mrs O'Dwyer provide old-fashioned hospitality and comfort at Barronstown House, a lovely old house furnished with antiques belonging to Mr O'Dwyer's ancestors. The house is situated in the heart of the Golden Vale overlooking the Galtee Mountains. Rooms are large and comfortable and there is a quiet spot on the landing, ideal for reading or playing cards. The TV lounge has the original fireplace. The motto of the house, "An Irish home – where every guest is a friend", certainly describes the wel-

come that guests receive here. A good base for exploring the Glen of Aherlow and the Rock of Cashel, and with salmon and trout fishing on the River Suir. The house is located 3 miles (4½ km) from Tipperary.

OWNERS Mr and Mrs J O'Dwyer   OPEN 1 May–1 September
ROOMS 1 double, 2 twin, 1 family   TERMS B&B IR£13.00 p.p.; reductions for children; single supplement IR£4.00; evening meal IR£10.00

Clonmore House

Galbally Road, Tipperary, Co Tipperary
Tel: (062) 51637

An immaculate, detached house set back from the main road on the edge of town. The bedrooms are tastefully decorated and colour-coordinated, with modern fitted wardrobes. Breakfasts are served in the attractive dining-room with pretty lace table-cloths. The spacious lounge/dining-room overlooks the gardens, which are available for guests' use. A fire is lit in the lounge on chilly days and guests may enjoy a hot drink in the evening; a pleasant spot to unwind in after a busy day of sightseeing. On fine days the sun lounge is a popular place. Mary Quinn is a delightful host who prides herself on personal service. There is no need to worry about parking or driving in town, as Clonmore House is just 5 minutes' walk away. Mary Quinn is pleased to advise on good local restaurants. Smoking in the lounge only.

OWNER Mrs Mary Quinn   OPEN 1 April–1 October   ROOMS 2 double, 3 twin, 1 family, (6 en suite)   TERMS B&B IR£13.00 p.p.; reductions for children

County Westmeath

Centrally located, this county has no dramatic features but it offers a peaceful and beautiful landscape, excellent fishing and lots of history.

The main attractions are its lakes, the four larger ones of Loughs Owel, Ennell, Derravaragh and Lene being within easy reach of Mullingar. Beautiful Lough Sheelin is further north and there are a number of small lakes too, as well as Lough Ree, an expansion of the Shannon which is now popular for sailing, cruising and coarse fishing. On many of the islands which dot the lakes are remains of early Christian churches.

Mullingar, the county town, is a thriving commercial centre and attractive market town. It is in one of the best cattle-raising districts of Ireland and is also a great centre for hunting, shooting and fishing.

Athlone is the largest town in the county, growing from its origins as a fording point of the Shannon to a busy market town, major road and rail terminus, and harbour on the inland waterways system. Athlone Castle, now housing a museum dealing with local history on the banks of the River Shannon, is a strongly fortified building with many interesting features. It has been a famous military post since its original construction in the thirteenth century.

Lough Derravaragh, one of the most beautiful in County Westmeath and offering good fishing, is associated with the most tragic of Irish legendary romances, when the Children of Lir were changed into swans by a jealous stepmother and spent 300 years on its dark waters.

Near Castlepollard is Tullynally Castle, seat of the Earls of Longford, with a spectacular façade of turrets and towers, and at Fore is the most historic Christian site in Westmeath. There are several ruins to see dating from the tenth century and later, amongst them St Fechin's Church, an unusual feature of which is the massive cross-inscribed lintel stone.

ATHLONE

Cluain-Inis

Summerhill, Galway Road, Athlone, Co Westmeath

Tel: (0902) 94202

A friendly, cosy bungalow located off the N6 Galway road 1 mile (1½ km) from town. The lounge is tastefully decorated with matching pink and red fabrics, attractive lights and wall lamps. Tea- and coffee-making facilities are also provided. The bedrooms are all on the ground floor and are clean and comfortable. Although there are no en suite rooms, there are 2 bathrooms for the exclusive use of guests. Four-course evening meals are available if prearranged with home-style, good old-fashioned cooking, using fresh local produce and home-baking. An ideal location for touring Clonmacnoise, Deer Park, with fishing and golf close by.

OWNER Kathleen Shaw   OPEN All year   ROOMS 1 double/twin/family   TERMS B&B IR£12.00 p.p.; reductions for children; single supplement IR£3.00

Riverdale House

Clonown Road, Athlone, Co Westmeath
Tel: (0902) 92480

A turn-of-the-century house pleasantly situated on the Connaught side of the River Shannon in its own grounds, just a few minutes' walk from the town centre. The bed-rooms and lounge are large and comfortable with traditional furnishings and the house has a warm, old-fashioned atmos-phere. Two of the bedrooms have a TV and all have hairdryers. The stones surrounding the marble fireplace in the lounge were specially made to preserve the character of the house. The front door has beautiful stained-glass depict-ing a peacock. Mr and Mrs Lyons have been established for over 25 years and were one of the first B&Bs in the area. They have built up an excellent reputation; most of their guests are repeat visitors or recommendations; advance reservations suggested. Riverdale House specialises in coarse-fishing holidays and is just 200 yards from the River Shannon; group rates and holiday packages are available upon request. South of the town lies the ancient monastic settlement of Clonmacnoise and there is an 18-hole golf course as well as tennis and walking trails close by. Take N6 west from Dublin to Athlone – Riverdale House is very close to the Shamrock Lodge Hotel.

OWNER Mrs Anne Lyons   OPEN All year   ROOMS 2 double, 2 twin, 1 single, 2 family (3 en suite)   TERMS B&B IR£13.00 p.p.; reductions for children; single supplement IR£4.00; evening meal IR £12.00

Shelmalier House

Cartrontroy, Athlone, Co Westmeath
Tel: (0902) 72245, Fax: (0902) 94612

A modern, spacious house standing in its own grounds with an attractive front garden. The 7 bedrooms are beautifully appointed with firm, comfortable beds, 2 of which are on the ground floor. All have hairdryers, telephones and 2 have TVS. Very much a family-run establishment with considerate hosts who do everything possible to ensure their guests' comfort. There is a spacious TV lounge. Guests may help themselves to tea and coffee in the sun-porch. Jim and Nancy Denby specialise in coarse-fishing holidays, but a warm welcome is extended to all visitors. Excellent evening meals are served, with the emphasis on fresh food and home-baking. There is an 18-hole golf course on the shores of Lough Ree, trail walks and a heated swimming pool within 10 minutes' walk. Shelmalier is a delightful house offering excellent value. No pets. Signposted off the N6 town route. Visa accepted.

OWNERS Jim and Nancy Denby   OPEN All year   ROOMS 3 double, 2 twin, 2 family (all en suite)   TERMS B&B IR£13.50 p.p.; reductions for children; single supplement IR£4.50; evening meal IR£11.00

HORSELEAP

Temple House

Horseleap, Co Westmeath
Tel: (0506) 35118

Temple House has been in the same family for 3 generations, set among mature trees and gardens on a 140-acre cattle and sheep farm. It was built on the site of a sixth-century monastery, hence the name. This lovely 200-year-old country house with its old-world atmosphere has marble washstands, fireplaces and brass beds. Bernadette is an excellent cook; evening meals are served family-style in the large dining-room, featuring farm-fresh meats and vegetables with delicious home-made desserts. After dinner, guests gather round the open fire in the lounge, often joined by Bernadette and Declan. All the bedrooms are now en suite, and a new games room and library were added in 1991. All-inclusive walking, cycling and relaxation holiday packages are available; rates upon request. A special 3-day half-board rate of IR£81.00 is also available. Fishing and golfing holidays at championship courses can be arranged for small groups. Reservations should be made as much ahead as possible. Vegetarians catered for if prearranged. There is a wine licence. An ideal location in which to relax, unwind and enjoy the best of Ireland. Access, Visa and Mastercard accepted. Situated 1 mile (1½ km) west of Horseleap village.

OWNERS Declan and Bernadette Fagan   OPEN 1 March–30 November   ROOMS 2 double/family (all en suite)   TERMS B&B IR£18.00 p.p.; reductions for children; single supplement IR£4.00; evening meal IR£12.00

MOATE

Cooleen House

Ballymore Road, Moate, Co Westmeath
Tel: (0902) 81044

This is a well-maintained and very attractive modern bungalow in a country setting of 1½ acres. The rooms are good-sized, tastefully furnished and decorated with comfortable beds. A warm welcome is received; guests are treated as one of the family, and tea or coffee are offered upon arrival at no charge. Breakfasts, which include fresh home-baked scones, are served in the lush conservatory on warm days. There is a guest lounge with a TV where peat fires burn in the evening. Bicycles are available and there are some lovely walks winding past the bog. For guests looking for a home-from-home atmosphere, Cooleen is an excellent choice. Pets by arrangement. Situated off the N6 heading west just before coming into Moate.

OWNERS Ethna Kelly   OPEN All year   ROOMS 2 double/twin (2 en suite)   TERMS B&B IR£12.50 p.p.; reductions for children; single supplement IR£4.00

MULLINGAR

Grove House

Blackhall, Mullingar, Co Westmeath
Tel: (044) 41974

Grove House is very centrally located and is found on a quiet cul-de-sac. Mrs Buckley is a delightful lady who runs an immaculate and friendly house. There is a comfortable lounge with a TV and fireplace, which is lit at the first sign of a chill in the air. A guest lounge and a tastefully furnished dining-room overlook the garden, full of mature shrubs, flowers and a fishpond. Gladys Buckley has created a real home-from-home atmosphere; guests often book in for a night or two and end up staying a week. Gladys enjoys cooking and serves fresh home-baked bread. Seamus Buckley helps out when needed and takes care of the lovely gardens. Light snacks are available upon request at reasonable prices as well as a cup of tea or coffee just about any time at no charge. Smoking is not permitted in the dining-room. No pets in the house.

OWNERS Gladys Buckley   OPEN All year, except Christmas
ROOMS 1 double/twin/family (1 en suite)   TERMS B&B IR£12.00-£14.00 p.p.; reductions for children; no single supplement

Hilltop

Navan/Delvin Road, Rathconnell, Mullingar,

Co Westmeath

Tel: (044) 48958

An exceptionally well-maintained, spacious, split-level house. Approached by a private gravel drive, the house sits in an elevated position with views of the Sheever Lough in the distance and of the city at night. The house was specifically designed for bed and breakfast; the bedrooms are all large, with a high standard of decor and with comfortable, firm beds. Breakfasts are served in the bright dining-room overlooking pretty countryside. One of the en suite bedrooms is on the ground floor and has its own entrance. Dympna and Sean are extremely hospitable and helpful and are happy to assist with itinerary planning. Hilltop has facilities for the angler, including a tackle room with fridges and drying facilities. Boat hire can also be arranged. No smoking in the dining-room. Evening meals must be ordered in advance. Situated 2 miles (3 km) from Mullingar on the N52 off the N4.

OWNERS Dympna and Sean Casey   OPEN 1 March–1 November
ROOMS 3 double, 2 twin, 1 family (all en suite)   TERMS B&B IR£14.00 p.p.; reductions for children; single supplement IR£5.00; evening meal IR£12.00

Keadeen

Irishtown, Longford Road, Mullingar, Co Westmeath
Tel: (044) 48440

There is a comfortable, easy-going atmosphere at Keadeen,
a well-maintained bungalow in a quiet location on the edge
of town. To quote Madge Nolan, "She has never had a
guest she didn't like", which could have something to do
with her tolerant, helpful attitude. The bedrooms are clean
and fresh, individually decorated in bright colours with
warm duvets and purple carpets. Additional en suite facilities have been added to one of the bedrooms; there are now
2 with their own bathrooms. Breakfast is served from 7 to
10.30 am and consists of home-made marmalades, preserves
and fresh-baked bread. Evening meals are available by prior
arrangement; vegetarians catered for. Local amenities
include golf, fishing, swimming and boating. No smoking in
the dining-room. No pets. Located 100 yards off the N4 past
the county hospital.

OWNER Mrs Madge Nolan   OPEN All year   ROOMS 1 double/twin/
family (2 en suite)   TERMS B&B IR£13.00 p.p.; reductions for
children; no single supplement; evening meal IR£10.00

Lough Owel Lodge

Cullion, near Mullingar, Co Westmeath
Tel: (044) 48714

Lough Owel Lodge is a most attractive country house
approached by a long private drive and standing in 50 acres
of farmland. The property extends down to the lake, there
are gillie and boats available, windsurfing, and several golf
courses are located nearby. The house is well appointed and
the spacious, well-furnished TV lounge overlooks the beautiful gardens and hard tennis court, which is available for
guests' use. The bedrooms are individually furnished and
comfortable; one has a four-poster bed. There are several
interesting pieces of antique furniture about. A delightful
property in a beautiful setting, an ideal haven of peaceful
seclusion and tranquillity. No smoking in the dining-room
or bedrooms. No pets. Approximately 2^1/$_2$ miles (4 km)
from Mullingar on the Sligo road.

OWNERS Martin and Aideen Ginnell   OPEN 1 March–1 December
ROOMS 1 double, 1 twin, 1 single, 2 family (3 en suite)

Pettiswood House

Mullingar, Co Westmeath
Tel: (044) 48397

An attractive 1940s country house set in 3 acres of beautiful landscaped grounds, approached by a tree-lined drive. The lawn furnishings are for guests' use. The bedrooms are fresh and clean and all have electric blankets. The elegant dining-room, furnished with antiques, is exceptionally pleasant. Sumptuous breakfasts are served with a wide choice of cereals, unlimited fruit juice, home-baked bread and a full-cooked breakfast. Evening meals are available but advance notice is required. Evening snacks are served in the TV lounge. There are several pieces of antique furniture about, including a very nice chaise-longue. Lovely walks, fishing, golf and boating are available close by. Located 1 mile (1½ km) from Mullingar.

OWNER Marie Cox   OPEN All year   ROOMS 1 double/twin/single (1 en suite)   TERMS B&B IR£12.00-£13.50 p.p.; reductions for children; no single supplement; evening meal IR£10.00

Woodlands Farm

Streamstown, Mullingar, Co Westmeath
Tel: (044) 26414

A charming 200-year-old farmhouse surrounded by orna-mental trees on a 120-acre dry cattle farm. Woodlands Farm is a marvellous spot for families; Mrs Maxwell has created a wonderful, informal, welcoming atmosphere. Guests are encouraged to explore the farm and there are free riding ponies for the children. The bedrooms are spacious and there are lots of antique furnishings, including a chaise-longue and a lovely dresser. Guests enjoy sitting round the log fires in the spacious lounge, which has a grand piano, and musical evenings are encouraged. Four of the bedrooms are on the ground floor, and though none are en suite, there are 2 bathrooms, 2 shower rooms and 4 toilets. Excellent evening meals are served, if prearranged, using fresh home-grown and local produce. Wine licence. Golf and fishing holidays can be organised. Seven miles (10½ km) from

Moate, 10 miles (15 km) from Mullingar, 2½ miles (4 km) off N6 at Horseleap.

OWNER Mrs M Maxwell OPEN 1 March–1 November ROOMS 2 double, 2 twin, 1 single, 1 family TERMS B&B IR£12.00 p.p.; reductions for children; no single supplement; evening meal IR£12.00

MULTYFARNHAM

Mornington House

Multyfarnham, Co Westmeath

Tel: (044)72191

Mornington House has been the home of 5 generations of the O'Hara family since 1856; tucked away on a slope above Lough Derravagh, it is surrounded by mature trees and parkland and ringed by the hills of north Westmeath. Mornington is an oasis of peace and tranquillity and an ideal location from which to explore the midlands; it is within 1½ hours' drive from Dublin. The original Manor, built on the site of an ancient castle, was extended in the late nineteenth century. Today, Mornington is a gracious family home still furnished with its original furniture and portraits. Succeeding generations of the family have added to the collection of family memorabilia. The house is centrally heated and the reception rooms have open fires. Anne and Warwick are charming hosts; Anne is an excellent cook, and superb evening meals are served in the candlelit dining-room, featuring fresh fruit, vegetables and herbs from the walled garden, with the best of local produce. The house is licenced, enabling guests to enjoy a glass of fine wine with their meal. The bedrooms are large, 2 have brass beds, one has its own bathroom – the others have en suite showers. A wing of the house is available for self catering. Not suitable for children. Smoking permitted only in the drawing-room. Signposted off the N4.

OWNER Warwick and Anne O'Hara OPEN 15 April–30 September ROOMS 3 rooms (all en suite) TERMS B&B IR£17.50-£22.50 p.p.; single supplement upon request; evening meal IR£16.00

Northern Ireland

County Antrim

County Antrim's attractions are many. The county town of
Belfast lies on the shores of Belfast Lough in a most attractive setting, surrounded by hills which can be seen from
most parts of the town. It became a thriving commercial
centre and port in the nineteenth century and now has a
population of some 400,000, nearly a third of the population
of Northern Ireland. Amongst the many sights to see in
Belfast is the Ulster Museum, which contains the treasures
from the wreck of the Spanish Armada vessel, the *Girona*.

The town of Antrim is set back from Lough Neagh, the
largest expanse of inland water in the British Isles and
famous for its eels. The main fishery is at Toomebridge.
One of the best ways to see the lough is from the Shane's
Castle Railway at Randalstown, Ireland's only working
narrow-gauge railway.

County Antrim's stretch of coastline is amongst the most
spectacular and scenic in Europe. Carrickfergus in the
soutn, the oldest town in Northern Ireland, is dominated by
its castle, and further north lies Larne, an important port
just a 70-minute ferry ride from Scotland. Beyond Larne the
coast road, built in the 1830s, affords breathtaking views of
the coast and cliffs; along this stretch it is possible to see the
formation of the earth's outer crust.

The coast road connects each of the nine famous glens,
green valleys running down to the sea, with rivers, water-
falls, wild flowers and birds. From south to north they are:
Glenarm, Glencloy, Glenariff, Glenballyeamon, Glenaan,
Glencorp, Glendun, Glenshesk and Glentaisie, which are
said to mean: glen of the army, glen of the hedges, plough-
man's glen, Edwardstown glen, glen of the rush lights, glen
of the slaughter, brown glen, sedgy glen, and Taisie's glen
(the legendary princess of Rathlin Island). The resort town
of Ballycastle is famous for its "Oul' Lammas Fair", which
once lasted a week and now takes place over two hectic days
at the end of August. Ballintoy, a picturesque Mediterra-
nean-looking fishing village, is one of the prettiest towns on
the coast and beyond it is one of the world's most amazing
natural wonders, the Giant's Causeway. This is made up of
a mass of basalt columns, altogether some 40,000 which are
tightly packed together, reaching heights of 40 feet, and
which disappear into the sea. They reappear at Staffa Island
on the Scottish coast and all kinds of legends are attached to
this natural phenomenon.

Colliers Hall

50 Cushendall Road, Ballycastle, BT54 6QR, Co Antrim
Tel: (02657) 62531

An interesting eighteenth-century stone-dashed farmhouse
offering comfort, excellent value and a homely atmosphere.
The 90-acre farm is mostly sheep and beef. The bedrooms
are spacious, with the wash-basins cleverly incorporated into
marble wash-stands, and all have tea- and coffee-making
facilities. The house is furnished with a mixture of traditional and antique furniture, and one room has handmade
beds. A large lounge with TV has its original marble fireplace
and is furnished with antiques. Of particular interest is the
china cabinet and beautiful marble clock which was a
wedding present given to Mrs McCarry's grandmother.
There are lovely walks through the woods, with views of the
Knocklayde Mountains and Glen Shesk Valley. An 18-hole
golf course is situated across the road. Located 2 miles (3
km) from Ballycastle. No pets.

OWNER Mrs Maureen McCarry   OPEN 1 April–1 September
ROOMS 1 double/twin/single/family (2 en suite)   TERMS B&B
£13.50–£16.00 p.p; reductions for children; single supplement
£1.50; evening meal from £10.00, high tea from £5.00

Drumawillan House

1 Whitepark Road, Ballycastle, Co Antrim
Tel: (02657) 62539

An attractive old whitewashed house standing in mature
gardens right on top of the hill above Ballycastle; here
visitors have wonderful views over the town to the sea and
Scotland beyond. The building was once a church school
and has been in Mrs Todd's family for some years. It is a
comfortable family home, attractively decorated. Smoking in
the lounge only and no pets.

OWNER Jeanette Jackson Todd   OPEN All year   ROOMS 1 double, 1
twin, 2 family   TERMS B&B £14.00–£19.00 p.p.; reductions for
children; evening meal from £9.50–£10.50

Fair Head View

26 Worth Street, Ballycastle, BT54 6BW, Co Antrim
Tel: (02657) 62822

A small, family-run bed and breakfast situated 2 minutes from the beach and tennis court, with the Ballycastle golf course a little further away. The bedrooms are clean and simply furnished, and there is a cosy TV lounge with a peat fire lit at the first sign of a chill in the air. With just 3 bedrooms, Mrs Delargy is able to offer her guests personal service, with cups of tea or coffee proferred upon arrival. Fair Head View offers good basic accommodation at reasonable prices. There is a public car park close by. No pets.

OWNER Mrs K Delargy   OPEN All year   ROOMS 2 double, 1 family   TERMS B&B £11.00 p.p.; reductions for children

BALLYMENA

Ardmore House

51/53 Thomas Street, Ballymena, BT43 6AZ, Co Antrim
Tel: (0266) 47772

Ardmore House is a tasteful conversion of 2 houses situated in a peaceful location on the north side of town, surrounded by its own grounds which include a lovely rose garden. Extremely high standards prevail: the bedrooms are immaculate, with pretty wallpapers and duvets; 4 bedrooms are on the ground floor. Breakfasts and evening meals are served in a most attractive dining-room. Vegetarians are catered for, and evening refreshments are offered at no extra charge. There are 2 lounges with TV, one of which is very spacious, with an antique couch. This is a very popular venue with business people and tourists, so early reservations are advised. Handicapped facilities available on the ground floor. Smoking in designated areas. No pets.

OWNER Mrs Ann Bamber   OPEN All year, except Christmas
ROOMS 2 double, 7 twin, 5 single   TERMS B&B £15.00 p.p.; reductions for children; single supplement £1.00; evening meal £6.00

Ballynagashel House

30 Cregagh Road, Ballymoney, Co Antrim
Tel: (02656) 41366/41208

This solid-looking, stone-built farmhouse has been in the Kirkpatrick family for 6 generations. Approached through a rather grand entrance and up a driveway which leads round to the farm buildings, the house has recently been repainted. The accommodation is simple yet comfortable, and there is a sauna, sun bed and jacuzzi bath. Mrs Kirkpatrick is a very friendly lady who also works part-time as a nurse. There are TVs in the bedrooms. The house is located 6 miles (9 km) from Ballymoney on the B16 road.

OWNER Mrs Barbara Kirkpatrick   OPEN All year, except Christmas
ROOMS 2 double, 1 twin, 1 family   TERMS B&B £15.00 p.p.;
reductions for children; evening meal £12.00, high tea £8.00

Moore Lodge

Vow Road, Ballymoney, BT53 7NT, Co Antrim
Tel: (02656) 41043

This most attractive eighteenth-century country house has been in the Moore family for 400 years. Located on the banks of the River Bann, the oldest part of the house dates from 1620 and the newest from 1901. Moore Lodge has been beautifully decorated and furnished, but has a pleasant, relaxed atmosphere exuding the feel of a family home. Guests have use of the drawing-room, cosy, lived-in study, or comfortable sitting-room off the kitchen, which is where breakfast is served. The bedrooms are very large and all have lovely views. There is a billiard room on the top floor and a cellar with a bar and ping-pong table. The estate comprises 200 acres, which are let out, and there is free fishing on the river; boats are available to explore the miles of navigable water. No children and no pets.

OWNER Sir William Moore   OPEN 1 May–1 August
ROOMS 2 double, 1 twin, 1 single (all en suite)   TERMS B&B from £40.00 p.p.

Ash-Rowan Town House

12 Windsor Avenue, Belfast, BT9 6EE, Co Antrim
Tel: (0232) 661758, Fax: (0232) 661983

Ash-Rowan Town House is a late Victorian property in a quiet, tree-lined avenue, situated 10 minutes from the town centre, the King's Hall, Balmoral golf course, Queen's University, the Ulster Museum and the Grand Opera House. The comfortable bedrooms have TVs, tea-makers, bathrobes, linen sheets, telephones, hairdryers, trouser presses and information leaflets. The 2 top-floor rooms are now en suite and the others have part bathrooms. This is a most attractive house, with interesting colours and furnishings, and it is cosy and friendly. Breakfasts only are served, but they are substantial, with freshly squeezed orange juice, cereals and home-baked bread, followed by a cooked breakfast. There are flowers and newspapers on the dining-room tables. Laundry services are available. Sam and Evelyn have thought of just about everything for their guests, combining all the facilities of a hotel with personal service at a reasonable price. Private parking. No pets. No smoking in the bedrooms.

OWNERS Sam and Evelyn Hazlett   OPEN All year, except Christmas   ROOMS double/twin/single (4 en suite)   TERMS B&B £28.00-£33.00 p.p.; reductions for children; single supplement £10.00-£13.00; evening meal £15.00

Malone Guest House

79 Malone Road, Belfast, BT9 6SH, Co Antrim
Tel: (0232) 669565

An immaculate, bright and sunny Victorian house close to the town centre and all amenities. Elsie McClure, a native of Belfast, is a gracious lady, formerly a nurse who travelled extensively in her profession, staying at B&Bs on her travels. When she opened up her establishment she wanted all the facilities she had found lacking; this has certainly been accomplished. Malone Guest House is a delightful, tastefully furnished house; the lounge has a rich wood fireplace, lots of books to read and is a pleasant spot to relax in after a busy day. The bedrooms vary in size but are well appointed, all with TVs and tea- and coffee-making facilities. No pets.

Not suitable for children. The private parking has been extended.

OWNER Mrs Elsie McClure   OPEN 1 January–1 December
ROOMS 6 twin, 2 single (8 en suite)   TERMS B&B £21.00 p.p.;
weekends £17.50 p.p.; single supplement £6.00; weekends £2.50

The Malone Lodge

60 Eglantine Avenue, Belfast BT9 6DY, Co Antrim
Tel: (0232) 382409

This new, small hotel is a conversion of 2 houses, which have been virtually gutted. Built of brick with columns of blue-metal bow windows, Malone Lodge is in the university area and convenient to the city centre. The bedrooms are comfortable and attractively furnished, using modern furniture. The hotel has a pleasant, friendly atmosphere and offers guests a small conference room, car park, sauna, lounge and dining-room. Children are welcome; there are high chairs and children's menus. The dining-room is open for breakfast, morning coffee, lunch, afternoon tea and evening meals. The bedrooms all have telephones, TVs, trouser presses, hairdryers, tea- and coffee-making facilities, and there are non-smoking rooms available. All major credit cards accepted.

OWNERS The Malone Lodge   OPEN All year   ROOMS: 33 rooms
double/single/family (all en suite)   TERMS £30.00-£45.00 p.p.;
meals à la carte

Montpelier

96 Malone Road, Belfast, Co Antrim
Tel: (0232) 381831/622147

On a main road not far from Queen's University and accessible to central Belfast, Montpelier is a substantial early Victorian house. Amongst others, the house has belonged to Lord Justice Gibson, Thomas Gilmore – a tea merchant – and in 1887, Reverend Hugh Hanna. Known as Roaring Hugh, his statue occupied the centre of Carlisle Circus. Mary Carberry, who lives a short distance away and is on hand for breakfast, lunch and evening meals, bought the house in 1990. The bedrooms are comfortable, one large double en suite located in the old stables at the rear of the building. The public rooms, however, still need some attention. Lunch and evening meals are available. There is no wine licence.

OWNERS Mary Carberry OPEN All year ROOMS 4 double, 1 single (1 en suite) TERMS B&B £30.00-£45.00 p.p.; evening meal £15.00

Oakhill Country House

59 Dunmurry Lane, Belfast, BT17 9JR, Co Antrim

Tel: (0232) 610658, Fax: (0232) 621566

Only 4 miles (6 km) from Belfast, this country house is approached up a windy, leafy driveway. The first impression is not promising, but walk to the side of the house and you will see that the garden is quite amazing – beautifully designed, immaculately kept and stretching away into the distance with trees shielding the property from the neighbouring park. The house extends back too, followed by greenhouses and outbuildings. The interior is beautifully decorated and furnished with an enormous formal drawing-room and dining-room, where May Nobles will put on a dinner party for a group. Unfortunately, overnight guests are not catered for and must forgo her excellent cooking. Upstairs the 2 front double bedrooms are elegantly furnished and decorated with bathrooms larger than the average-sized en suite bedroom. Breakfast is served in a pretty breakfast room, or in summer in the conservatory – garden views in every direction. A truly delightful, peaceful spot close to Belfast. No pets.

OWNERS May Noble OPEN All year, except Christmas ROOMS 2 double, 1 suite, 1 twin (3 en suite) TERMS B&B from £35.00 p.p.

Stranmillis Lodge

14 Chlorine Gardens, Belfast, Co Antrim

Tel: (0232) 682009, Fax: same

Stranmillis Lodge is a new guest house, begun in 1991 by two sisters-in-law, who both have families and family homes outside Belfast and take it in turns to run the business. They have done an excellent job in doing up the house to a high standard of comfort. Simply furnished, each bedroom has an en suite bathroom, TV, telephone, trouser press, hairdryer and tea- and coffee-making facilities; a daily newspaper is also provided. There is a pleasant panelled lounge with open fire, and both breakfast and evening meals are served by arrangement in the panelled dining-room. The house stands on a bend in the road in the Stranmillis/Malone area close to Queen's University and handy for shops, restaurants and the city centre. Some car parking is available. Pets are not allowed.

OWNERS Mrs Barton and Mrs Barton   OPEN All year   ROOMS 5 twin, 1 single (all en suite)   TERMS B&B £28.00-£40.00 p.p.; evening meals à la carte

Windermere House

60 Wellington Park, Belfast, BT9 6DD, Co Antrim
Tel: (0232) 662693

A spacious Victorian house situated on a quiet tree-lined street 1 mile (1¹/₂ km) from the town centre. The rooms vary in size from modest to spacious and are clean and comfortable. All bedrooms have TVs. Four of the single rooms are on the top floor with bathrooms one floor down. Agnes and Anna are friendly, outgoing ladies with a good sense of humour. They both lecture at the University of Ulster on hotel catering and management. Evening meals are served if prearranged; home-style cooking; light snacks are available. There's a comfortable guest lounge. Private parking. Good bus service to town centre. No pets. Smoking only in the lounge. Visa and Access cards accepted

OWNERS Agnes and Anna Murray   OPEN All year, except Christmas ROOMS 2 twin, 4 single, 1 triple, 1 family (2 en suite)   TERMS B&B £15.00–£22.00 p.p.; reductions for children; evening meal £10.00, snacks from £3.00

BUSHMILLS

Auberge de Seneirl

28 Ballyclough Road, Bushmills, Co Antrim
Tel: (02657) 41536

This famous French restaurant is housed in what was once an old school house. Auberge de Seneirl has pleasant views and is close to the scenic Antrim coast and the Bushmills distillery. The building has been extended and renovated in a rather dark, French rustic style. The focus is on the restaurant and the food, but to help those who come from far away to enjoy their meal, there are 5 comfortable, attractively decorated rooms, all en suite, with one suite. There's also an indoor swimming pool, sauna and sunbed. Mr Defres comes from Provence and Mrs Defres lectures in catering. No pets. Diners Club accepted.

OWNER Mr and Mrs B E Defres   OPEN All year, except Christmas   ROOMS 5 en suite rooms, 1 suite   TERMS B&B £18.50-£29.00 p.p.

Montalto Guest House

5 Craigaboney Road, off Priestland Road, Bushmills, BT57 8XD, Co Antrim
Tel: (02657) 31257

A large nineteenth-century farmhouse on 100 acres of mixed farming in an elevated position, with beautiful views of the surrounding countryside and the sea. A superb combination of a beautiful setting with a most accommodating host. Montalto was one of the first B&Bs in the area. The spotless bedrooms are simply furnished and the house, which is bright and airy, has a lounge and conservatory. There are plans to add a couple of shower rooms. Of special interest is the monk seat in the hallway. There is a kitchen for guests' use. Montalto is just a few minutes to the old Bushmills Distillery, Dunluce Castle and the Giant's Causeway, with golf, fishing and lovely walks close by. Located off the Bushmills-Coleraine road B17 beside Dunluce Manor. Pets outside.

OWNER Mrs Dorothy Taggart   OPEN 1 March–1 October ROOMS 2 double/single   TERMS B&B from £15.00 p.p.; reductions for children; single supplement £1.00

White Gables

83 Dunluce Road, Bushmills, Co Antrim
Tel: (02657) 31611

A modern whitewashed house perched on the clifftop with spectacular views, just off the main road. White Gables is very close to Dunluce Castle and is only 4 miles (6 km) from the Giant's Causeway and 2 miles (3 km) from the Bushmills Distillery. The rooms are very comfortable and well furnished and all have lovely views. The pleasant sitting-room, where informal meals are shared with the family, and the dining-room, where breakfast and evening meals are served, also enjoy the same view. This is a very popular place, so early bookings are recommended. No smoking in the bedrooms and pets outside only.

OWNER Mrs Ria Johnston OPEN 1 April–1 September ROOMS 3 double, 1 single (3 en suite) TERMS B&B £17.50 p.p.; evening meal £10.00

CUSHENDALL
Glendale
46 Coast Road, Cushendall, BT44 0RX, Co Antrim
Tel: (02667) 71495

An attractive white-dashed house on the outskirts of the village, approached by a private drive, in a peaceful location with views of the Lurig Mountains and the sea. The house is well maintained and comfortably furnished. Mary O'Neill is an accommodating host and Mr O'Neill, who works on the Stranraer ferries, enjoys outlining sightseeing itineraries for guests. Breakfasts only are served, but there are several venues for eating in the area.

OWNER Mrs Mary O'Neill OPEN 1 April–1 September ROOMS 2 double, 1 family TERMS B&B £13.00 p.p.; reductions for children

DUNDONALD
The Cottage
377 Comber Road, Dundonald, Belfast, BT16 0XB,
Co Antrim
Tel: (0247) 878189

An absolutely charming, low, whitewashed 250-year-old cottage lying on the road to Comber from Belfast, just outside Dundonald, in open countryside with lovely views in both directions. There is a most attractive small rear garden, and one enters the house through a pretty conservatory covered with an enormous passion flower plant which seems to cover half the house as well. It is owned by the Muldoons, who bought the cottage about 14 years ago as a mostly derelict building and have restored it to a delightful small country retreat. The cottage justifiably became a very popular place to stay, listed as Belfast but out in the countryside. It has been very prettily decorated and furnished throughout, completely in keeping with its cottage atmosphere. The bedrooms are small, all with antique double beds, pretty wallpaper and materials, and the large breakfast room/lounge with TV and open fireplace is a lovely room. Full of character, it is a relaxing, comfortable house with a most delightfully friendly owner. All bedrooms are on the ground floor. Smoking is not permitted.

OWNER Elizabeth Muldoon   OPEN All year   ROOMS 2 double
TERMS B&B £16.00 p.p.

LARNE

Cairnview

13 Croft Heights, Ballygally, Larne, Co Antrim
Tel: (0574) 583269

A modern house in an area of newer buildings standing above the Coast road, with views of the sea from the front terrace and the side of the house. There is an open-plan sitting-room and dining-room. Convenient to Larne, which is only 4 miles (6 km) away and 500 metres from the beach. Breakfast only is served. No smoking and no pets.

OWNER Mrs Jennifer Lough   OPEN All year   ROOMS 2 double/
family (2 en suite)   TERMS B&B from £15.00 p.p.; reductions for children and senior citizens; single supplement available

MUCKAMORE

The Beeches

10 Dunadry Road, Muckamore, Co Antrim
Tel: (08494) 33161

Standing in quite a sizeable garden, this Edwardian country house is just off the A6 between Antrim and Templepatrick, 5 miles (7^1/$_2$ km) from Belfast airport. The Allens, a very friendly couple, offer simple, comfortable accommodation and, with a previous Taste of Ulster award, good home-cooked food. Two of the bedrooms are in the main part of the house and the remaining 3 in a new purpose-built extension. All rooms have tea- and coffee-making facilities, TVs, hairdryers and trouser presses. Lunch is available, as well as evening meals. No smoking in the bedrooms and no pets. Visa accepted.

OWNER Mrs Allen   OPEN All year, except Christmas   ROOMS 4
double, 1 single, 1 twin (all en suite)   TERMS B&B £25.00-£30.00 p.p.; reductions for children; evening meal £10.50

Alexandra

11 Lansdowne Crescent, Portrush, BT56 8AY, Co Antrim
Tel: (0265) 822284

Right on the sea-front and minutes from the centre of town, the Alexandra is a well-maintained, immaculate Victorian house. The front is a blaze of colour in summer with pretty window boxes and tubs full of flowers. The house is warm and comfortable and the bedrooms are well appointed; some have sea views. There is one very large en suite family room, and the rooms at the top of the house have been enlarged. Most of the house has recently been refurbished. Mr Taylor, the owner, was looking for a new business when a friend suggested bed and breakfast. He spent quite a long time searching for the right place before finding the Alexandra. After months of hard work, the spic-and-span house was open for business. He is ably assisted by his 2 daughters. There's a very large, well-furnished lounge which overlooks the sea. Lovely walks close by. Plenty of street parking available. No pets.

OWNER Mr Robert Taylor OPEN All year ROOMS 2 double, 2 single 4 family (1 en suite) TERMS B&B from £15.00 p.p.; reductions for children; single supplement available; evening meal from £7.00

Ardnaree

White Rocks, 105 Dunluce Road, Portrush, BT56 8NB, Co Antrim
Tel: (0265) 823407

A modern villa-style house on the Causeway road, 1½ miles (2½ km) from Portrush. Ardnaree, meaning "top of the hill", certainly describes the location. This must be one of the best views in Northern Ireland; it overlooks the ocean, the Donegal hills and an 18-hole championship golf course. The bedrooms are fairly small but they are clean and comfortable, all with TVs. There's a guest lounge with TV and a bright dining-room where substantial breakfasts are served at separate tables. Elsie Rankin worked in a hotel before opening up her home to visitors and she certainly knows how to make guests feel at home. Established over 20 years now, this is a popular venue so early reservations are recommended. There is one ground-floor bedroom. Smoking in the lounge only. Pets outside.

OWNER Mrs Elsie Rankin   OPEN All year   ROOMS 3 double, 1 twin, 1 single (2 en suite)   TERMS B&B £15.00-£17.00 p.p.; single supplement £2.00

Ballymagarry House

46 Leeke Road, Portrush, BT56 8NH, Co Antrim
Tel: (0265) 823737

Ballymagarry House, meaning "house of the enclosed garden", stands on the site of the home of the Earls of Antrim who moved here after the kitchen in Dunluce Castle, the ruins of which are just below the house, fell into the sea. A converted sixteenth-century barn is the central feature of the house, now an enormous drawing-room with a large brick fireplace. The rest of the house has been built around it, slowly evolving over a period of about 4 years. The ruins of the walled garden stand in the grounds, purchased when the Leckeys learned that this historical site was to be torn down for farmland. Alyson Leckey, who recently gave up working for Ulster TV, has applied her creative energy into making the house unusual and interesting in decor and furnishings. There is a great playroom for small children and a play area outside, which children are invited to share with Alyson and Paul's 2 small boys. Paul, a keen golfer, would be happy to advise on golf courses. Alyson is an excellent cook and prepares imaginative meals; the breakfast selection is a speciality. On clear days there are views of the Glens of Antrim and the sea. No smoking in public rooms and no pets. Off the Ballybogey Road, or the Coast Road, 2 miles (3 km) from Portrush.

OWNERS Alyson Leckey   OPEN 1 March–1 October   ROOMS 2 twin /suites   TERMS B&B from £17.50 p.p.; reductions for children; evening meals by arrangement

Maddybenny Farm

18 Maddybenny Park, Portrush, BT52 2PJ, Co Antrim
Tel: (0265) 823394

Maddybenny Farm, meaning sanctified or holy post, dating from the 1600s, was built as a plantation house on lands belonging to the Earl of Antrim. The first Presbyterian

Minister, Rev. Gabriel Cornwall, lived here. Added onto over the years at 3 different phases, the house floor plan is unique in that the integral part of the house is in the centre and one can walk completely around the house from the inside. The house is approached up a long track and stands in a wonderful, rural position. It is part of a big complex of buildings: the farm, stables, and soon-to-be self-catering cottages. Newly opened is the riding school, with tuition available for guests by an international rider. Maddybenny Farm is a comfortable, relaxed place – a bright and spacious house – with the dining-room and drawing-room recently refurbished. Rosemary White, the owner, is a marvellous host with a wonderful sense of humour. She also serves the best breakfast in Ireland, a claim backed up by her Irish Breakfast award: fresh trout, haddock, fruit, hot and cold cereals, fresh fruit, home-made scones, fresh-baked breads – the menu goes on and on. It is a feast, to be sure. Maddybenny has a games room and is very near the Royal Portrush Golf Club, 6 other courses, the Giant's Causeway and beaches. Pets outside only.

OWNER Mrs Rosemary White   OPEN All year, except Christmas
ROOMS 1 double/twin/family (2 en suite)   TERMS B&B £16.50
p.p.; reductions for children; single supplement £5.00

County Armagh

County Armagh is the smallest and most varied county in Northern Ireland, ranging from magnificent mountain scenery in the south to rich fruit-growing country in the north, interspersed with small lakes and dairy farms.

Armagh, the ancient capital of Ulster and former great centre of learning, has been the spiritual capital of Ireland for 1,500 years and is the seat of both Protestant and Catholic archbishops. There is little left to see of its early days, the architecture today being predominantly Georgian. The two cathedral churches are prominent features of the city. The Church of Ireland stands on the hill where St Patrick built his stone church, and the twin spires of the Catholic Cathedral of St Patrick, which was finished in 1873, rise from the opposite hill.

In the south of Armagh the mountains of Slieve Gullion contain an unspoilt area of small villages and beautiful scenery. Crossmaglen has the largest market square in Europe and has become the centre of the recently revived lace-making industry. There is an enormous open-air market every Sunday at Jonesborough.

Whilst driving down some country lane you might come across the great Armagh game, road bowls, which is shared with the county of Cork. The object is to hurl a metal bowl weighing $1^3/_4$ lbs (1 kg) as far as possible, covering several miles in the shortest number of shots. Children are dispatched ahead to warn motorists.

The Orchard of Ireland, the rich fruit-growing county in the north east, is at its best in May, Apple Blossom Sunday being in late May.

ARMAGH

Clonhugh Guest House

College Hill, Armagh, BT61 9DF, Co Armagh

Tel: (0861) 522693

Guests are well taken care of here by Mrs McKenna, a kindly lady who welcomes guests as friends. Clonhugh House is a wisteria-covered 1930s residence set back off the road in a lovely garden. Mrs McKenna is very interested in antiques, evidenced by the antique furnishings, paintings, china and her collection of over 100 teapots. The bright, airy bedrooms are nicely decorated, and there is one ground-floor en suite room suitable for wheelchair access. There are no set times for breakfast, which is served in the attractive dining-room with its original fireplace. Tea and biscuits are served in the evening in the cheery lounge, where guests are often joined by Mrs McKenna. Within walking distance of town and all amenities. No smoking in the bedrooms. No pets.

OWNER Mrs P McKenna OPEN All year ROOMS 2 double, 2 twin, 1 family (1 en suite) TERMS B&B £12.00-£15.00 p.p.; reductions for children

Padua House

63 Cathedral Road, Armagh, BT61 7QX, Co Armagh

Tel: (0861) 523584, Fax: (0861) 527426

Guests are made to feel like part of the family at Padua. Mr and Mrs O'Hagan are a friendly, welcoming couple who thoroughly enjoy their visitors. The family lounge is shared with guests who are encouraged to join the owners after a busy day's touring. A hot drink is almost always available, and the O'Hagans are always happy to assist guests with itineraries, recommendations on places to eat, etc. The accommodation is clean and basic; all the bedrooms have a TV. Padua House, built with red brick, is opposite the playing fields and beside St Patrick's Cathedral. Substantial breakfasts are served in the dining-room, which has a beautiful antique chaise-longue. Street parking and limited private parking available. No smoking in the bedrooms and no pets.

OWNER Kathleen O'Hagan   OPEN All year   ROOMS 1 double/twin/family   TERMS B&B £10.00 p.p.; reductions for children

RICHHILL

Ballinahinch House

47 Ballygroobany Road, Richhill, BT61 9NA, Co Armagh
Tel: (0762) 870081

On a 120-acre working beef and arable farm, this beautiful early Victorian house has an old-world atmosphere. The rooms are all spacious and there are antique and traditional furnishings throughout. The comfortable bedrooms are individually decorated and furnished, one with a coronet (decorative bed addition). The lounge is large, as is the dining-room, which has the original black slate fireplace. Exceptionally high standards prevail throughout this lovely home with its informal and welcoming atmosphere. The owners, Mr and Mrs Kee, are a delightful couple who have been lovingly restoring the house to its original splendour. A peaceful location with lovely walks close by. There is a car park to the front of the house. No smoking and pets outside only. To locate Ballinahinch, turn off the A3 at Junction B131, take second road on the right, continue on over the crossroad, house is approximately 1 mile (1½ km) on the left.

OWNER Mr and Mrs J E Kee   OPEN 1 April–1 October   ROOMS 2 double, 1 twin, 1 single   TERMS B&B £13.50–£14.00 p.p.; reductions for children

County Down

A county rich in monuments of antiquity, County Down has been subject to many invasions throughout its history, the fiercest one of all from the Vikings in the ninth century.
    Legend has it that St Patrick landed here in AD 432 where

the Slaney River flows into Strangford Lough. In the 30 years between his arrival in Ireland and AD 461 when he died in his abbey at Saul, St Patrick converted the Irish to Christianity.

The Ards Peninsula, bordered by Strangford Lough to the west and the sea to the east, is a narrow strip of land with a bracing climate, the sunniest and driest part of the North. It has some charming villages and towns which were first settled by the Scots and English. Bangor was a famous centre of learning from the sixth century until it was devastated by the Vikings in the ninth century. It was from here that the missionaries St Columbanus, St Gall and many others set off to bring Christianity to the rest of Europe.

The breezy Coast road runs from Bangor past Ballycopeland – the only working windmill in Ireland – past the pretty village of Kearney to the attractive town of Portaferry, where the five-mile-long ferry ride to Strangford affords lovely views up Strangford Lough. The Lough is a famous bird sanctuary and wildlife reserve and the small rounded hills, called drumlins, that cover North Down are to be found in Strangford Lough, appearing as small islands. Amongst the historic places to visit are Castle Ward, built by the first Lord Bangor in 1765, and Mount Stewart, the childhood home of Lord Castlereagh, a former British foreign secretary. Three out of the four Cistercian abbeys in medieval County Down were built around the lough – Inch Abbey, Grey Abbey and Comber.

Downpatrick, at the southern tip of Strangford Lough, is an attractive Georgian town and the burial site of St Patrick, which is in the graveyard of the Church of Ireland Cathedral.

The Mourne Mountains, the best-known mountains in Ireland, cover a small self-contained area, just 15 miles (22½ km) long and 8 miles (12 km) wide, with 12 rounded peaks. The barren peak of Slieve Donard, climbing steeply to 2,796 feet, dominates this peaceful landscape, which is a paradise for walkers. From the summit you can see the Isle of Man, the Belfast hills and Lough Neagh. Two big artificial lakes that supply Belfast's water are surrounded by a huge dry stone wall over 6 feet (2m) high and 22 miles (33 km) long. The Mourne Wall Walk attracts thousands of walkers from all over the world each June.

The coast south from Newcastle, a lively seaside resort, was notorious for smuggling in the eighteenth century. Newry was once a prosperous mercantile town with large townhouses and public buildings, and the earliest Protestant church in Ireland, St Patrick's Parish Church.

BANBRIDGE

Lisdrum House

189 Newry Road, Banbridge, BT32 3NB, Co Down
Tel: (08206) 22663

Lisdrum is situated in an elevated position with lovely views
of the Mourne Mountains. Built in 1930, the house is set in
beautiful grounds with shrubs and flowers on 25 acres of
land. The accommodation, which is attached to the main
house, comprises a bedroom with a double and single bed,
separate bathroom, and a small, cosy sitting-room with TV,
telephone and tea-maker. Breakfasts are served in the flat.
Elizabeth Campbell is interested in genealogy and is willing
to assist guests with ancestry tracing. No smoking in the flat.
No pets. Situated on the main road from Banbridge to
Newry.

OWNER Mrs Elizabeth Campbell   OPEN All year, except Christmas
ROOMS 1 double/family (all en suite)   TERMS B&B £13.00 p.p.;
reductions for children

BANGOR

Beresford House

45 Queen's Parade, Bangor, BT20 3BH, Co Down
Tel: (0247) 472143

Set in a very quiet location on a cul-de-sac, Beresford House
is part of a Victorian terrace with splendid views over the
harbour and marina. Mrs Anderson is a dietician and
specialises in having boxers stay with her who train in
Belfast; she takes care of their diets, providing all the meals.
There is a cheerful, bright dining-room and a sitting-room.
No smoking in the bedrooms or dining-room and no pets.

OWNER Mrs J Anderson   OPEN All year   ROOMS 6 double, 4 twin,
6 single (5 en suite)   TERMS B&B £13.50-£17.50 p.p.; evening
meals à la carte

Carrig-Gorm

27 Bridge Road, Helen's Bay, Bangor, BT19 1TS,
Co Down
Tel: (0247) 853680

A rambling, old whitewashed house standing in about 2

acres of grounds on the edge of St Helen's. It is thought the oldest wing of the house dates back around 300 years, and the newest, which includes the elegant, recently refurbished drawing-room, from 1870. The house has a rather worn, faded appearance but exudes a friendly atmosphere. There are sea views from both bedrooms; breakfast only is served in the dining-room, and guests tend to sit around the open fire in the well lived-in, panelled, large entrance hall. No smoking in the bedrooms and no pets.

OWNER Elizabeth Eves   OPEN All year, except Christmas
ROOMS 2 twin   TERMS B&B £16.00 p.p.

Shelleven House

59/61 Princetown Road, Bangor, BT20 3TA, Co Down
Tel: (0247) 271777

Occupying the last of a row of houses, this Victorian double terraced house stands above the city and coast, with sea and town views from the upper floors. Brian and Frances, a very pleasant couple, have run the guest house for the last 10 years and take pride in its cleanliness and standard of decor. Meals are served in the dining-room, if arranged in advance, and a curious door separates this room from the lounge. The rooms all have bathrooms, TVs, radio alarms, tea- and coffee-making facilities, hairdryers and irons. No smoking in the dining-room and no pets.

OWNER Brian and Frances Davis   OPEN All year   ROOMS 4 double/twin/family (all en suite)   TERMS B&B £20.00-£25.00 p.p.; reductions for children; evening meal £12.50

DOWNPATRICK

Havine Farm Guest House

51 Ballydonnell Road, Downpatrick, BT30 8EP, Co Down
Tel: (0396) 85242

A comfortable eighteenth-century stone-dashed farmhouse with 125 acres of land for beef and sheep. The bedrooms are small and cosy, with wooden sloping ceilings and tea- and coffee-making facilities. Mrs Macauley tries to think of everything for her guests' comfort: sewing kits, house gowns, slippers, etc. Little wonder that this is a highly acclaimed farmhouse which has received an award for hospitality. Meals are imaginative and nicely presented, with fresh home-cooking including delicious desserts and home-made gooseberry pickle. Evening snacks are also offered, and tea and home-made cakes. There are 2 lounges, one with a TV and one for relaxing or reading in. There are no fancy frills, but Havine is a place you will look forward to returning to. Pets outside only. No smoking in the bedrooms. Downpatrick Road from Clough 2¼ miles (3½ km), turn right at Tyreel – house is 2 miles (3 km) along on left.

OWNER Mrs Myrtle Macauley OPEN All year, except Christmas ROOMS 2 double, 1 single, 1 family TERMS B&B £12.50-£13.00 p.p.; reductions for children; evening meal £9.00-£10.00

Tyrella House

Downpatrick, BT30 8SU, Co Down
Tel: (0396) 85422

A large elegant country house with a porticoed, classical façade, standing in 300 acres of grounds stretching down to the sea; Tyrella House owns a private beach. David, whose father bought the property in the late 1940s, takes care of the cattle and sheep farm. Sally looks after their 2 small children and likes to hunt. The grounds include a private event course and also a point-to-point course, which is used a couple of times a year. Guests are welcome to bring their own horses, if booked in advance, and there are miles of beach to explore. Croquet and tennis on a grass court are also available. Most of the house dates from around the sixteenth century, with the front part added in the early nineteenth century. The house has a welcoming feeling with a large hallway and stairs leading up to the 3 large double rooms, 2 with en suite bathrooms and featuring pre-war fittings. Guests are welcome to use the comfortable drawing-room with open fire, and evening meals are served by candlelight in the elegant dining-room. There is also a TV room. No smoking and no pets. Bookings should be made in advance and it is advisable to get directions.

OWNER David and Sally Corbett OPEN All year, except Christmas ROOMS 3 double (2 en suite) TERMS B&B £35.00-£40.00 p.p.; evening meal from £16.00

DROMORE

Sylvan Hill House

76 Kiltown Road, Dromore, BT25 1HS, Co Down

Tel: (0846) 692321

A listed one-and-a-half-storey Georgian house built in 1781, standing in beautiful gardens with mature trees and panoramic views of the Mourne and Dromara mountains. The house was recently completely refurbished. The 3 very large bedrooms, all with tea-makers, overlook the garden and furnishings are a mixture of antique and traditional, with decor in soft pastel colours. Mr and Mrs Coburn join their guests for meals. Mrs Coburn is a gourmet cook, and all breads and desserts are home-made. A special treat at breakfast is her elder-flower marmalade. An absolutely wonderful opportunity to experience gracious living in a peaceful and tranquil atmosphere. To find the house, go north from Dromore, turn left off the A1 up Connolystown Road, drive up Kilntoen Road; the house is half a mile on the right.

OWNER Elise Coburn   OPEN All year   ROOMS 2 double, 1 twin, 1 family   TERMS B&B £15.00-£17.00 p.p.; evening meal £10.00

GROOMSPORT

Sandeel Lodge

18 Sandeel Lane, Orlock, Groomsport, BT19 2LP,

Co Down

Tel: (0247) 883139

The approach to Sandeel Lodge is up a bumpy gravel road several hundred yards long, but it is worth the ride. Sandeel is situated in a shoreline position with magnificent views and surrounded by lovely grounds. The house, which is new, was built as a retirement residence for Mr and Mrs Allen; however, they missed their contact with people and opened up their beautiful home as a bed and breakfast. The bedrooms are beautifully furnished, tastefully decorated and one has its own jacuzzi. There is a lovely lounge where guests can sit in the evening and watch the ships pass by. A real plus is the heated swimming pool and sun lounge. There are lots of interesting objects of art, a Royal Doulton collection and antique furnishings. Very popular with business people and tourists, so early reservations are essential. Off the main

Donaghadee/Groomsport road, left into Orlock, first entrance is Sandeel Lane marked "National Trust", continue on to last house on the right.

OWNER Mrs Maureen Allen   OPEN All year   ROOMS 2 double/twin (all en suite)   TERMS B&B £25.00-£30.00 p.p; reductions for children; evening meal £10.00-£12.00

Tanner Cottage

5 Main Street, Groomsport, Co Down

Tel: (0247) 464534

This absolutely charming home is on the one main road which runs through the small village of Groomsport, overlooking the harbour, sea and Antrim hills. Beautifully decorated and furnished and immaculately kept, Tanner Cottage has a warm and friendly atmosphere and delightful owners. The pretty bedrooms all have tea- and coffee-making facilities, a trouser press and a hairdryer. The large drawing-room is in the front of the house, but guests often end up in the owners' charming sitting-room. The dining-room is at the back of the house, with a small conservatory where guests can have breakfast in warm weather. At the back of the main house is an outside toilet and small house, where in pre-war days the owners would spend the summer while they let out the cottage. Beyond is an attractive garden featuring a well, and there is also a garage for 4 cars. No smoking in the bedrooms and no pets.

OWNER Mr and Mrs L Walker   OPEN All year, except Christmas   ROOMS 1 double/twin (all en suite)   TERMS B&B £15.00-£20.00 p.p.

HOLYWOOD

Ardshane Country House

5 Bangor Road, Holywood, BT18 0NU, Co Down

Tel: (02317) 2044, Fax: (02317) 7506

A turn-of-the-century Edwardian large brick family home standing in most attractive mature gardens and approached up a driveway off the main road at the Bangor end of Holywood behind the Presbyterian church. Ardshane means "Hill of John" and it is built on the 800-year-old camp site of King John's army. It is a restful, spacious and elegant house, beautifully appointed with every comfort. The bedrooms are large, with modern bathrooms, showers, hairdryers, trouser presses, TVs and tea- and coffee-making facilities. There is a TV lounge and an elegant dining-room with a marble fireplace where à la carte as well as table d'hôte evening

meals are served at separate tables by waiters and waitresses dressed in Edwardian clothes. The young, informal and fun-loving owner used to run the house in partnership with her mother as a retirement home and has recently turned the property into a guest house. Left over from these days is the wheelchair lift; consequently the house is well adapted for those in wheelchairs. Ardshane has a wine licence. Visa, Access and Eurocard accepted.

OWNER Judith Caughey   OPEN All year   ROOMS 3 double, 3 twin, 2 single, 1 family (8 en suite)   TERMS B&B £35.00-£45.00 p.p.; reductions for children; evening meal £12.00-£16.00 and à la carte

KILKEEL

Heath Hall

160 Moyadd Road, Kilkeel, BT34 4HJ, Co Down
Tel: (06937) 62612

A turn-of-the-century stone-built farmhouse set in 16 acres of farmland with sheep and cattle. Health Hall is ideally situated, with views of the sea and Mourne Mountains. The interior of the house was completely renovated a few years ago. New windows were installed and the house was attractively decorated. The lounge has the original marble fireplace and there is a TV. There is also a snooker room. The house was formerly run as a bed and breakfast by Mrs McGlue's mother-in-law and has a good reputation for offering good value meals and accommodation. There is no licence, but guests are welcome to bring their own wine. Some of the rooms have harbour views. Evening meals must be prearranged and light lunches are also available. No smoking in the bedrooms and pets outside only. Located on the main Hilltown Road 1¹/₂ miles (2¹/₂ km) south of Kilkeel.

OWNER Mrs Mary McGlue   OPEN 1 April–1 October   ROOMS 2 double, 1 single   TERMS B&B £11.50 p.p.; reductions for children; evening meal £6.00, light lunch £3.00

Wyncrest Guest House

30 Main Road, Kilkeel, Co Down
Tel: (06937) 63012

This small 16-acre farm lies on the main road on the edge of
the village of Ballymartin, between Kilkeel and Newcastle.
Wyncrest has been in the Adair family for some years and
was recently renovated, giving it a modern appearance. It is
close to the sea and is a comfortable house with simple
decor. Mrs Adair is a most friendly lady who in 1991 won
both the Taste of Ulster award and the National Galtee
Breakfast award. There is a sitting-room, and evening meals
are served in the large dining-room. No smoking in the
bedrooms and no pets.

OWNER Mrs Irene Adair   OPEN Easter–1 October   ROOMS 3
double/twin (4 en suite)   TERMS B&B £14.00-£16.50 p.p.;
reductions for children; single supplement £2.50-£5.00; evening
meal £12.00

NEWCASTLE

Golf Links House

109 Dundrum Road, Newcastle, BT33 0LN, Co Down
Tel: (03967) 22054

Golf Links is situated in a residential area, 5 minutes' walk
to town. It is adjacent to and overlooking the Royal County
Down golf course. This must be one of the best value bed
and breakfasts in Newcastle, and this is obviously recognised
by people visiting the area as it is full most of the time. Very
early reservations are recommended. The bedrooms are a
good size, simply furnished, clean and comfortable. Mrs
McPolin started with 3 rooms, but was so successful from
the beginning that additional rooms were added. Although
there are 14 bedrooms, a homely atmosphere has been
retained. The three-course evening meals are also good
value; good-sized portions, lots of fresh vegetables and
home-made desserts. There is a large, sunny lounge and a
front patio with furniture. No pets. No smoking in the
bedrooms.

OWNER Mrs Eileen McPolin   OPEN All year, except Christmas
ROOMS 2 double, 4 twin, 5 family, 2 single (all en suite)
TERMS B&B £12.00 p.p.; reductions for children; no single
supplement; evening meals from £6.00

The Briers

39 Middle Tullymore Road, Newcastle, BT33 0JJ,
Co Down

Tel: (03967) 24347/24067

A 200-year-old farmhouse, once part of Lord Roden's estate
and set in 2 acres, at one time a tied cottage. Located half a
mile off the main road and 1½ miles (2½ km) from Newcastle, with just the twittering of birds and visiting squirrels
and rabbits to break up the silence. The Briers is a low,
whitewashed and very pretty house decorated with colourful
hanging flowers. The house was almost totally derelict until
6 years ago when it was lovingly restored. There are thick
stone walls, beamed ceilings and the original fireplace made
from local stone. The delightful bedrooms have a mixture of
pine and antique furnishings with matching fabrics. Three
rooms are now en suite and there are plans to add on a few
more. The upstairs twin bedroom is very spacious and has a
beamed pitched roof. The single en suite room is on the
ground floor. There is a lovely garden, a newly planted
arboretum and a sun porch for guests' use. Horse riding and
fishing are available close by. There is no licence, but guests
are welcome to bring their own wine. No pets. Not suitable for
children under 12. Located ½ mile (¾ km) from Newcastle.

OWNER Mrs Mary Bowater   OPEN All year   ROOMS 2 double, 1
twin, 1 single (3 en suite)   TERMS B&B £17.50 p.p.; evening
meals from £10.50, lunch from £3.50

NEWTOWNARDS

Rockdene

4 Springvale Road, Ballywalter, Newtownards, BT22 2PE,
Co Down

Tel: (02477) 58205

A spotless, cosy bungalow in a superb location facing the
sea. The bedrooms are on the first floor and the bathroom,
with a shower and bath, is on the ground floor. There are no
wash-basins in the rooms, but with just 2 rooms it does not
seem to matter. Mrs Dickson is a most accommodating
host; cups of tea are offered upon arrival and in the evening
and are included in the price. Excellent breakfasts are served
in the dining-room overlooking the bay; vegetarian and
special diets are catered for if prearranged. Evening meals
are by special arrangement, but there are several eating

establishments within walking distance. Easily located during the spring and summer when the front garden is full of roses. No pets.

OWNER Mrs F Dickson   OPEN All year, except Christmas
ROOMS 1 double/twin   TERMS B&B £12.00 p.p.; evening meal £6.00

PORTAFERRY

Mrs Marie Adair's

22 The Square, Portaferry, BT22 1LW, Co Down
Tel: (02477) 28412

A spotless house located in the town square within walking distance of the ferry, shops and restaurants. The bedrooms are large and modestly furnished. The family unit has a 3-bed room and an adjoining single. There's a comfortable TV lounge. The house appears much larger than it is from the front, as all of the bedrooms are in an extension to the rear of the house. Street parking available. No smoking in the bedrooms. No pets.

OWNER Tommy and Marie Adair   OPEN 1 April–1 October
ROOMS 1 double/twin/single/family   TERMS B&B £11.00 p.p.; reductions for children; no single supplement

ROSTREVOR

Still Waters

14 Killowen Road, Rostrevor, BT34 3AF, Co Down
Tel: (06937) 38743

Still Waters is in a superb position with wonderful views of the Cooley Mountains, Carlingford Lough and the sea. Mr McCabe is an expert gardener, as evidenced by the many beautiful shrubs and flowers; there is a pleasant sun-porch with plants. Mr and Mrs McCabe are an interesting couple who lived in Africa for several years before returning to Ireland. They started doing bed and breakfast as a hobby, but with the combination of their great hospitality and the superb location it quickly became a full-time business. There is a comfortable guest lounge with a TV and a quiet area for reading, both overlooking the view. The garage has been converted as private quarters for the owners; guests therefore have the run of the house. All of the bedrooms are on the ground floor. No pets. Located 3 miles (4½ km) from Rostrevor.

OWNER Eileen McCabe OPEN 1 March–1 October ROOMS 3
double TERMS B&B £12.00 p.p.; reductions for children; single
supplement available

County Fermanagh

County Fermanagh is lakeland – one third of the county is
under water – and is traversed by the Erne River which
meanders its way across the forested county into a huge lake
dotted with drumlins. A paradise for fishermen, boat enthusiasts and other water-related activities, Lough Erne is a
magnificent 50 mile (75 km)-long waterway offering
uncongested cruising opportunities with 154 islands and
many coves and inlets to explore. It has an interesting mix of
pagan and Christian relics and traditions that have withstood the centuries.

The medieval town of Enniskillen is built on a bridge of
land between Upper and Lower Lough Erne and its origins
go back to prehistory when it was on the main highway
between Ulster and Connaught. The County museum,
housed in the castle keep, displays the brilliant uniforms,
colours and Napoleonic battle trophies of the famous
Inniskilling regiments who fought at Waterloo.

Amongst the many islands to visit, Devenish is particularly interesting, with its perfect twelfth-century round
tower, tiny church and remains of a fifteenth-century
Augustinian abbey. In the cemetery of the largest island,
Boa, are two ancient stone Janus idols, thought to date
from the first century. Belleek is famous both for its fishing
and its china, which comes mostly in the form of objets
d'art. Two of Northern Ireland's most attractive Georgian
houses are to be found in Fermanagh – Castle Coole, a
neo-classical mansion with Paladian features, built in 1795
for the Earl of Belmore, and Florence Court House, seat of
the Earls of Enniskillen, which has wonderful rococo
plasterwork.

BALLINAMALLARD

Jamestown

Magheracross, Ballinamallard, Co Fermanagh

Tel: (0365) 81209

An attractive country house dating from the 1760s and set
in a lovely location in the heart of Fermanagh's lakeland. A

wing of the house and the gracious stableyard were added in the early 1820s. The Ballinamallard River runs through the estate, providing excellent fly-fishing, and shooting for pheasant, duck, snipe and woodcock can be arranged nearby. The garden includes a tennis court and croquet lawn, and there are pleasant walks along the river bank. Stabling is available for guests' horses. There are 3 comfortable bedrooms, an elegant, formal dining-room, where evening meals are served by arrangement, and a relaxing drawing-room. No pets in the house.

OWNERS Arthur and Helen Stuart   OPEN All year, except Christmas   ROOMS 2 double (all en suite)   TERMS B&B £25.00 p.p.; evening meal from £15.00

BELCOO

Corralea Forest Lodge

Belcoo, BT93 5DZ, Co Fermanagh
Tel: (036586) 325

The best thing about this guest house is the location and view. It is in a superb position standing in 50 acres of forested land on the shores of Upper Lough Macnean, with glorious uninterrupted views over the lough to the hills beyond. All rooms share the same views. The bedrooms, which are spacious and functional, with TVs, have sliding doors out onto a terrace. The property has its own private landing stage and boats are available for hire. There are also 6 self-catering chalets in the grounds, sika deer roam the estate, and in the mid 1970s, 37,000 trees were planted. When the Catteralls came here 14 years ago and built the house, the property was just a derelict farm. There is a large TV lounge and a dining-room where evening meals are available if booked in advance. There is no licence, but guests may bring their own wine. No pets are allowed. The house can be found about 3 miles (4¹/₂ km) outside Belcoo on the road to Garrison.

OWNERS Mr and Mrs Peter Catterall   OPEN 1 April–1 September
ROOMS 4 twin (all en suite)   TERMS B&B £17.00 p.p.; reductions for children; single supplement £3.00; evening meal £10.00

DERRYGONNELLY

Navar Guest House

Derryvary, Derrygonnelly, Co Fermanagh
Tel: (036564) 384

An immaculately kept, low, whitewashed modern house
with black trim and front garden, standing just above the
Enniskillen to Derrygonnelly road. The Loves built this
house about 14 years ago, and it has been designed so the
guests have one part of the building and the owners the
other part. Mrs Love is a most friendly, outgoing lady who,
apart from running the B&B, also teaches. Her husband,
whose chief love is fishing (he fished twice for Ireland),
helps out in the house and runs their 300-acre farm. One
hundred and fifty acres of this is hill land, where rough
shooting for pheasant, snipe, woodcock and duck is available. There is good game fishing for salmon and trout and,
of course, Mr Love is more than happy to offer advice and
help to fishermen. The house is most attractive inside; there
is a large entrance hall with Italian tiles and a large comfortable lounge with TV and open fire. There is also a separate
lounge with a piano and computer, particularly popular with
children who are welcome here. All the bedrooms are on the
ground floor. Evening meals are served at 7 pm if booked in
advance and packed lunches are also available. Pets outside
only. The house can be found 8 miles (12 km) west of
Enniskillen on the Derrygonnelly road.

OWNER Patrick and Joan Love   OPEN All year   ROOMS 1 double, 2
twin, 2 family (2 rooms en suite)   TERMS B&B £14.00 p.p.;
reductions for children; evening meal from £6.50

ENNISKILLEN

Brindley Guest House

Tully, Killadeas, Enniskillen, BT74 6DN, Co Fermanagh
Tel: (03656) 28065

A purpose-built guest house, about 8 years old. This large,
whitewashed building is in an elevated position with wonderful views of Lower Lough Erne and the islands. There is
an attractive dining-room where evening meals are served at
6 pm if arranged in advance. A small TV lounge leads to a
conservatory where tea- and coffee-making facilities are
available. Three of the bedrooms are on the ground floor

and there is a ramp leading up to the front door. No smoking and no pets. The house is signposted off the Enniskillen to Kesh road at Killadeas.

OWNER Mr and Mrs Deane Flood   OPEN All year, except Christmas   ROOMS 3 double, 3 twin, 2 family (6 en suite)   TERMS B&B from £16.00 p.p.; reductions for children; single supplement £4.00; evening meals £10.00

Riverside Farm Guest House

Gortadrehid, Culkey, Enniskillen, Co Fermanagh
Tel: (0365) 322725

A most welcoming, warm, friendly house and an angler's paradise in a secluded position in pretty farmland. The house, which is on a 65-acre beef farm, belonged to Ollie Fawcett's grandfather, the oldest part being over 100-years old; modern stucco and windows give it the appearance of beng a more modern building. Mollie, who is a trained cook and used to be in charge of a canteen, has been running the bed and breakfast for the last 20 years. The house is simply furnished with a good ratio of bathrooms to bedrooms, a TV lounge with solid-fuel fire and video, and a dining-room where evening meals are served if ordered in advance. There is no licence, but guests are welcome to bring their own wine. The Sillies River, at the bottom of the farm, holds the world's record for coarse fishing. The farm has over a mile of private fishing and there is an excellent outbuilding for storage and fridges to keep bait fresh. There is one ground-floor bedroom and a ramp into the house. Pets outside only. The house can be found on the A509 3 miles (4¹/₂ km) from Enniskillen. Visa accepted.

OWNERS Mary Isobel Fawcett   OPEN All year   ROOMS 1 double, 2 twin, 2 single, 1 family (1 en suite)   TERMS B&B £12.00-£15.00 p.p.; reductions for children; evening meal from £7.00

FLORENCECOURT

Tullyhona Farm Guest House

Marble Arch Caves Road, Florencecourt, BT92 1DE, Co Fermanagh
Tel: (036582) 452

When the Armstrongs bought the property 12 years ago there was just a tiny cottage. This has been added on to over the years until it has reached its present state of a sizeable guest house. Mrs Armstrong has always been in the catering business, and it had been her dream to one day have her own guest house. A lot of thought has been put into exactly what she wanted and how she wanted to run it. A friendly, chatty, hard- working mother of 3, Mrs Armstrong loves to have families and children, for which this property is ideally suited. There is plenty of space outside. There are flexible meal times and special child menus, a baby-sitting service, play house, and lambing tours at Easter on the quite extensive beef and sheep farm. For adults the house is very close to Florence Court House and the Marble Arch Caves, which have only recently been developed as a tourist site; there are farm and forest walks, some fitness equipment, pheasant shooting, fishing, golf and hill walking. There is a quite sizeable restaurant where lunches, teas and evening meals are served until 7 pm and which is available to both residents and non-residents. Breakfast is buffet style and Tullyhona has barbeque evenings. The focus is on home-cooking and baking and special diets are catered for. The lounge is a large, pleasant room where tea is served at 10 pm and where the only TV set is located. Smoking is permitted only in the sun lounge. Pets outside.

OWNER Mrs Rosemary Armstrong   OPEN All year   ROOMS 2 double, 2 twin, 3 family (4 en suite)   TERMS B&B £14.00-£17.00 p.p.; reductions for children; single supplement £2.00; à la carte meals available all day

IRVINESTOWN

Fletchers Farm

Drumadravey, Irvinestown, Co Fermanagh
Tel: (03656) 21351

A low, whitewashed building about 2 miles (3 km) from Irvinestown on the road to Lisnarick. This 72-acre farm, supporting a suckling herd, has belonged to the Knoxes for the last 20 years. They always wanted to build a new house on the site, which they finally did about 3 years ago, and then Mrs Knox, who works full time as a nurse, also started doing B&B, which she loves. The property is immaculately kept, with the farmyard behind the house and pleasant farmland views. The house has been comfortably furnished and all bedrooms are on the ground floor. Evening meals are served by prior arrangement, and there are good hotels nearby. The bedrooms have tea-making facilities, hairdryers, trouser presses and electric blankets. The lounge has a TV and open fire. Smoking in the lounge only. Pets are not allowed in the bedrooms.

OWNER Myrtle Knox OPEN All year ROOMS 2 double, 1 twin, 1 family (3 en suite) TERMS B&B £12.00 p.p.; reductions for children; evening meal £8.00

KESH

Ardess House

Kesh, Co Fermanagh

Tel: (03656) 31267

The house is located in the tiny hamlet of Ardess, a couple of miles out of Kesh, and is approached up a winding driveway with the house at the top of a hill. It is a rather run-down looking, old, square, grey stucco building, built in 1780 as the rectory for the church opposite and with lovely views. The Pendrys bought it in 1984 and they have done a great deal of work on restoring the house; they are still continuing with projects. Dorothy Pendry was a teacher in a girls' school in Belfast and did weaving and spinning as a hobby. Now she has turned the basement of the house into small workshops, where courses on different crafts are taught partly by herself and other tutors. There is also a small shop. The students who attend the courses get full board in the house. Those not attending courses can order evening meals if they wish, cooked by Dorothy using home-grown vegetables. Evening meals are served at 7.30 pm. for both family and guests. Guests are also welcome to join in the activities in the craft centre. The kitchen is the preferred place for breakfast, but there is a dining-room as well and a drawing-room. The bedrooms have been freshly decorated and good-sized bathrooms have been added. They are large, airy rooms, with high ceilings and wonderful views and furnished with antiques. Smoking is not encouraged. Pets by arrangement. Follow the signs to Kesh; turn off onto the B72 before you reach the village.

OWNER Dorothy Pendry OPEN 1 January–1 November ROOMS 3 double, 1 twin (4 en suite) TERMS B&B £17.50 p.p.; reductions for children; single supplement £1.00; evening meal £10.00, lunch £3.50

Manville Guest House

Aughnablaney, Letter, BT93 2BB, Co Fermanagh
Tel: (03656) 31668

Manville House is set in an idyllic location with a superb view of Lower Lough Erne and Boa Island. Standing in its own grounds, it is hard to pin down the exact date of its origins as it has been added to and modernised over the years. The house is clean, comfortable and simply furnished, and an ideal location for tourists and anglers, with seasons for brown trout and salmon and fishing all year for pike, perch, rudd and bream, which are plentiful. There are boats and engines for hire. There is a lounge with a TV and a separate dining-room. Evening meals are not served, but there is no shortage of good eating establishments in the area. Manville House is one of the first B&Bs in Letter, and Mrs Graham is a congenial host, always happy to give advice and recommend restaurants. Pets by arrangement.

OWNERS Mr and Mrs R H Graham   OPEN All year, except Christmas   ROOMS 5 double/twin/family   TERMS B&B £13.00 p.p.; reductions for children; no single supplement

LISBELLAW

Aghnacarra House

Carrybridge, Lisbellaw, Co Fermanagh
Tel: (0365) 87077

The Ensors came here from Coventry and, after scouring the countryside, finally settled on this site where they purpose-built a guest house designed with the angler in mind. Dave Ensor is a great fisherman and he spends most of his time making sure his guests get just the fishing they want. The house has tackle storage space, and bait can be ordered in advance ready for a guest's arrival. Previously Dave was in the plumbing and building trade, and the couple built the house themselves; the name Aghnacarra means "hill of the fort", although the house is not actually on a hill. Set in 2½ acres of lawns, gardens and a lake, there is a nice view from the terrace which runs the length of the house, overlooking farmland and the lake. The house stands beside a country road in the small village of Carrybridge, halfway between the 2 major Erne loughs. The house is clean, freshly decorated and comfortably furnished, with TV lounge and a dining-room. Evening meals, if ordered in advance, are served at 7 pm; special diets are catered for and lunch and packed lunches are also available. There is no licence, but guests are welcome to bring their own. There are 4 ground-floor bedrooms. Pets are not allowed.

OWNERS Dave and Norma Ensor   OPEN All year   ROOMS 3 triple, 1 family (2 en suite)   TERMS B&B£12.00-£13.00 p.p.; reductions for children; evening meal £7.50

County Londonderry

Before the present troubles Londonderry was probably best known for the tune "Londonderry Air". The city of Londonderry, situated on a hill on the banks of the Foyle estuary, acquired its name when the City of London sent money and builders to rebuild it in the seventeenth century. The seventeenth-century walls, about a mile (1½ km) round and 18 feet (5½ m) thick, have withstood several sieges and are still complete, giving magnificent views of the surrounding countryside. The city still preserves its medieval layout, and amongst the historic buildings is the 1633 Gothic Cathedral of St Columb. From the quay behind the Guildhall hundreds of thousands of Irish emigrants left Derry for America during the eighteenth and nineteenth centuries, amongst them the families from whom Davy Crockett and President James Polk are descended.

The Mussenden Temple, built by the eccentric Earl Biship of Derry as testimony of his affection for Mrs Mussenden, stands on a windswept headland on the coast at Downhill; adjacent, the castle itself, now in ruins but still exuding an aura of romance and grandeur, is certainly worth visiting. One of Ulster's finest fortified farmhouses can be seen at Bellaghy, and whiskey is produced at Bushmills, near Coleraine, the town allegedly founded by St Patrick.

CASTLEROCK

Carneety House

120 Mussenden Road, Castlerock, Coleraine, BT51 4TX, Co Londonderry

Tel: (0265) 848640

An attractive farmhouse on the A2, on the edge of Castlerock, standing in a beautifully kept, compact front garden. The house has been in Mr Henry's family for some time and is 300-years old, with additions. The entrance is through a porch/conservatory into this comfortable family home. It is immaculately kept and attractively decorated and furnished. Mrs Henry is an attractive young mother of 2 who also runs an outside catering business. Her husband takes care of the dairy and beef farm. The dining-room, with one table at which breakfast only is served, is a cosy room with a nice fireplace and family silver, and the drawing-room has a piano, TV and open gas fire. There are TVs in all the bedrooms. Stabling is available, and pony trekking, golf and forest and beach walks are close by.

OWNER Mrs Carol Henry   OPEN All year   ROOMS 2 double, 1 twin (1 en suite)   TERMS B&B £15.00 p.p.; reductions for children

COLERAINE

Blackheath House

112 Killeague Road, Blackhill, Coleraine, BT51 4HH,
Co Londonderry
Tel: (0265) 868433

This fine old house is set in 2 acres of gardens and was built in 1791 as a rectory. It was at one time home of Archbishop William Alexander, whose wife Cecil wrote "There is a Green Hill Far Away" and "All Things Bright and Beautiful". The present owners were originally teachers in London and took over the house when it was derelict. Now it is difficult to imagine the state it once was in, as they have done a wonderful job in creating a warm, comfortable house, beautifully furnished and decorated. All bedrooms have TVs and hairdryers. There is a breakfast room, and the drawing-room is a gracious room with a grand piano, a warm, open fire and shelves to each side reaching to the ceiling full of collectable items; the room has a pleasant lived-in feeling. Joey and Margaret are a friendly, relaxed couple with 2 teenage children. Margaret is in charge with an assistant chef of the kitchen. Macduff's Restaurant was the first part of the house to be open to the public. It is located in the basement and has its own entrance. The restaurant has the atmosphere of a cellar, with its low ceilings and arches, and is most attractively furnished with pink table cloths, flowers on every table, green chairs and, with only a few tables, a cosy, intimate atmosphere. It offers country-house cooking using freshly grown produce, local game, salmon and seafood. There is a full licence and an indoor heated swimming pool. Not suitable for children. No pets. Blackheath House can be found 4¹/₂ miles (6¹/₂ km) north of Garvagh just off the A29. Visa and Access cards accepted.

OWNERS Joey and Margaret Erwin   OPEN All year, except Christmas   ROOMS 4 double, 1 twin (4 en suite)   TERMS B&B £30.00 p.p.; evening meal à la carte

Camus House

27 Curragh Road, Coleraine, BT51 3RY, Co Londonderry
Tel: (0265) 42982

Camus House may have been built on the site of an old monastery. It is the oldest house in the area, a listed building dating from 1685. The house is in a charming setting close to the River Bann and Mrs King owns a mile of river frontage. The  lovely old ivy-covered house is approached by a driveway through park-like grounds and has a pretty front garden. Mrs King's parents bought the house in 1914. The land is now let out and, when her 2 children moved away from home, she started doing bed and breakfast. Mrs King is a most friendly, characterful lady and does all the work herself. Her passion is fishing, and this is a great fishing family. Her daughter, who works for Ulster Television, fished for Ireland. The house has a lot of character and is comfortably furnished as a family home. In winter guests use Mrs King's own sitting-room, a cosy room with an open fire. However, there is another sitting-room and a nice old dining-room where breakfast only is served. The bedrooms are large, fresh and bright and simply furnished. Mrs King was the recipient of the Galtee Breakfast award 1991. There is a partial central heating. Not suitable for children under 14. No pets. No smoking in the dining-room.

OWNER Mrs Josephine King   OPEN All year   ROOMS 1 double/family/twin   TERMS B&B £15.00-£16.50 p.p.

Greenhill House

24 Greenhill Road, Aghadowey, Coleraine, BT51 4EU,
Co Londonderry
Tel: (0265) 868241

A nice old Georgian country house standing in its own grounds of trees, lawns and shrubs, with lovely views over farmland to distant hills. The Hegartys bought the house about 12 years ago, mostly because they wanted the land, now a 150-acre beef and arable farm. The house was derelict when they bought it and they have gradually been doing it up. Mrs Hegarty was a teacher but now devotes her time to running the bed and breakfast; she is a most friendly and cheerful lady. The bedrooms are large, well equipped and furnished with tea- and coffee-making facilities and minute shower rooms, cleverly disguised. There is a large lounge and dining-room with 2 tables. Evening meals can be served by arrangement. No pets. The house lies off the B66 to Ballymoney, just off the A29, 3 miles (4¹/₂ km) north of Garvagh and 7 miles (10¹/₂ km) south of Coleraine. Visa, Access and Eurocard accepted.

OWNER Mrs James Hegarty   OPEN 1 March–1 October   ROOMS 2 double/twin/family (6 en suite)   TERMS B&B £20.00 p.p.; reductions for children; single supplement £5.00; evening meal £12.50

Inchadoghill House

1 Agivey Road, Aghadowey, Coleraine, BT51 4AD,
Co Londonderry
Tel: (0265) 868232/868259

An old brick farmhouse, standing back from the A54, 9 miles (13¹/₂ km) south of Coleraine, in a pleasant lawned front garden, part of a mixed farm. The house has been in the same family for 5 generations and was built by them. Mrs McIlroy is helped in the business by her daughter-in-law who lives next door. They offer comfortable, simple farmhouse accommodation. The dining-room has a piano and family memorabilia in the dresser, a TV lounge, and one of the bedrooms is very small. No pets.

OWNERS Mamie and Ann McIlroy   OPEN All year   ROOMS 2 double, 1 family   TERMS B&B £12.00 p.p.; reductions for children; single supplement available

Killeague House

Blackhill, Coleraine, BT51 4HJ, Co Londonderry
Tel: (0265) 868229

From the outside Killeague House looks quite modern, with newly applied stucco and the addition of arches and a garage. This square house standing in its own garden is, however, about 300-years old. The farm buildings adjacent serve the 120-acre dairy farm. It is a comfortable house with a friendly atmosphere and a lot of steps to negotiate. The bathroom is downstairs and the pleasant dining-room, with 2 tables, family silver on the sideboard and cabinets filled with china and glass, is in the basement. The decor is individual in taste; one bedroom has dark built-in cupboards around the bed, and the TV lounge has both an organ and piano. Evening meals are served by arrangement. No smoking; pets by arrangement. The house can be found on the A29, 5 miles (7¹/₂ km) south of Coleraine.

OWNER Mrs Margaret Moore OPEN All year ROOMS 1 double, 1 single, 2 family (2 en suite) TERMS B&B from £14.00 p.p.; reductions for children; single supplement £2.00; evening meal £9.00

EGLINTON

Longfield Farm

132 Clooney Road, Eglinton, BT47 3DX, Co Londonderry
Tel: (0504) 810210

A spacious old house in a pleasant garden with lawn and shrubs, separated by a field from the main Londonderry to Limavady road. The farmyard, which serves the 200-acre farm of potatoes, beef and cereals, is to the back of the house. It is a comfortable family home with a lived-in feeling and a cosy lounge with open fire, used in winter. In summer the large lounge with piano is preferred, and the dining-room also has a TV. The bedrooms are a good size and there are 2 bathrooms between the 3 bedrooms. Longfield Farm is well placed for visiting Donegal and Londonderry. No smoking in the bedrooms.

OWNER Mrs E M Hunter OPEN 1 April–1 October ROOMS 1 double/single/family TERMS B&B £12.00 p.p.; reductions for children; single supplement £2.00

LIMAVADY

Ballyhenry House

172 Seacoast Road, Limavady, BT49 9EF, Co Londonderry
Tel: (05047) 22657

An attractive house built around the turn of the century, close to the sea, on the B69 between Limavady and Castlerock. The house was built by Mr Kane's grandfather, who subsequently sold it. Mr and Mrs Kane bought it back when they got married. The acreage at that time was 53 acres and with prudent acquisitions it now exceeds 500 acres. The land is very flat and fertile and the fields are enormous, some in excess of 100 acres. Mr Kane died about 5 years ago, and the farm is now managed by the 2 sons and their uncle. It is an extremely successful operation, and they have won all kinds of awards. Mrs Kane is a most friendly lady who prepares excellent evening meals if arranged in advance. The rooms are nicely proportioned and pleasantly decorated and furnished, with some good pieces of furniture. There is a dining-room, TV lounge, snooker room and a pub within 100 yards, which serves food some evenings. The bedrooms have hairdryers and trouser presses. Smoking downstairs only and pets outside.

OWNER Rosemary Kane   OPEN All year   ROOMS 1 double/twin/ family (1 with private shower)   TERMS B&B £15.00 p.p.; reductions for children; evening meal £8.50

LONDONDERRY

Robin Hill

103 Chapel Road, Londonderry, BT47 2BG,
Co Londonderry
Tel: (0504) 42776

A country setting right in the heart of the city. Robin Hill was built as a Presbyterian manse 115 years ago and is a large square house standing in an acre of gardens and park-like grounds right on top of a hill, with wonderful views of the city and hills. The Muirs have been here for about 7 years. Mrs Muir is a teacher and Mr Muir looks after the 2 small children and runs the bed and breakfast. This is a warm, comfortable family home with large rooms, freshly decorated and with new carpets and double-glazed windows. There is a TV lounge, dining-room and small sitting-

room. Evening meals can be served if booked in advance.
Non-smoking rooms are available. No pets.

OWNER Malcolm and Gemma Muir   OPEN All year   ROOMS 1
double/twin/single/family   TERMS B&B £12.50 p.p.; reductions for
children; evening meal £5.00

PORTSTEWART

Oregon Guest House

168 Station Road, Portstewart, BT55 7PU,

Co Londonderry

Tel: (0265) 832826

About half a mile from the sea and within walking distance
of the city centre, this guest house lies on the outskirts of
Portstewart, just off a fairly busy main road. The house is
immaculately kept with a high standard of furnishings and
fresh, bright rooms prettily decorated with floral curtains
and bedcovers. The small, cosy, panelled dining-room, with
pretty floral china and flowers on tables, overlooks the sunny
patio with pond and small fountain. There is a comfortable
TV lounge and off it a supplementary dining-room, very
bright, with windows all around. One of the double rooms
has a corner bath, separate shower, bidet and sauna. All
bedrooms have TVs and hairdryers. Evening meals are served
if ordered in advance and all rooms are on the ground floor.
No smoking in the bedrooms. No pets. The house is located
half a mile south of Portstewart on the B185.

OWNER Mrs Vi Anderson   OPEN All year   ROOMS 3 double, 2
twin, 2 family (5 en suite)   TERMS B&B £17.50-£20.00 p.p.;
reductions for children; evening meal £10.00

County Tyrone

The least populated of the six counties and the heart of
Ulster, Tyrone is bordered to the north by the Sperrin
Mountains, bare hills with fertile green valleys. The main
towns are Omagh, the county town, Cookstown and
Dungannon, chief seat of the O'Neills. It has a textile
industry and crystal factory.

The meaning of the Beaghmore stone circles, consisting
of seven Bronze Age ceremonial stone circles and cairns, is
still unknown. This is just one of many Neolithic sites. The
Ulster-American Folk Park at Camphill, Omagh, which

recreates the America of pioneering days, grew up round the cottage where Thomas Mellon was born in 1813.

Also in County Tyrone is the ancestral home of Woodrow Wilson. The farm is still occupied by Wilsons, who will show callers round the house.

BALLYGAWLEY

The Grange Guest House

15 Grange Road, Ballygawley, BT70 2LP, Co Tyrone
Tel: (06625) 68053

Situated on the edge of Ballygawley, this old house, dating from 1720, had a thatched roof until 10 years ago. It stands in a lovely, large walled garden of lawns surrounded by flower beds and has now the appearance of a more modern house, with white stucco and new windows. Mrs Lyttle is a very friendly, older lady and the house has a pleasant, family lived-in feeling. The smallish lounge has a piano and TV, and the attractive dining-room, from which stairs lead to the next floor, has lots of character, is full of knick-knacks and has sideboards decorated with silver and china. There is one ground-floor bedroom with bathroom next to it and smoking is not permitted in the bedrooms. Pets outside only.

OWNER E Lyttle   OPEN 1 April–1 November   ROOMS 1 double/twin/family (3 en suite)   TERMS B&B £12.50 p.p.; reductions for children; single supplement available; evening meal £7.50

DUNGANNON

Grange Lodge

7 Grange Road, Dungannon, BT71 7EJ, Co Tyrone
Tel: (08627) 84212

An attractive country house just off the Dungannon to Moy road set in pleasant lawned gardens. The Browns, who also own a retail concern in Dungannon, bought the house about 6 years ago and have done a great deal to bring it up to a very high standard of comfort. It is a spacious house with large, well-proportioned rooms and the bedrooms all have TVs and tea- and coffee-making facilities. There is a large, somewhat formal drawing-room and a cosier, smaller den with TV, which is normally the preferred sitting area for guests. Other facilities include a tennis court and a panelled snooker room with piano. Grange Lodge offers its guests comfort and a friendly atmosphere in peaceful surroundings; however, a stay here would not be complete without sampling Norah Brown's cooking. She is quite superb and a perfectionist, both in terms of the extremely high standard of the food itself and the way in which it is presented. Evening meals are served in the elegant dining-room, with separate tables covered in white table-cloths and decorated with pretty flowers and candles. The dining-room is open to non-residents on Friday and Saturday evenings, and bookings are absolutely essential. Not suitable for children under 12, and smoking is only permitted in the den. There is no licence, but guests are welcome to bring their own wine. Visa and Access cards accepted.

OWNER Ralph and Norah Brown   OPEN All year, except Christmas
ROOMS 2 double, 1 twin (2 en suite)   TERMS B&B £25.00-£30.00 p.p.

Muleany House

86 Gorsetown Road, Moy, Dungannon, BT71 7EX,
Co Tyrone
Tel: (08687) 84657

A substantial, porticoed whitewashed building, purpose-built 9 years ago, close to the town of Moy. Mrs Mullen is a most friendly, chatty lady who does her own baking and enjoys meeting her guests. The bedrooms are good sized with tiny shower rooms, and although all are en suite there are 2 extra public bathrooms with bathtubs. An excellent place for children, Muleany House offers a laundry facility, baby-sitting service, and a large games room with pool table, small organ and open fire. There is also a smaller lounge with a TV and a dining-room where evening meals are served between 6 and 6.30 pm if ordered in advance. There is no licence, but guests are welcome to bring their own wine. Two bedrooms are on the ground floor. The house can be found about 2 miles (3 km) from Moy; from the B106 to Benburb, take the right fork towards Ballygawley.

OWNERS Mary and Brian Mullen   OPEN All year   ROOMS double/ twin/family (9 en suite)   TERMS B&B £12.00-£15.00 p.p.; reductions for children; single supplement £3.00; evening meal £7.00-£10.00

Al-Di-Gwyn

103 Clabby Road, Fivemiletown, BT75 0QY, Co Tyrone
Tel: (03655) 21298

This large, colour-washed building, in a good centre for touring, stands just off the road between Fivemiletown and Clabby. Originally it was a 3-roomed bungalow, but it has been added on to over the years. The rooms are functional and there is one small TV sitting-room and a larger TV lounge. There is one ground-floor room with en suite shower room and a ramp and wide doors leading into the house. No smoking in the bedrooms. Pets outside only.

OWNER Mrs Vera Gilmore   OPEN 1 January–1 November
ROOMS 3 double, 4 twin, 4 family (9 en suite)   TERMS B&B
£15.00-£16.00 p.p.; reductions for children; single supplement available

MOY

Charlemont House

4 The Square, Moy, Dungannon, BT71 7SG, Co Tyrone
Tel: (08687) 84755/84895

A lovely Georgian townhouse occupying a corner site on the long central square of the most attractive small town of Moy, which lies half way between Armagh and Dungannon. Until recently it was owned by a doctor and has been taken over by the McNeice family, who have been associated with innkeeping in Moy for many generations. A sign to one side of the house reads "Enquire at Tomney's Bar and Lounge or Moy Reproductions", which are located just a few doors down the square. The bar is quite an amazing place, completely authentic, with small, dark rooms and a great atmosphere. The house is also amazing. It has been left just as it was when the doctor's family lived there – Victorian furnishings and furniture. The lounge has old floral wallpaper, pinkish chintzes, black-and-pink patterned carpet, black furniture, including piano, romantic pictures and all kinds of glass and china. The house has elegant proportions with the breakfast room in the basement, a less flamboyant room with Aga cooker and pottery adorning the high shelf around the room. The property stretches right down to the River Blackwater at the back, reached through a courtyard. Here guests can sit out on fine days, surrounded by old coach houses (destined to be converted into bedrooms), then through an archway to a pretty, partly walled, compact garden with more tables and chairs. The bedrooms have TVs and tea- and coffee-making facilities, and there are 2 sitting-rooms.

OWNERS Mr and Mrs L McNeice   OPEN All year   ROOMS 5 double, 4 single   TERMS B&B £12.50-£15.00 p.p.; reductions for children

OMAGH

Bankhead

9 Lissan Road, Omagh, BT78 1TX, Co Tyrone

Tel: (0662) 245592

A small house, built by the Clements in 1970, with farm buildings to the rear. The beef and sheep farm consists of 27 acres and is located about 1½ miles (2½ km) outside Omagh on the Ballygawley Road. The bedrooms are simply furnished but fresh and bright; there is a small, neatly kept TV lounge with an open fire and the dining-room has a TV and sitting area. Outside, the terrace is pleasant for sitting out on fine days, with farmland views, and guests have use of a garden. Smoking is not allowed in bedrooms and pets are not permitted. All the bedrooms are on the ground floor. Bankhead is a quarter of a mile from the golf course.

OWNER Mrs S C Clements   OPEN All year   ROOMS 2 double, 1 twin   TERMS B&B £11.00 p.p.; reductions for children

Greenmount Lodge

58 Greenmount Road, Gortaclare, Omagh, BT79 0YE,

Co Tyrone

Tel: (0662) 841325

The house stands in a lovely park-like setting in a very quiet position on a 70-acre beef and sheep farm, with old farm buildings to the rear of the modern, low house. Greenmount Lodge specialises in wedding receptions and is open to non-residents for evening meals on Fridays and Saturdays. There is little atmosphere but the bedrooms are quite pleasant and a reasonable size, although the bathrooms are minute. Evening meals are available if arranged ahead and are served at 6.30 pm. The house can be found 7 miles (10½ km) from

Ballygawley on the Omagh road, turning west at the Travellers' Rest and travelling a further mile. No smoking in the bedrooms.

OWNER Frances Reid   OPEN All year   ROOMS 1 double, 1 twin, 3 family (all en suite)   TERMS B&B £15.00-£17.00 p.p.; reductions for children; evening meal from £8.00-£12.00

STRABANE

Mrs Jean Ballantine's

38 Leckpatrick Road, Artigarvan, Strabane, BT82 0HB, Co Tyrone

Tel: (0504) 882714

A family home just off the B49 Strabane to Dunnemana road, with lovely distant views of farmland and hills. This modern house has a friendly atmosphere and 3 small bedrooms as well as 2 bathrooms. There is a fairly large TV lounge with an open fire and the family dining-room with one table where evening meals can be served by arrangement. Smoking is not encouraged. Pets outside only.

OWNER Mrs Jean Ballantine   OPEN All year, except Christmas ROOMS 1 double/twin/single   TERMS B&B £11.00 p.p.; reductions for children; evening meal £5.00

Area Maps

DROGHEDA ▲ Baltray

N51

N2

N1

▲ Navan ▲ Duleek

N51

N52

M E A T H

N3

N41

N6

▲ Dunshaughlin

N2 ▲ Santry

DUBLIN

Newcastle ▲ N7

N81

Dun Laoghaire

DUBLIN

K I L D A R E Naas

Bray

N7 ▲ Kildare N9

N78

N11

N81

▲ Roundwood

Glendalough ▲ ▲ Annamoe

W I C K L O W ▲ Ashford
▲ Wicklow

N9 ▲ Castledermot ▲ Kiltegan

N11

▲ Rathvilly

N80

Carlow ▲ Arklow

Castlecomer

N78

C A R L O W

N80

▲ Bagenalstown

N10 ▲ Bunclody

N80

N10

N9

Enniscorthy

KENNY

W E X F O R D

▲ Thomastown

tonyford

N8

▲ New Ross

N25

N25

WEXFORD ▲

▲ Foulkesmill

▲ Rosslare

RFORD

N25

Ballymaclode

Rossduff ▲

Dunmore East

amore

Area 2

▲ Tipperary = Guide entry

| 0 | 5 | 10 | 15 | 20 | 25 Miles |

| 0 | 10 | 20 | 30 | 40 Kilometres |

Area 3

Ballycastle ▲

Killala ▲   ▲ Inishcrone

Crossmolina ▲   ▲ Ballina

ACHILL
ISLAND

M A Y O

Achill
Sound

▲ Newport

▲ Westport
N84

N60

▲ Louisburgh
N59

N84

N59

▲ Kylemore   Clonbur ▲

CONNEMARA

▲ Clifden   N59

▲ Cashel   Oughterard ▲   ▲ Annagh

N59

N84

Moycullen ▲   N6

Spiddle ▲   **GALWAY**

▲ Salthill

N67

THE
BURREN

▲ Lisdoonvarna

▲ Ennistymon
▲ Lahinch

N67

▲ Milltown Malbay   Ennis ▲

N67

N68

N68

| 0 | 5 | 10 | 15 | 20 | 25 Miles |

| 0 | 10 | 20 | 30 | 40 Kilometres |

▲ Tipperary = Guide entry

Area 4

▲ Tipperary = Guide entry

0   5   10   15   20   25 Miles

0   10   20   30   40 Kilometres

Index of towns and cities